CW00647567

£11.95

FRONT COVER: Dashel Drasher

PHOTOGRAPHS: Mark Cranham - cranhamphoto.com; John Grossick - grossick.co.uk; Dan Abraham; Seamus Durack; Carl Evans; Tim Holt; Tattersalls Ireland - www.tattersalls.ie

ISBN: 978-1-872437-68-2

CONTENTS

WELCOME

By Paul Ferguson

Beginning the season knowing that Ruby Walsh won't be riding at the Cheltenham Festival come the spring – or anywhere in between, for that matter – is a strange feeling.

Walsh has been synonymous with the festival for the past two decades, with the first of his 59 winners coming aboard *Alexander Banquet* in the 1998 Champion Bumper. The 11-time leading jockey at the meeting, he rode seven winners in both 2009 and 2016, and his final Cheltenham Festival winner came in last year's Supreme Novices' Hurdle, aboard *Klassical Dream*. I was delighted to be on course when he bowed out following the victory of *Kemboy* in the Punchestown Gold Cup, and the iconic 40-year-old will be sorely missed.

Walsh wasn't the only high-profile jockey to retire in the spring, with *Jumpers To Follow* contributor Noel Fehily announcing his retirement following the victory of *Eglantine du Seuil* in the Dawn Run, and nine days later signed off by riding *Get In The Queue* to win the valuable sales bumper at Newbury. His CV is also chock full of Grade 1 winners, including a brace of Champion Hurdles, a Queen Mother Champion Chase, and a couple of King Georges.

With Fehily hanging up his boots, it is time for a revamp in the *A View From The Saddle* section of this year's book, and I'm delighted to welcome Jonathan Burke, Aidan Coleman and Jonjo O'Neill Jnr into the fray. They are joined by regulars Jamie Codd, Brian Hughes, Jerry McGrath, Harry Skelton and Nick Scholfield, each of whom selects their 10 horses to follow for the season ahead.

For those of you who haven't read *Jumpers To Follow* previously, the first – and main – section of the book is made up of my 40 Leading Prospects for the season. Twenty-three of this year's 40 will be competing in the novice hurdle division, and with 38 of the 40 being aged either five or six, you can see that the idea behind the book is to unearth up-and-coming talent. Of the other 17, several will be embarking on their first season over fences, and whilst I will be hoping that some will develop into Grade 1 novice chasers, I have included a clutch of horses rated around the 130 mark who could improve for facing fences. Given the number of former Point-to-Point horses to feature amongst this year's 40, I have included the form in that sphere – in the form figures – for the first time. The Point-to-Point form is illustrated in red.

Now in its thirteenth year, other regular sections return this year, such as *Across The Sea* (additional horses to follow from Ireland) and *Around The Yards*, where I personally pick out horses from almost 60 yards from up and down the country. New additions this year include *Top-Class Performers*, where I take a look at the genuine Grade 1 performers in England and Ireland, and the *Point-to-Point Graduates* section has been given a revamp. The main addition to this year's publication, however, is the introduction of the *Big-Race Trends*, which is a spin-off of the long-running *Cheltenham Festival Betting Guide*, which I wrote for the first time this year. Hopefully, adding these trends and in-depth analysis for a dozen big races will prove informative throughout the season and, if you have never read the Cheltenham equivalent, will give you a feel for what you can expect from that publication.

I would like to thank everyone who helped in putting together this year's edition of *Jumpers To Follow*, including all owners and trainers who have kindly answered my questions/emails etc. Thank you to all eight jockeys who kindly took their time to provide readers with insight into horses they are looking forward to this season, and to my colleagues at Weatherbys, who have once again done a fine job with the design. Finally, thanks to the photographers, whose excellent photos help break up my endless text, and, of course, to Cornelius Lysaght. Racing correspondent for the BBC, he has kindly written this year's Foreword.

Also, thank you to everyone who has bought a copy of this year's book and I sincerely hope you enjoy the pages which you are about to read. I also hope that you find it informative, interesting and value for money, and that it helps you back the odd winner or two along the way.

Good luck for the season,

Paul Ferguson
@paulfergusonJTF

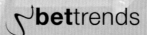

FOREWORD

By Cornelius Lysaght

I take part in a fiercely-competitive 'Twelve-To-Follow' tipping competition during the National Hunt season administered in his own unique style by the Newmarket trainer John Berry. During 2018/19, I'm ashamed to report that my finishing position was not so much down the field, as hopelessly tailed off.

It would be nice to be able to conclude that the list was dripping with potential only to be dogged by wretched luck, but it's more honest to admit its compiler failed. That said, as stick inevitably flew around from my fellow runners and riders, I insisted that I was, in true Dick Francis-style, giving myself a 'quiet run' in order to 'get handicapped' for the future.

With that insistence in mind, my nose will barely be out of Paul Ferguson's latest *Jumpers To Follow* in the run-up to the start of the 2019/20 competition, and I'm sensing all sorts of successes ahead. Now in its thirteenth year, and for the first time consisting of a vast 160 pages of detail, *Jumpers To Follow* really is a must-have for enthusiasts of jumping.

The fact is that many of us have had our heads turned by the Flat since that April end-of-season afternoon at Sandown when Richard Johnson and Bryony Frost received their jockey-trophies and Altior set a new jumps world record with a nineteenth success on the trot. An element of re-adjustment will therefore be required in preparation for the months ahead – which is exactly where Paul's opus bursts to the front.

And mention of Altior reminds us that the Nicky Henderson-trained superstar received rave reviews as long ago as the 2014/15 edition having scooted up in a Market Rasen bumper on what was then his sole start.

With the skills, organisation and dedication that the author hopes to see weekly from Everton, his – and my – favourite football team, he's been on a scouting mission for clues hoping to continue a, thank goodness, rather more consistent run of form than that of the 'Blues'.

Altior featured in the 'Leading Prospects' section which contains 40 more names this time: those of us who've witnessed admiringly the meteoric rise of trainer Olly Murphy will be pleased to read expectations of bigger, better things from the string he supervises in the months ahead.

'Around The Yards' does exactly what it says on the tin, with comprehensive evaluations of horses of varying degrees of darkness from either side of the Irish Sea. Having recovered from the shock of finding no mention of the 10-year-old Craiganboy – of which I have a tiny share – in the analysis of Nick Alexander's upwardly-mobile Scottish operation (!), I noted that it's anticipated that the Graeme McPherson-trained Ask Ben which beat us into a (um, distant) second at Ayr in January will further 'advertise' the form.

And there is so much more information: from the Sales-ring, the Point-to-Point field, the stats department, and the saddle from where some of our favourite jockeys offer an insight which will hopefully go some way to disproving the old adage that theirs are the worst tips.

Jumpers To Follow should ensure all of us have a lucrative and enjoyable season: best wishes for that – and if you're part of the John Berry competition, look out!

Cornelius Lysaght
@CorneliusRacing

Moonlighter - one to look forward to over fences for Jane Williams this season

LEADING PROSPECTS

**Form figures in red indicate
Point-to-Point form**

AL DANCER

6yo Al Namix - Steel Dancer (Kaldounevees)

Trainer:
Nigel Twiston-Davies

Owner:
Walters Plant Hire Ltd

Optimum Conditions:
2m+ on any ground

Career Form Figures:
2314/11110

Twice placed in bumpers for Christian Williams, Al Dancer went on to win at Bangor and finish fourth at Aintree for Nigel Twiston-Davies, but he flourished over hurdles last season and could step forward again now he is sent over fences.

A tall son of Al Namix with bags of scope, he had Windsor Avenue and Tedham in behind when winning at Carlisle, and beat another subsequent winner under his penalty at Ffos Las.

Pitched into handicap company at Cheltenham's November meeting, Al Dancer was fitted with a hood (had worn one at Aintree) having been keen in his earlier races. Off an appealing looking mark of 129, he duly bolted up and, again, the second won next time.

Given his recent record in the race, it wasn't surprising that Twiston-Davies then targeted the Betfair Hurdle, and after the Equine Influenza outbreak he won the rearranged contest at Ascot. Despite a 12lb rise in the weights, he again ran out a very impressive winner, once more travelling very powerfully throughout. It might not have been as strong a Betfair as normal, but Getaway Trump (4th) advertised the form by winning twice during April.

Things didn't go to plan in the Supreme and he dropped away from two out, but I'm sure this wasn't his true running and the fact that we didn't see him again suggests all was not right. He can leave that behind and could easily make up into a leading contender for the Arkle.

ANDY DUFRESNE

5yo Doyen - Daytona Lily (Beneficial)

Trainer:
Gordon Elliott

Owner:
John P. McManus

Optimum Conditions:
2m+ on easy ground

Career Form Figures:
1/1-

Sadly, we only got to see the exciting Andy Dufresne once last season – was declared a non-runner at Fairyhouse over Easter due to the good ground – but he remains a very bright prospect and can certainly make his presence felt over hurdles this winter.

Famed for being sold by Gordon Elliott's travelling head lass Camilla Sharples, he ran out a taking winner of a Borris House maiden Point in March of last year, prior to him being purchased by JP McManus. That form looks quite strong, with the runner-up shaping well on his debut for Colin Tizzard, and Conflated – a faller when beaten in third – won a Clonmel bumper for Elliott and Gigginstown.

Sent to Down Royal for his debut under Rules, Andy Dufresne was extremely keen in the early part of the race, and as a consequence Derek O'Connor elected to allow him to stride on. He dictated matters and strode clear to beat Golden Spread by 10 lengths despite those early exertions. The runner-up advertised the form by winning his next two starts, before taking his chance in the Grade 1 at Punchestown.

Andy Dufresne looks to possess the class to develop into a Graded novice hurdler this winter, and despite the obvious strength in depth in the division within the Elliott stable, he could easily be towards the top of the pecking order. He might appreciate an extra half-mile over hurdles, provided he relaxes with experience.

BIRCHDALE

5yo Jeremy - Onewayortheother (Presenting)

Trainer:
Nicky Henderson

Owner:
John P. McManus

Optimum Conditions:
2m4f – 3m on decent ground

Career Form Figures:
1/11P-

Despite being pulled-up in the Albert Bartlett when last seen, Birchdale remains a high-class prospect for the staying novice chase division this season.

Having beaten another of this year's *Leading Prospects*, Blazer's Mill, in a maiden Point at Tyrella, he made a winning debut for Nicky Henderson and JP McManus, in a maiden hurdle at Warwick. He eased his way into contention, took up the running two out, and despite running down the final flight, readily picked up to beat a clutch of subsequent winners.

After missing the Leamington Novices' Hurdle, he took his chance in the Classic Novices' Hurdle, when he was left in front at the last, by the fall of Brewin'upastorm. My initial feeling was that the faller had the race won, but whatever way you look at it, the pair had drawn right away from a decent field, marking themselves down as two very smart novices.

Upped in trip for the Albert Bartlett, Birchdale travelled really well throughout, and with the exception of the winner, was going best turning for home. He quickly stopped, however, suggesting either something was wrong or, more likely, it was too stiff a test at that stage of his career.

Still only five, he can leave that behind on his return when I expect him to take high-rank among the British-trained stayers. Quick enough to start off over 2m4f, Newbury's Berkshire Novices' Chase might well be an option before he goes up in trip.

BLAZER'S MILL

5yo Westerner - Creation (Definite Article)

Trainer:
Olly Murphy

Owner:
Mrs J. A. Wakefield

Optimum Conditions:
2m+ on any ground

Career Form Figures:
2/1-

Trainer Olly Murphy was responsible for a smart crop of novice hurdlers last season and Thomas Darby, Itchy Feet and Brewin'upastorm all performed with great credit at Cheltenham and (in the case of the last-named pairing) Aintree. The fact that his only novice hurdle runners at both meetings all finished in the first four shows that Murphy isn't prepared to send young horses to either festival unless he believes them up to the task, and he has a strong-looking team again for this season.

Quite whether Blazer's Mill ends up being festival material only time will tell, but he certainly rates as a nice prospect for the novice hurdle division, judged on his sole appearance under Rules to date. Sent off at prohibitive odds, he defied greenness to win a Fontwell bumper in mid-February, beating Mount Windsor by 3½ lengths. We didn't get to see him again, but the runner-up franked the form by winning twice, and his Irish Point-to-Point form reads well, too. Beaten a length by Nicky Henderson's Birchdale (see above), the son of Westerner jumped well at Tyrella, only to be caught after the last.

A half-brother to War Creation and Taniokey, Blazer's Mill has the pace to start off over the minimum trip and seems versatile in terms of ground. He should have little trouble in adding to his tally now he is sent hurdling.

 LEADING PROSPECTS

BLUE SARI

4yo Saddex - Blue Aster (Astarabad)

Trainer:
Willie Mullins

Owner:
John P. McManus

Optimum Conditions:
2m+ on soft ground

Career Form Figures:
12-

Willie Mullins enjoyed a red-letter day on Thyetes Day at Gowran Park in late-January, winning the final three races. Invitation Only justified favouritism under Ruby Walsh in the big race, before smart hurdler Cilaos Emery won the beginners' chase, and it was Blue Sari who completed the treble in explosive fashion in the concluding bumper.

Allowed to stride on before the home turn, Blue Sari grabbed the stands' side rail and wound things up from two out. He quickly drew clear and was full of running as he crossed the line, marking himself down as a potentially exciting prospect. The runner-up, Front View, would later advertise the form by winning the four-year-old bumper at the Punchestown Festival and his owner, JP McManus, was quick to snap up Blue Sari after that impressive debut.

It was originally thought that he would be aimed at Limerick's valuable four-year-old bumper, but was instead targeted at the Champion Bumper, in which he went down by just three-quarters of a length to Envoi Allen. Held up, he made smooth progress coming down the hill only for the winner to make his move first. He chased hard on the run to the line, but was unable to get by the more experienced winner.

It was a fine effort for a four-year-old, and when he returns he can be expected to take high rank over hurdles on soft ground.

BOLD PLAN

5yo Jeremy - Kings Orchid (King's Theatre)

Trainer:
Evan Williams

Owner:
Mr & Mrs William Rucker

Optimum Conditions:
2m4f+ on soft ground

Career Form Figures:
12/3312-

Bold Plan kept himself in good company throughout last season and could be the pick of a nice bunch of five-year-olds that belong to his connections.

Having shaped with plenty of encouragement at Newbury on debut – when a staying-on third, just 2½ lengths off Grade 2 winner Mister Fisher – he then chased home Rouge Vif (another subsequent Grade 2 winner) at Southwell, when he probably cost himself second place by trying to match strides with the winner. Oakley (2nd) also franked that form, by winning both subsequent starts.

Given a couple of months off, he appreciated the step up in trip when getting off the mark at Taunton. He was receiving 7lb from Southfield Stone – who was three-from-three at the track to that point – and having travelled well for Sean Bowen, he picked him up after the last. Again, the runner-up went on to land the Grade 2 Dovecote Novices' Hurdle on his next start.

Bold Plan's final start came in a competitive handicap hurdle at Uttoxeter on Midlands Grand National Day and he finished a clear second, behind Poker Play. Forced wide to challenge, he ran a sound race and remains on a fair mark (132) should connections persist down the staying handicap hurdle route. However, jumping appears to be his forte – he jumped really well when beating New Age Dawning (now rated 133) by eight lengths in an Irish Point – and would rate a smart prospect for novice chases.

BREWIN'UPASTORM

6yo Milan - Daraheen Diamond (Husyan)

Trainer:
Olly Murphy

Owner:
Mrs Barbara Hester

Optimum Conditions:
2m – 2m4f on any ground

Career Form Figures:
1/14/14F42-

The only one of last year's *Leading Prospects* to retain their place, Brewin'upastorm might only have won once from five starts, but performed with great credit after his smooth win at Huntingdon and now rates a smart prospect for novice chases. He travelled with purpose en route to beating several subsequent winners on debut, before being inconvenienced by the lack of pace in the Challow at Newbury.

He then headed to Cheltenham on trials day, and having attempted to make all, he was still in front when taking a nasty final-flight fall. Thankfully none the worse, he headed to the festival where he again travelled powerfully, in the Ballymore. Held up a long way off the pace, he made stealthy headway and loomed up on the approach to two out. He never really looked like getting on terms with the front pair on the run to the last, however, with his stamina possibly being stretched.

Sent to Aintree for the Mersey, he again shaped well in defeat and, once more, possibly didn't see out the trip as well as the winner; he again travelled smoothly and looked the likely winner when jumping the last. Reserve Tank went on to advertise the form at Punchestown.

Brewin'upastorm isn't short of speed and being ridden more aggressively over 2m might be the route to take. He could well develop into an Arkle contender.

CHAMP

7yo King's Theatre - China Sky (Definite Article)

Trainer:
Nicky Henderson

Owner:
John P. McManus

Optimum Conditions:
2m4f+ on any ground

Career Form Figures:
12/2/111121-

Twice a winner at short odds during May last year, Champ reappeared at Newbury's Winter Carnival and despite appearing to race far too freely, ran out a most impressive winner.

That victory came in handicap company and from a mark of 139, so following an 11lb rise, he reverted to novice company in the Challow over the same course and distance. Sent off even-money favourite for the Grade 1, the lack of pace didn't pose him any problems and he quickened up smartly to lead on the run to the last. He saw the race out well to beat Getaway Trump (won twice in April, latterly in a handicap off 147), with Brewin'upastorm back in fourth.

Like the fourth, Champ contested the Ballymore at Cheltenham, where he found only City Island too good. He did little wrong, perhaps just beaten by a stronger stayer having again raced exuberantly. On to Aintree, where I was slightly surprised to see him contest the 3m½f Sefton Novices' Hurdle. The relatively sedate gallop played to his strengths, however, as he cruised through the contest for the deputising Mark Walsh. Still on the bit as he hit the front two out, he was punched out after the last to record a second Grade 1 success.

Expected to be sent chasing, the seven-year-old won't have a problem in dropping back in trip, and it could be that the JLT ends up being his Cheltenham target, although he appears right at home on a flat track.

CHANTRY HOUSE

5yo Yeats - The Last Bank (Phardante)

Trainer:
Nicky Henderson

Owner:
John P. McManus

Optimum Conditions:
2m+ on easy ground

Career Form Figures:
U/11-

A maiden Point winner at the second time of asking, Chantry House changed hands for £295,000 on the back of his victory at Tattersalls Farm. Still in the lead and going well when coming down three out on debut, he defied greenness (ran wide on the home bend) to get off the mark and duly proved popular at the sale just five days later.

The Yeats gelding was declared to run in bumpers at both Kempton and Newbury (non-runner on each occasion due to the ground) before we got to see him make a successful winning debut for Nicky Henderson, at Warwick. Well-supported, he was sent off odds-on and never really looked like he wouldn't justify favouritism. Covered up in mid-field, the five-year-old eased into contention and only had to be nudged out to score comfortably. The runner-up had twice earlier filled the same spot and appeared the one to beat on form beforehand, whilst the fifth home, Story of Friends, gave the form a boost when winning a bumper and a maiden hurdle during May.

Chantry House was given a couple of entries over hurdles at the Punchestown Festival, but the ground was presumably deemed too quick for him once again. When he returns, he will have no problem getting 2m4f, but doesn't look short of speed and is one who I am particularly looking forward to seeing again. He could be very exciting.

DANNY WHIZZBANG

6yo Getaway - Lakil Princess (Bering)

Trainer:
Paul Nicholls

Owner:
Mrs Angela Tincknell

Optimum Conditions:
3m+ on easy ground

Career Form Figures:
P1/11-

A winner at the second time of asking in Irish Points, Danny Whizzbang had just two runs over hurdles last season for Paul Nicholls, but rates a really nice prospect for staying novice chases this winter.

A maiden winner at Hereford in November, the son of Getaway was quite keen and pulled himself to the front at an early stage. Despite looking a little tired in the closing stages, he kept on well to win what was just an ordinary event in workmanlike fashion.

Declared for a Grade 2 at Cheltenham the following month, he had to be pulled out (didn't eat up) and we then had to wait until March until next seeing him. Dropped back a couple of furlongs to contest an extended 2m7f novices' hurdle at Exeter, he again made all and ran out an authoritative winner, this time beating better opposition.

A mark of 139 would look stiff enough on the face of it, but it is likely to prove irrelevant at this stage, as he will almost certainly be sent chasing in the autumn and could really flourish over fences. He jumped well when winning his Point for Colin Bowe, beating Ask Ben, who won twice over hurdles for Graeme McPherson and is now rated 133. A strong stayer, he appeals as the type who will relish galloping tracks such as Chepstow or Newbury.

DASHEL DRASHER

6yo Passing Glance - So Long (Nomadic Way)

Trainer:
Jeremy Scott

Owner:
Mrs B Tully and Mr R Lock

Optimum Conditions:
2m4f on good-to-soft ground

Career Form Figures:
106/3341111-

Beaten on his first three starts over hurdles last winter, Dashel Drasher went on to win four times between January and April, and now rates a lovely prospect for the novice chase division.

Having looked in need of the run behind Kateson on debut, he shaped with plenty of promise in a couple of competitive races at Newbury over 2m½f, before flourishing over an extra half-mile after the turn of the year. He galloped on really strongly when getting off the mark at Chepstow, before following up under a penalty at Ascot, showing a fine attitude.

Clearly enjoying himself under more positive tactics, he again made all and showed improved form to complete the hat-trick at Newbury. After skipping Aintree, Jeremy Scott opted for Cheltenham's April meeting for Dashel Drasher, who completed the four-timer with plenty in hand. He hurdled well – as he had done at Ascot – and looked to have the race sewn up before the home turn.

Despite missing the spring festivals, he still managed to obtain an official rating of 145 over hurdles and was on a sharp upward curve when last seen. If he continues his progression upon his return, this thoroughly likeable individual could easily develop into a Graded-class novice chaser, and his style of racing ought to stand him in good stead in small-field contests. Newbury's Berkshire Novices' Chase could be an ideal early-season target.

DLAURO

6yo Lauro - Gergovie de Bussy (Bad Conduct)

Trainer:
Joseph Patrick O'Brien

Owner:
Lloyd J Williams

Optimum Conditions:
2m4f+ on soft ground

Career Form Figures:
1/1

Purchased for £410,000 in February 2018, Dlauro wasn't seen until mid-May of this year, but the wait was worthwhile, as he ran out a thoroughly convincing winner of a Punchestown bumper. Despite easing significantly in the market during the build-up to the race, the six-year-old travelled purposefully for Derek O'Connor and could be spotted going ominously well in behind with half-a-mile to run. Angled out inside the final three furlongs, he breezed to the front in an instant and bounded clear. He won by 11 lengths in the end, but it was the race-winning move on the home bend which I found so impressive.

The winner of maiden Point at Belharbour when trained by Donnchadh Doyle, the placed horses from that race didn't exactly enhance the form under Rules last term but he was again easy on the eye. He moved well on the front end that day and jumped well, too, appearing to have the opposition beaten soon after three out. Eased right down to score by six lengths at the line, you would expect him to come into his own over 2m4f or further over hurdles this season, and he clearly has no problem in handling decent ground.

By an unfashionable sire, Dlauro wouldn't have the flashiest of pedigrees, but he has now created a lasting impression on two occasions, and his hurdling debut is something to really look forward to this autumn.

EDEN DU HOUX

5yo Irish Wells - Maralypha (Louveteau)

Trainer:
David Pipe

Owner:
Prof. Caroline Tisdall

Optimum Conditions:
2m1f+ on soft ground

Career Form Figures:
1/11-

The winner of a maiden Point at Monksgrange when trained by James Doyle, Eden du Houx created an instant impression on his debut under Rules, when successful in a soft-ground bumper at Plumpton in early-December.

A powerful mover, the son of Irish Wells pulled his way to the front leaving the far side, at which point Tom Scudamore allowed him to stride on. Still green in the closing stages, he kept on well and scored with something to spare.

Having made most to win his Point, similar tactics were adopted when he headed to Ascot just 18 days later, for what appeared a strong Listed event. Ears pricked, Eden du Houx clearly enjoyed himself out in front and dictated matters throughout. Due to the slow pace, plenty still held chances turning in, but he kept on in a likeable manner to maintain his 100% record.

That form worked out well, with The Glancing Queen (3rd) winning a Grade 2 at Aintree, Enrilo (4th) winning at Kempton, and Montego Grey (5th) victorious at Market Rasen. It had been expected that Eden du Houx would take his chance in the Champion Bumper, but he was instead given plenty of time to strengthen and the patience of his connections might well be rewarded in novice hurdle company this season. He appeals as the type to have improved physically for his summer break.

ELDORADO ALLEN

5yo Khalkevi - Hesmeralda (Royal Charter)

Trainer:
Colin Tizzard

Owner:
J P Romans & Terry Warner

Optimum Conditions:
2m+ on soft ground

Career Form Figures:
23/1U-

Eldorado Allen burst on to the scene last November, when beating one of last year's *Leading Prospects*, Sevarano, in a soft-ground maiden hurdle at Sandown. The highlight of the performance was his hurdling and he had impressed in that department when finishing third at Auteuil the previous March. Having travelled up powerfully, he comprehensively outjumped the runner-up two out and ran out a very impressive winner.

Although the second failed to get his head in front, he did split the Ballymore third, Bright Forecast, and the smart Dashel Drasher next time out at Newbury, whilst six of the next seven horses home won no fewer than 12 races between them, so that piece of form is rock-solid. One of those in behind, West To The Bridge (6th), caused a 40-1 upset at Aintree in December, in a race in which Eldorado Allen was sent off odds-on. He didn't get very far, however, as he was hampered at the very first flight, enough to force Tom O'Brien out of the saddle.

Frustratingly, he picked up an injury which kept him off the track for the remainder of the season, but he is expected to return in the autumn when connections will have to decide whether to send him over fences or head for something like the Greatwood Hurdle. A mark of 145 probably won't prove beyond him, especially on soft ground, but he jumps like a chaser and remains a very exciting prospect.

EMITOM

5yo Gold Well - Avenging Angel (Heron Island)

Trainer:
Warren Greatrex

Owner:
The Spero Partnership Ltd

Optimum Conditions:
2m4f+ on soft ground

Career Form Figures:
1/11112-

Aside from Paisley Park and, possibly, If The Cap Fits, there doesn't appear too much strength in depth to the British staying hurdle division at present. With Champ set to head down the novice chase route, the door could be ajar for Emitom to step forward.

Currently only rated 147, he has 22lb to find with Paisley Park as things stand, but Emma Lavelle's Stayers' Hurdle winner began last season on a mark of 140, so it is not out of the question. Plus, after just one run over 3m, Emitom is completely unexposed as a stayer, and although he lost his unbeaten record in the Sefton at Aintree, he ran with credit in a race which wasn't run to suit.

The five-year-old had earlier made a winning return in an Ascot bumper, before beating subsequent Grade 2 winner Lisnagar Oscar – with ease – at Ffos Las. He followed up by winning a weak race at Lingfield, before giving sale-topper Interconnected 10lb and a beating over 2m4½f at Newbury.

Given his current mark, the Betfair Exchange Stayers' Handicap Hurdle at Haydock would appeal as the ideal starting point, although it wouldn't surprise me if Warren Greatrex followed the same path as he did with Cole Harden. He also finished runner-up in the Sefton, before winning Wetherby's West Yorkshire Hurdle on his reappearance. Emitom remains highly progressive and relishes soft ground.

ENEMY COAST AHEAD

5yo Malinas - Penang Princess (Act One)

Trainer:
Tom George

Owner:
McNeill Family

Optimum Conditions:
2m on decent ground

Career Form Figures:
1-

Jockey Adrian Heskin, who is the retained rider for owners the McNeill Family, missed a good chunk of last season through injury, and one young horse who I suspect that he will be looking forward to getting aboard is the once-raced Enemy Coast Ahead.

The five-year-old made a winning racecourse debut in a bumper at Stratford in late-March, when partnered by Tom George's son, Noel. Held up just worse than mid-field for the first half of the race, the Malinas gelding moved smoothly into contention and was still on the bridle when cruising to the front on the home bend. Asked to quicken up, he did just that and quickly shot clear, putting the race to bed in a matter of strides. Pushed out, he strode right away to score by an eased-down ten lengths. The form is difficult to evaluate, although the third home had earlier finished much closer when twice placed and, visually, the winner was very impressive.

Given the pace he showed, Enemy Coast Ahead might be at his best when the emphasis is on speed at this stage, and with that in mind, could be one to catch in the early part of the season. That said, his pedigree suggests he will handle softer ground and he looks a nice type for novice hurdles.

LEADING PROSPECTS

ENVOI ALLEN

5yo Muhtathir - Reaction (Saint des Saints)

Trainer:
Gordon Elliott

Owner:
Cheveley Park Stud

Optimum Conditions:
2m+ on easy ground

Career Form Figures:
1/1111-

Cheveley Park Stud invested heavily in National Hunt stock prior to last season and were rewarded with a brace of Cheltenham Festival winners, and an Aintree winner for good measure. So used to success at the top level on the Flat, they saw their red, white and blue silks carried to victory on day one at Cheltenham by A Plus Tard, and Envoi Allen made it two winners in as many days when successful in the Weatherbys Champion Bumper.

In fairness, the owners had paid £400,000 to secure him 13 months earlier, following a ten-length maiden Point success for Colin Bowe, and he quickly made his mark under Rules, winning bumpers at Fairyhouse and Navan (Listed) in December.

He completed the hat-trick in workmanlike fashion in the Grade 2 at the Dublin Racing Festival, before maintaining his 100% record at Cheltenham. He stayed on really strongly on the run to the line and shapes as though he will relish an extra half-mile once sent hurdling.

The Champion Bumper form has already been franked, with Abacadabras (4th) going close at Punchestown and The Glancing Queen (5th) winning the mares' Grade 2 at Aintree, and connections of the good-looking Envoi Allen will be hoping that he is back at Cheltenham in March. Prominent in the betting for all three novice hurdles, the Ballymore would appeal as the most likely target at this stage.

FAUSTINOVICK

5yo Black Sam Bellamy - Cormorant Cove (Fair Mix)

Trainer:
Colin Tizzard

Owner:
Taylor & O'Dwyer

Optimum Conditions:
2m+ on soft ground

Career Form Figures:
2/2-

Representing the connections of one of last year's *Leading Prospects*, Lostintranslation, the imposing Faustinovick made a hugely encouraging debut under Rules at Newbury in March, when runner-up to subsequent Grade 2 winner McFabulous.

Held up by Robbie Power, the Black Sam Bellamy gelding was keen in the early part of the race and still had eight horses in front of him as the field straightened up for home. Despite showing distinct signs of greenness and not enjoying the clearest of passages, he ran on well when the gap finally came and the penny dropped, finishing six lengths behind the penalised winner. He also looked to have quite a pronounced knee action, so it might be that he will improve for meeting easier ground this season.

The ground was certainly easier when he finished runner-up in a maiden Irish Point last March, again beaten six lengths. Runner-up to impressive Down Royal bumper winner Andy Dufresne, Faustinovick again appeared to race a shade keenly but jumped well in the main and was just getting the better of long-time leader Conflated – a bumper winner for Gigginstown House Stud – when he came down two out.

When he returns, he looks capable of winning a bumper before going over hurdles, should connections persist down that route. Once he learns to relax, he could well develop into a really nice type and his long-term future certainly lies over fences.

FONTSANTA

6yo Flemensfirth - Day's Over (Overbury)

Trainer:
Emma Lavelle

Owner:
Tim Syder

Optimum Conditions:
3m on any ground

Career Form Figures:
14/551-

The winner of a Fontwell bumper the season before last, Fontsanta has been a headstrong individual in the past – wore a hood on both bumper starts – but is learning to relax now and ended last season with an emphatic 11-length success at Hereford.

He made his debut over hurdles in a competitive novice event at Newbury just before Christmas (sent off 100-1), and having been anchored out the back by Aidan Coleman, gradually worked his way into the race; it was an encouraging introduction.

Given a similar ride at Chepstow next time, he again travelled like a nice prospect and finished on the heels of another of this year's *Leading Prospects*, Minella Bobo. Three of the quartet who finished in front of him won next time out (the runner-up won twice) and Fontsanta also got off the mark on his next – and final – start.

Well-supported in the market, the six-year-old had clearly benefited from those two initial runs. Ridden a shade closer on this occasion, he sat in behind travelling really well and cruised into the lead on the home bend. Without having to be asked any sort of question, he sauntered clear to score in some style.

Officially rated 134 after just those three hurdles starts, he will be heading down the novice chase route when he returns, and the imposing son of Flemensfirth looks built for fences.

GET IN THE QUEUE

5yo Mount Nelson - Amarullah (Daylami)

Trainer:
Harry Fry

Owner:
Paul & Clare Rooney

Optimum Conditions:
2m4f+ on any ground

Career Form Figures:
111-

Harry Fry has now saddled the winner of the valuable Goffs UK Spring Sale Bumper at Newbury for each of the past three seasons. The victory of Get In The Queue in March will long be remembered for being the final ride in the illustrious career of jockey Noel Fehily, who bowed out on a winning note, with the son of Mount Nelson completing a hat-trick of his own.

A winner at Uttoxeter on debut, the five-year-old marked himself down as a horse with an extremely bright future when following up by 16 lengths at Exeter, under a penalty. Visibility was poor (to say the least) that day, but Get In The Queue could be spotted going well at the top of the home straight and reappeared from the gloom in splendid isolation. He gave the runner-up 16lb and he won at Wetherby next time, whilst the third home also won on his next start, so the form looks strong.

Sent off at prohibitive odds at Newbury, he was quite workmanlike on this occasion, but shouldered a double-penalty and both the fourth and sixth won over hurdles during May to advertise the form.

He shapes as though he will want an extra half-mile once sent jumping in the autumn, but seems versatile with regards to ground conditions and should make his mark at a high level this season.

 LEADING PROSPECTS

GYPSY ISLAND

5yo Jeremy - Thieving Gypsy (Presenting)

Trainer:
Peter Fahey

Owner:
John P. McManus

Optimum Conditions:
2m+ on decent ground

Career Form Figures:
1211-1

A winner at Ballinrobe last August, Gypsy Island was sporting the silks of JP McManus when running in a maiden hurdle at Navan in late-November. Held up, she was set quite a task and only just failed. In hindsight, that defeat might well have been the making of her, as she reverted to bumpers and won another three.

A smooth winner at Naas in March, Gypsy Island took her form to another level on her final two outings, starting with an 11-length success in a Listed event at Fairyhouse. The race looked a strong event and she travelled like a dream into the straight, still on the bridle when taking up the running. Pushed out, she drew right away to score in emphatic fashion, and the form would be advertised by Colreevy (3rd), who won the Grade 1 against the boys at Punchestown.

Gypsy Island herself went on to Punchestown, where she again won in the manner of a potentially high-class mare. Ridden with utmost confidence, she came from way off the pace to join issue as they turned in, and quickly put the race to bed. The placed horses filled the frame at Aintree, so the form looks solid, and the winner can be expected to make up into a very smart novice hurdler. The Dawn Run at Cheltenham is the obvious spring target, although as she should get further, the 2m4f Grade 1 at Fairyhouse over Easter is another likely option.

HONEYSUCKLE

5yo Sulamani - First Royal (Lando)

Trainer:
Henry de Bromhead

Owner:
Kenneth Alexander

Optimum Conditions:
2m4f+ on decent ground

Career Form Figures:
1/1111-

Henry de Bromhead enjoyed Cheltenham Festival success with both A Plus Tard and Minella Indo in March, but was dealt a big blow in the build-up to the meeting, when Honeysuckle was ruled out of the Dawn Run.

The five-year-old headed the market at the time, following three wins from three starts over hurdles. Impressive in beating Moskovite (won her next two) on debut over 2m4f at Fairyhouse, she successfully dropped back in trip to win in Listed company at Thurles, where she beat Sassy Diva (winner of a handicap next time). She completed the hat-trick in the Grade 3 Solerina Novice Hurdle, when she had Tintangle (close-up third at Cheltenham) back in third and subsequent Grade 3 winner, Robin de Carlow, in fourth.

After missing the festival, Honeysuckle maintained her unbeaten record in Grade 1 company at Fairyhouse on Easter Sunday. Back up to 2m4f, she moved well and the result looked inevitable when she took up the running. Held together until after the penultimate flight, she quickened right away to win in authoritative fashion.

The obvious race to aim at this season would be the OLBG Mares' Hurdle, but given her Point-to-Point background, chasing is likely to be seriously considered. She jumped well when beating Annie Mc (winner of the Mares' Final at Newbury) by 15 lengths at Dromahane and if heading down the novice chase route, could well be up to taking on the boys, in receipt of the sex-allowance.

INTERCONNECTED

5yo Network - R de Rien Sivola (Robin des Champs)

Trainer:
Dan Skelton

Owner:
Darren & Annaley Yates

Optimum Conditions:
2m4f+ on decent ground

Career Form Figures:
F1/2-

Following his record-breaking sale during May (£620,000), you will struggle to hear or read the name of Interconnected without his price-tag being mentioned. To put it into context, he would need to win the Ballymore, the RSA, and then a King George and a Gold Cup to recoup the money that Darren Yates has spent on him. Quite whether the five-year-old can scale those heights is debatable, but there is no doubting his potential and he remains one of the brightest young National Hunt prospects.

Following his big-money purchase, the five-year-old was sent north to Philip Kirby, but it was announced in early-July that the owner was moving his jumps horses to Dan Skelton, highlighting a lack of luck – and being superstitious – as the main reason.

A 20-length winner of a Point-to-Point for Sophie Lacey – which prompted the now-defunct owners Grech & Parkin to shell out £220,000 in March 2018 – Interconnected only saw the track once for Nicky Henderson last season, when a highly promising second behind Emitom at Newbury.

A tall, good-looking son of Network, he is a half-brother to the useful Little Miss Poet and is very much a chaser on looks. However, given that he remains a maiden, it will be a surprise if he doesn't spend the full season in novice hurdle company and he could well take fairly high rank. The Leamington Novices' Hurdle – a race which his new trainer has won twice in the past five years – is a likely mid-season target.

L'AIR DU VENT

5yo Coastal Path - Bleu Perle (Pistolet Bleu)

Trainer:
Colin Tizzard

Owner:
Brocade Racing

Optimum Conditions:
2m+ on decent ground

Career Form Figures:
F1-

Colin Tizzard and Brocade Racing have teamed up for big-race success over the years with the likes of Hey Big Spender, Golden Chieftain and, of course, 2018 Cheltenham Gold Cup winner Native River. Whilst it is impossible to make comparisons with that trio at this stage of his career, L'Air du Vent did something which that trio were unable to, in that he was successful in a bumper, at Bangor in April.

A faller on his sole start between the flags (when travelling well, in behind Nicky Henderson's impressive Kempton Bumper winner Shishkin), the son of Coastal Path – who is a half-brother to Si C'Etait Vrai – was sent off favourite for the second division of a good-ground bumper. It didn't look the strongest race on paper (three non-runners due to the ground) and both the bunch finish and slow time would suggest it wasn't strongly run, but L'Air du Vent impressed with how he moved under Jonjo O'Neill Jnr. Still on the bridle when poking his nose in front up the inside rail, he showed a nice turn of foot to put the race to bed and won with plenty to spare.

Much tougher tasks lie ahead, but he created a really good impression at Bangor, and aside from Master Debonair – who scored at Listed level before finishing fifth at Aintree – L'Air du Vent was Tizzard's only bumper winner last season.

MALONE ROAD

5yo Kalanisi – Zaffarella (Zaffaran)

Trainer:
Gordon Elliott

Owner:
Cheveley Park Stud

Optimum Conditions:
2m+ on easy ground

Career Form Figures:
1/11-

Before Envoi Allen had made his debut under Rules, the same connections had seen another expensive purchase (£325,000) win a brace of bumpers. A maiden Point winner at Loughanmore for Stuart Crawford, Malone Road ran out an impressive winner of a bumper at Down Royal's big meeting in early-November. The five-year-old made all at a relatively sedate pace and quickly asserted, once asked to pick up. He drew seven lengths clear of Valdieu, who subsequently won a bumper and a maiden hurdle.

It was a similar story at Punchestown just 15 days later, although Jamie Codd was happy to take a lead on this occasion. He tracked his main market rival Mt Leinster, but once taking over on the home bend, Malone Road once again drew clear in the manner of a very smart prospect. The runner-up was beaten a similar distance by Envoi Allen at Leopardstown in February, whilst we didn't get to see the winner again, who met with a setback (knee injury) shortly after that second success.

A half-brother to both Ravenhill Road and Windsor Avenue, he looks to possess more speed than that pair and should have little trouble in winning a maiden hurdle over the minimum trip on his return. Connections will then, no doubt, be keen to keep him and Envoi Allen apart whenever possible, with both looking exciting prospects for the novice hurdle division.

MCFABULOUS

5yo Milan - Rossavon (Beneficial)

Trainer:
Paul Nicholls

Owner:
Giraffa Racing

Optimum Conditions:
2m+ on easy ground

Career Form Figures:
1711-

A winner on debut at Chepstow last October, McFabulous stayed on strongly to beat Ask Dillon and Lisnagar Oscar, having raced prominently throughout. The placed horses both went on to win twice over hurdles, the latter scoring in Grade 2 company before finishing fifth in the Albert Bartlett and third in the Sefton.

Given a break after disappointing at Cheltenham in November (falsely run race in which he reportedly struggled coming down the hill), McFabulous returned to action at Newbury when more positive tactics were once again employed and again displayed a fine attitude to fend off a host of challengers up the home straight.

Sent to Aintree for the Grade 2 the following month, he had no trouble in handling the softer ground. Coming from off the pace, he came wide up the home straight and again showed a very willing attitude to beat Thebannerkingrebel (already won twice over hurdles) by a length.

Being a half-brother to the high-class Waiting Patiently and the ill-fated Walking In The Air, McFabulous is bred to relish another half-mile or more, and his running style also suggests that he won't have a problem going up in trip. It could also be that he is at his best with some juice in the ground and is certainly one to look forward to over hurdles.

MIDNIGHT RUN

5yo Well Chosen - Knockamullen Girl (Alderbrook)

Trainer:
Joseph Patrick O'Brien

Owner:
Gigginstown House Stud

Optimum Conditions:
2m+ on decent ground

Career Form Figures:
121-

It was announced during May that powerful owners Gigginstown House Stud would be winding down their operation and would no longer be in the market for purchasing young stock. Whilst this will clearly have a detrimental impact on the bloodstock market and, potentially, on the sport as a whole in Ireland, it will be a number of years before their famous silks will no longer be seen on course. As ever, they have plenty to look forward to this season, and one youngster who could make a big splash for them is dual-bumper winner Midnight Run.

The son of Well Chosen – who is a full-brother to Willie Mullins' three-time Grade 1-placed Carefully Selected – won a Galway bumper before being purchased by Gigginstown and made a pleasing debut for his new owners at Navan in mid-December. Despite being beaten, he shaped really well behind subsequent Champion Bumper winner Envoi Allen, pulling five lengths clear of Run Wild Fred, who went on to win bumpers at Fairyhouse and Limerick.

Midnight Run returned to winning ways at Naas in February, where he travelled all over his rivals and ran out a convincing winner. His brother actually won the same race 12 months earlier and looks to possess the ability to make up into a smart novice hurdler. Given his pedigree, he might want 2m4f or further in time.

MINELLA BOBO

6yo Oscar - Line Kendie (Bonnet Rouge)

Trainer:
Rebecca Curtis

Owner:
Moran, Outhart, McDermott, Hyde & Hill

Optimum Conditions:
2m6f+ on any ground

Career Form Figures:
1/6241-

Rebecca Curtis did well with Drovers Lane in novice chases last season, and Minella Bobo looks cut from a similar cloth. Like his stablemate, he is a son of Oscar and a former winning Irish Pointer who progressed steadily over hurdles, and it wasn't until Stratford in mid-April that he got off the mark.

Having travelled well in a Newbury bumper on his debut for current connections, the grey finished runner-up to Nadaitak (winner of the Grade 2 River Don) at Doncaster, with Weakfield (winner of a handicap off 109) a further 19 lengths back in fourth. He again travelled best for a long way, and it was a similar story when fourth at Chepstow, where he finished in front of easy Hereford winner Fontsanta.

Liosduin Bhearna finished runner-up at Chepstow and following a couple of handicap wins is now rated 132. Minella Bobo had beaten that rival in his maiden Point at Inch and his season ended on a winning note, when winning a weak event by 18 lengths. Thankfully, the handicapper left him on a mark of 126, and with another summer to strengthen up, plus the prospect of improvement for jumping fences, it will be disappointing if he can't make his mark this term. He is one to catch in a novices' handicap first time out and it wouldn't surprise me if he headed to Hereford for the race which Drovers Lane won last season.

 LEADING PROSPECTS

MOONLIGHTER

6yo Midnight Legend - Countess Camilla (Bob's Return)

Trainer:
Jane Williams

Owner:
Mrs Jane Williams, Huw & Richard Davies

Optimum Conditions:
2m4f+ on easy ground and a galloping track

Career Form Figures:
16/31F7-

A bumper winner at Bangor, Moonlighter returned to the North Wales track and made an encouraging debut over hurdles last October, finishing third in a race that worked out reasonably well. The imposing six-year-old appreciated the extra three furlongs when getting off the mark at Ascot, impressing with how he travelled and jumped.

Lizzie Kelly opted to make all at Ascot and the pair always looked in control. Asked to stretch in the home straight, he really came up at the final two flights and was always holding the runner-up. On the back of that likeable performance, Moonlighter headed to Newbury for a competitive-looking novices' hurdle and, despite shouldering a penalty, was in the process of running another big race when crashing out at the second-last. There were plenty of future winners in behind Tidal Flow that day and Moonlighter looked sure to play a hand in the finish.

His final outing came back at Ascot in January, when he faded and was beaten a long way. Held up, he made a big move halfway down the back and it could be that the way the race unfolded didn't suit. He was also extremely keen, so I'm prepared to put a line through the run, and judged on his earlier form he is one to look forward to over fences. From a mark of 133, Moonlighter is another to note in novices' handicap company.

MR GREY SKY

5yo Fame And Glory - Lakil Princess (Bering)

Trainer:
Kim Bailey

Owner:
Mr P. J. Andrews

Optimum Conditions:
2m4f+ on soft ground

Career Form Figures:
11-

Last season, trainer Kim Bailey broke the 50-winner marker for the first time in four years, and nine of his 51 winners came in bumpers, which bodes well for the future. Two of those nine victories came courtesy of the dual-Haydock scorer Mr Grey Sky.

The five-year-old seemed aptly named when making a winning racecourse debut at the Merseyside track, on what was a horrid afternoon in early-December. The light was fading and the ground was heavy, but Mr Grey Sky moved well and joined issue with Ebony Jewel early in the home straight. After a protracted battle with the eventual runner-up, he finally mastered him inside the final half-furlong and won going away, with the remainder of the field well strung out. Ebony Jewel was subsequently sold to Nick Alexander and bolted up in a bumper at Ayr on his first start for the stable.

Mr Grey Sky had already made it two-from-two by that point, returning to Haydock to defy a penalty just 25 days later. Again the ground was testing, and as he had on debut, he stayed on really well, doing his best work late on.

A half-brother to fellow *Leading Prospect* Danny Whizzbang, there is plenty of stamina in his pedigree, so he is likely to want a trip over hurdles, and being by Fame And Glory, he shouldn't have a problem in handling a sounder surface.

NICKOLSON

5yo No Risk At All - Incorrigible (Septieme Ciel)

Trainer:
Olly Murphy

Owner:
Tim Syder

Optimum Conditions:
2m4f+ on any ground

Career Form Figures:
1-

Of Olly Murphy's 82 winners last season, 14 were achieved in bumpers and one who is likely to be high up the pecking order is Ayr scorer Nickolson. A five-year-old by an improving young sire, No Risk At All, he made a winning debut in February, having been well supported beforehand.

Ridden patiently, Fergus Gregory moved Nickolson up into fourth down the far side and was still travelling powerfully as the field turned for home. Briefly short of room as the tempo increased, he was given time to regain his balance and was switched inside by his young rider. He found his stride once angled out and was in front by the furlong marker, before only needing to be punched out to win with a bit in hand.

The form of his success wouldn't amount to much at this stage, but he got the job done in a likeable manner, especially considering he was hampered early in the straight when seemingly about to press on. When he returns, I would expect Nickolson to head straight over hurdles and given both the way he finished his race and the fact that he is bred to get further, he should come into his own over 2m4f or beyond.

As was the case last season, Murphy seems to have a nice bunch of youngsters to send hurdling, and Nickolson can form part of that strong novice hurdle team.

OVERTHETOP

5yo Flemensfirth - Dawn Bid (Mazaad)

Trainer:
Olly Murphy

Owner:
What the Elle

Optimum Conditions:
2m4f+ on any ground

Career Form Figures:
11-

Another to look forward to in novice hurdles for Olly Murphy is Overthetop, who first took my eye when studying the catalogue for the Tattersalls Cheltenham sale last December. The son of Flemensfirth – who is a half-brother to both On Raglan Road and No No Manolito, a horse who featured in *Jumpers To Follow* after an impressive debut success in a bumper – had won a four-year-old Point under Jamie Codd at Ballindenisk.

Held up, he was still a long way off the pace approaching two out, but really picked up late on and was upsides thanks to a fine leap at the final fence. The placed horses went on to win three times between them, so the form looks decent.

Overthetop made his debut for current connections in a good-ground bumper at Warwick in late-April. Again held up, he raced wide down the far side and was forced four-wide into the straight, but he galloped on strongly and pulled away inside the final 100 yards. Given how the race unfolded, it was a good performance to win, and he promises to be suited by 2m4f or further once sent jumping.

The fourth-placed horse, The Swagman, advertised the form by winning at Newton Abbot, and Overthetop looks yet another nice young prospect from Warren Chase. He seems versatile in terms of ground and ought to have learnt plenty for that Warwick run.

LEADING PROSPECTS

PHOENIX WAY

6yo Stowaway - Arcuate (Arch)

Trainer:
Harry Fry

Owner:
John P. McManus

Optimum Conditions:
2m4f+ on any ground

Career Form Figures:
1/521-

We only got to see Phoenix Way on three occasions last season, and after an encouraging debut when fifth at Bangor, he finished a sound second at Sandown, where he made a serious error at the final flight down the far side. Given plenty of time to recover, he kept on well up the hill to the line, finishing in front of plenty of subsequent winners (seven of the eight horses who finished behind him went on to win no fewer than 12 races between them).

Phoenix Way himself won next time, when appearing to appreciate the step up in distance at Plumpton. Again ridden patiently, he latched onto the leading group on the run to two out and was upsides with a big leap at the last. He stayed on well to score with something to spare and, again, the race would work out well. Runner-up Third Wind won his next two including the EBF Final, whilst the third, fourth, fifth, eighth and ninth won eight races between them subsequently.

Kept off the track for the remainder of the season, the son of Stowaway is expected to return to action in the autumn, when he could either head down the handicap hurdle route or – more likely – head over fences. An impressive winner on his sole run in Irish Points, he is a smart chasing prospect, and from a mark of 133 is one to keep onside, whichever route is chosen.

RATHHILL

6yo Getaway - Bella Venezia (Milan)

Trainer:
Nicky Henderson

Owner:
John P. McManus

Optimum Conditions:
2m+ on any ground

Career Form Figures:
2/14-

Rather like Phoenix Way, Rathhill is another who wasn't seen after the first weekend of January, with his season curtailed following a disappointing run in the Grade 1 Tolworth Novices' Hurdle. The son of Getaway was struggling a long way from home and left the impression that he failed to give his running.

The six-year-old – who finished an eye-catching second in an Irish Point – had earlier won what turned out to be a very competitive Newbury maiden, and won it in impressive fashion. Ridden with confidence and patience by Barry Geraghty, he was finessed into contention on the run to the final flight. Still on the bridle after the last, he only had to be nudged out to score in the manner of a potentially smart prospect, and those in behind franked the form. The runner-up failed to win, but stablemate Pistol Whipped (3rd) won at Fakenham; Dashel Drasher (4th) won four times; Umndeni (5th) won twice; and So Lonely (8th) won three times in the spring.

Given the impression he created that day, Rathhill remains a very bright prospect and it is hoped that he returns in that kind of form when he reappears this season. Yet to be handed a mark by the assessor, this might well determine which route is taken; a mark in the low 140s could tempt his connections to have a tilt at something like the Greatwood, although he is unlikely to be rushed and might be one for later in the season.

RESERVE TANK

5yo Jeremy - Lady Bellamy (Black Sam Bellamy)

Trainer:
Colin Tizzard

Owner:
The Reserve Tankers

Optimum Conditions:
2m4f+ on decent ground

Career Form Figures:
37111-1

Having had just the two starts before Christmas, Reserve Tank improved considerably in the second half of last season, with his four victories culminating with a second Grade 1 success at Punchestown. The winner of Aintree's Mersey Novices' Hurdle prior to that, Colin Tizzard stated that his five-year-old had been suffering with ulcers after his disappointing second run at Newbury and was deliberately freshened up, with a spring campaign in mind.

A chasing type on looks, he had shaped with promise on debut at Chepstow and returned from more than three months off to beat Elusive Belle (won again afterwards) over 2m at Sandown. He stayed on really strongly from two out and duly relished the step up to 2m5f when following up at Kempton. Again, stamina won the day.

Different tactics were deployed at Aintree, where he raced prominently and fended off a strong field. A couple of lengths clear two out, he again stayed strongly to see off Brewin'upastorm, and it was a similar story in Ireland where he took up the running three out and again showed a fantastic attitude to repel the challenge of Sams Profile.

His hurdling was very fluent at the business end of both Grade 1s and that should stand him in good stead as he heads over fences. He should take high rank in the novice chase division and could well follow a similar path to that taken by Lostintranslation last season.

RIBBLE VALLEY

6yo Westerner - Miss Greinton (Greinton)

Trainer:
Nicky Richards

Owner:
David Wesley Yates

Optimum Conditions:
2m+ on decent ground

Career Form Figures:
161-

The black and white silks of David Wesley Yates were made famous a few years ago by the high-class grey Monet's Garden, and the owner might just have another smart prospect on his hands in the shape of Ribble Valley.

Like Monet's Garden, the six-year-old is trained by Nicky Richards, and won twice, from three starts, in bumpers last term. The son of Westerner was ridden quietly when making a successful debut at Ayr last November. Having been eased into contention, Ribble Valley took up the running a couple of furlongs out and quickened up impressively, to score by seven lengths. The third advertised that form by winning next time, whilst Ribble Valley headed south to Cheltenham for his second start.

Only sixth of nine (just ½-a-length ahead of McFabulous), it was a messy race and certainly wasn't run to suit. Given the best part of two months off, he returned to Ayr and bounced back to winning ways, scoring comfortably. It was a similar performance to the one he had put up on debut and whilst he was probably entitled to win as he did, it was a decent effort under a penalty.

He looks to possess plenty of pace, so ought to start off over the minimum trip over hurdles and he rates a smart prospect for novice hurdles in the north. If he proves up to that level, he could be one for Aintree in the spring.

SHISHKIN

5yo Sholokhov - Labarynth (Exit To Nowhere)

Trainer:
Nicky Henderson

Owner:
Mrs J Donnelly

Optimum Conditions:
2m+ on good-to-soft ground

Career Form Figures:
3/11-

Twenty-four hours (well, 25½ to be precise) after Al Boum Photo carried the yellow and black chequered silks of Joe Donnelly to success in the Cheltenham Gold Cup, Shishkin did the same in the bumper at Kempton. In a race that Nicky Henderson has dominated (won it four times in the previous seven years, including with Mister Fisher in 2018), the Sholokhov gelding was sent off at odds-on to make a winning debut under Rules, and whilst it might not have been the strongest of races by the track's standards, he ran out a very taking winner.

A lengthy, unfurnished five-year-old, Shishkin made all and really picked up once asked to go about his business halfway up the home straight, and appeared full of running as he crossed the line.

Beaten into third on his Point debut, he got off the mark at the second time of asking in that sphere, scoring by eight lengths when ridden more positively. Out of a half-sister to the classy Voler La Vedette, Shishkin is bred to get a trip, but has a keen way of going and looks to have the pace to start over 2m, before going up in distance as and when Nicky Henderson sees fit. Given his physique, he appeals as the type to have done well for another summer at grass and will make a chaser in time.

SILVER HALLMARK

5yo Shirocco - Gaye Sophie (Environment Friend)

Trainer:
Fergal O'Brien

Owner:
Mr & Mrs William Rucker

Optimum Conditions:
2m4f+ on good-to-soft ground

Career Form Figures:
13-

Mr & Mrs Rucker – who have had some fine chasers down the years, none more so than State of Play – enjoyed 12 winners during the 2018-19 season, and they look to have a few really nice prospects for this season, one being the Fergal O'Brien-trained Silver Hallmark.

Given that I have already included McFabulous and Faustinovick amongst this year's *Leading Prospects*, it is safe to say that I thought the Newbury bumper in which he finished third looked to be a strong event. Held-up out the back, Silver Hallmark made up considerable ground up the home straight and – unsurprisingly, given his pedigree – was doing his best work late on.

A half-brother to the ill-fated mud-lover Gayebury, he is going to thrive once sent over 2m4f or beyond, and his Irish Points form reads really well, too. The winner of a strongly-run event at Tattersalls Farm last December, he beat Willie Butler (won a bumper for Neil King), with The Brass Man (bumper winner for Mags Mullins before joining Tom George) nine lengths away in third.

The trainer-owner combination has enjoyed some fantastic days with Alvarado and will be hoping that this grey son of Shirocco can fill the void, following his retirement at Cheltenham on New Year's Day. He looks capable of winning a bumper on his reappearance, although he will come into his own once upped in trip over hurdles.

TARADA

6yo Kayf Tara - Kerada (Astarabad)

Trainer:
Oliver Sherwood

Owner:
Mr Trevor Hemmings

Optimum Conditions:
2m4f+ on any ground

Career Form Figures:
221-

One of the nicest-looking horses I saw in the flesh last season, Tarada really took the eye when I saw him at Carlisle last November, ahead of his racecourse debut in a soft-ground bumper. He ran a sound race to chase home I K Brunel, ahead of his connections – who are renowned for their staying chasers – wasted no time in getting him over hurdles.

He jumped for the first time in public in a 2m3½f novices' hurdle at Chepstow in January and again shaped well, splitting Dashel Drasher (won his next three starts) and Walk In The Mill, who had won the Becher Chase on his previous start and would go on to finish fourth behind Tiger Roll in the Grand National.

Some seven weeks later, the scopey Tarada got off the mark at Fontwell. It wasn't the strongest of races in truth and he was entitled to win as he did, but he stayed on strongly to score by 10 lengths. Forced to miss the remainder of the season, he could be slightly later in returning to Oliver Sherwood's Rhonehurst stables, but hopefully that won't prevent him from continuing his progression when he reappears, as he remains completely unexposed. The six-year-old remains a lovely long-term prospect and it is hoped that he is sent chasing sooner rather than later.

THE GLANCING QUEEN

5yo Jeremy - Glancing (Kayf Tara)

Trainer:
Alan King

Owner:
Dingwall, Farrell, Hornsey & Murray

Optimum Conditions:
2m+ on any ground

Career Form Figures:
1/1351-

The winner of a maiden Point at Horse & Jockey in March of last year, The Glancing Queen made her debut under Rules in a Listed bumper at Cheltenham and defied her inexperience to beat Mega Yeats (won twice over hurdles) and Royal Illusion (twice a winner on the Flat), having travelled well in behind. She finished really strongly to score by one-and-a-quarter lengths.

The daughter of Jeremy – who is easily identifiable, given the big white blaze on her face – then faced the geldings on her next two starts, firstly at Ascot in December. Third behind Eden de Houx, she again travelled really well and despite receiving 3lb from all of her rivals, it should be remembered that she was shouldering a 4lb penalty.

Back to Cheltenham, she finished a respectable fifth in the Champion Bumper, before she won the Grade 2 – back against her own sex – at Aintree. She once again travelled like a dream and was still on the bridle when taking up the running two out. She kept on really well, and the form was advertised when Shantewe (5th) won at Hexham, whilst the placed horses filled the frame behind Gypsy Island at Punchestown.

Versatile in terms of ground, The Glancing Queen will get further in time, but certainly doesn't look short of pace and is likely to start off over the minimum trip. At this stage, connections surely have one eye on the Dawn Run at the Cheltenham Festival.

  LEADING PROSPECTS

THURLOE
THOROUGHBREDS

Since its establishment in 1995, Thurloe Thoroughbreds has gained a well-founded reputation for managing successful and enjoyable racing syndicates.

Thurloe partnerships, embracing both the Flat and National Hunt, have had victories at many of the sport's leading meetings with triumphs at Royal Ascot, Goodwood, the Epsom Derby meeting, York's Ebor fixture, Newmarket and Cheltenham.

Its stars have included the 2002 Champion Sprinter Kyllachy, dual Tote-Gold Trophy winner and top-class hurdler Geos, the fine sprinter, Baltic King, now at stud and the Group-class fillies Nanoushka, Ruby Rocket and Waterway Run.

Contact Us
Nicky and James Stafford
The Green, Shalbourne, Wiltshire, SN8 3PT
Tel: 01672 871776   Mob: 07967 555212
racing.thurloe@btopenworld.com
www.thurloethoroughbreds.com

Klassical Dream - will head down the Champion Hurdle route this season

ACROSS THE SEA

Form figures in red indicate Point-to-Point form

28

ALLAHO

5yo No Risk At All – Idaho Falls (Turgeon)

Trainer:
Willie Mullins

Owner:
Cheveley Park Stud

Optimum Conditions:
2m5f–3m on decent ground

Career Form Figures:
2/413-2

The Irish look to have a really strong bunch of 2m4f–3m novice chasers this season, and one of them is the Willie Mullins-trained Allaho, who twice hit the frame behind Minella Indo in Grade 1s during the spring.

Prior to that, the son of No Risk At All – who had finished runner-up in a Listed hurdle race in France before joining his powerful connections – had beaten the Albert Bartlett winner in the Grade 3 Surehaul Mercedez-Benz Novice Hurdle at Clonmel. That was a fine effort on what was his first start over hurdles in Ireland, having finished fourth in a bumper at Leopardstown over Christmas. He then shaped really well – for an inexperienced horse – in the Albert Bartlett and at Punchestown, and he might appreciate being dropped back a shade in distance over fences.

A tall, lengthy individual, Allaho certainly has the look of a chaser and should do well in novice company this season, as should stablemate **Carefully Selected**, who finished just one place behind him in the Irish Daily Mirror Novice Hurdle. Twice placed in Grade 1 bumpers, he made a belated winning reappearance over hurdles at Limerick, and given that he is seven, it is likely that the former winning Pointer will head straight over fences. He looks a thorough stayer, and although the RSA would be the more obvious target, Patrick Mullins might have one eye on the National Hunt Chase for him.

BATTLEOVERDOYEN

6yo Doyen – Battle Over (Sillery)

Trainer:
Gordon Elliott

Owner:
Gigginstown House Stud

Optimum Conditions:
2m–2m4f on decent ground

Career Form Figures:
1/111P-

Purchased for £235,000 in April 2017 on the back of a three-length maiden Point success at Loughanmore (beat Court Liability, who won his first four starts under Rules), we didn't get to see Battleoverdoyen until last November, when he won a bumper at Punchestown.

Given the time off and his age, he was immediately switched to hurdles and looked a potential star when scoring by 13 lengths at Navan. Prominent throughout, he took up the running halfway through the 2m maiden and really began to lengthen away approaching the second-last. He powered clear to score with any amount in hand, with his hurdling a particular highlight.

Straight into Grade 1 company, Battleoverdoyen maintained his 100% record in the Lawlor's of Naas Novice Hurdle in early-January. Upped half-a-mile in trip, the six-year-old again jumped well – particularly two out – and stayed on strongly to beat Sam's Profile by the best part of three lengths.

Sent off favourite for the Ballymore, he never looked comfortable at Cheltenham and it is possible that the track didn't suit. After just one start there, it is hard to be conclusive, but given the earlier impression created, I would expect Battleoverdoyen to bounce back in novice chase company this season. Not short of speed, he would be quick enough to win over the minimum trip and probably doesn't need to go further than 2m4f at this stage.

BIGBADANDBEAUTIFUL

5yo Big Bad Bob – Playing Around (Act One)

Trainer:
Gordon Elliott

Owner:
Andrew Bedford

Optimum Conditions:
2m4f+ on decent ground

Career Form Figures:
32-1

A big – and aptly-named – mare with a stout pedigree, Bigbadandbeautiful showed progressive form in bumpers last season and duly got off the mark at Clonmel in mid-May. Given her earlier form, she was entitled to win, but could hardly have created a better impression, scoring with the minimum of fuss. She tracked the pace until the two-furlong marker, when taking over and striding right away, without having to be asked any sort of question by Jamie Codd.

Earlier in the campaign, she had finished third behind stablemate The Very Man on debut and then chased home Santa Rossa in the mares' Grade 2 event at the Dublin Racing Festival. On both occasions she stayed on really strongly, suggesting that she could improve considerably over longer distances, once sent hurdling.

A half-sister to Kim Bailey's Dandy Dan (won three times over fences last season, between 3m and 3m2f), the grey is bred to want a trip and her pedigree also suggests that she will be at her best on a sound surface.

Another mare from the stable to note is Punchestown Festival winner **Ard Abhainn**. The daughter of Jeremy could be aimed at the Listed Mucklemeg bumper at Gowran, before she goes hurdling, whilst fellow festival winner **Festival d'Ex** – who won the Goffs Land Rover Bumper by ten lengths – also deserves a mention. He looks a stayer and forms part of a very strong novice hurdle team in the Elliott stable.

CHACUN POUR SOI

7yo Policy Maker – Kruscyna (Ultimately Lucky)

Trainer:
Willie Mullins

Owner:
Mrs S Ricci

Optimum Conditions:
2m on decent ground

Career Form Figures:
1253/1-1

Almost three years to the day after finishing third behind King's Socks in a four-year-old chase at Enghien, Chacun Pour Soi made his debut for Willie Mullins and Rich Ricci, in a 2m beginners' chase at Naas.

Sent straight to the front by Paul Townend, the lightly-raced seven-year-old jumped with aplomb, and having strode clear down the far side, kept the gallop up all the way to the line, to score in emphatic fashion.

On to Punchestown, and with Townend riding the Arkle winner Duc des Genievres and Ruby Walsh having retired some 24 hours earlier, it was Robbie Power who steered him to another impressive victory, this time in the Grade 1 Ryanair Novice Chase. Held-up on this occasion, he again jumped really well and had joined issue with his stablemate on the turn for home. Kicked clear two out, he had too much speed for JLT winner Defi du Seuil from the back of the last and made it two-from-two in Ireland.

To beat two Cheltenham Festival winners on the back of just that one run suggests that Chacun Pour Soi could be something special, and with the prospect of Altior going up in distance, it could be that he emerges as a serious contender for the Champion Chase. Mullins believes he will stay further, too, so his future looks very bright, provided that he can be kept sound.

 ACROSS THE SEA

CITY ISLAND

6yo Court Cave – Victorine (Un Desperado)

Trainer:
Martin Brassil

Owner:
Sean & Bernardine Mulryan

Optimum Conditions:
2m4f+ on any ground

Career Form Figures:
2/11D111-6

Having originally thought that City Island could develop into a Stayers' Hurdle contender, it would now appear that Martin Brassil's six-year-old is being considered for a novice chase campaign, and he is yet another smart prospect in what promises to be a deep division.

Having later been disqualified from a maiden hurdle which he won at Galway in August, the son of Court Cave beat Dallas des Pictons (won his next two starts) at Leopardstown over Christmas. Kept to a low level, his Ballymore prep came in a weak-looking novice event at Naas, which he duly won with the minimum of fuss.

Despite having been kept away from the Graded events on home soil, City Island was still sent off 8-1 – and just fourth in the market – at the festival. He travelled really well for Mark Walsh, staying on strongly to fend off Aintree winner Champ by two lengths.

Clearly not at his best at Punchestown, he looks quick enough to begin his chasing career over 2m4f on his return. He could actually be kept to intermediate trips for the time being, and should he be out early in the season, the Drinmore could become his first major target. The Flogas Novice Chase would be another likely Grade 1 target, whilst the Hatton's Grace would appeal as the obvious starting point, should there be a re-think and he were to remain over hurdles.

CONCERTISTA

5yo Nathaniel – Zagzig (Selkirk)

Trainer:
Willie Mullins

Owner:
Simon Munir & Isaac Souede

Optimum Conditions:
2m+ on decent ground

Career Form Figures:
2-

A good-ground winner over ten furlongs on the Flat in France, Concertista made her debut over hurdles in the Dawn Run Novices' Hurdle at Cheltenham and very nearly caused a huge shock.

Sent off at 66-1, the five-year-old – rather like the winner – came from a long way off the pace and made stealthy headway down the far side. Still on the bridle when getting even closer two out, she travelled supremely well into the home straight and was produced to lead jumping the final flight. It appeared as though her challenge had been timed to perfection, only for her stablemate Eglantine du Seuil to get up on the line, providing Noel Fehily with a final Cheltenham Festival winner.

Despite the starting price of the front two, there was no suggestion of this run being a fluke, especially given how she travelled through the race. The form was also well advertised, with the first and sixth filling the places behind Honeysuckle at Fairyhouse. That pair also franked the form again at Punchestown, with the winner finishing third behind Reserve Tank and Elfile winning the Listed mares' novice hurdle by ten lengths.

When she returns, Concertista will be very difficult to beat in a mares' maiden and her season is likely to be geared around attempting to go one place better in the Dawn Run. She is open to any amount of improvement after just the one run.

DALLAS DES PICTONS

6yo Spanish Moon – Nadia des Pictons (Video Rock)

Trainer:
Gordon Elliott

Optimum Conditions:
2m4f–3m on decent ground

Owner:
Gigginstown House Stud

Career Form Figures:
41/1421120-

Twice a winner of AQPS races in France when trained by Alain Couetil, Dallas des Pictons developed into a smart novice hurdler last season, and although he failed to cope with the rise in class in the Sefton Novices' Hurdle, he remains a smart prospect for fences.

The son of Spanish Moon was reported to have lost his action at Aintree and was also a shade disappointing on his debut in Ireland, when only fourth at Naas. He soon left that behind, chasing home subsequent Ballymore winner City Island at Leopardstown, before getting off the mark over 2m4f at Punchestown.

Upped to 3m, he returned to Leopardstown for the Dublin Racing Festival, where he stayed on well to win the William Fry Handicap Hurdle, off a mark of 130. This prompted an antepost gamble for the Martin Pipe at Cheltenham, in which he travelled like a dream, despite the drop in trip. He finished runner-up in the end, but still shaped like a future Grade 1 performer to my eyes, and when he returns, he could well develop into a leading contender for top honours in the novice chase division.

Gigginstown and Gordon Elliott also have **Commander of Fleet** for the same division, whilst it is expected that **Samcro** and **Felix Desjy** will also now head over fences. The former is a thorough stayer, whilst the other pair will be campaigned over shorter. That is a strong-looking crop of novice chasers.

KLASSICAL DREAM

5yo Dream Well – Klassical Way (Septieme Ciel)

Trainer:
Willie Mullins

Optimum Conditions:
2m+ on easy ground

Owner:
Mrs Joanne Coleman

Career Form Figures:
P324P/111-1

Fourth in the Grade 1 Prix Cambaceres when trained in France, Klassical Dream has won all four starts for Willie Mullins, three of which were achieved at the top-level.

A winner at Leopardstown over Christmas, he returned to the same track to narrowly defeat stablemate Aramon in the Chanelle Pharma Novice Hurdle. He travelled really powerfully in the hands of Ruby Walsh and skipped clear with a fast leap two out. Headed after the final flight, the five-year-old knuckled down in determined fashion to get back up.

He clearly took another big step forward when running out a really impressive winner of the Supreme Novices' Hurdle, having played up a little beforehand. He again travelled with real zest and having pulled himself upsides, he jumped on at the fourth-last. Seemingly in control on the run to the second-last, he picked up strongly as they turned for home and lengthened right away up the hill, to score in fine style. It could well be that he enjoyed the softer ground on this occasion.

On to Punchestown, where he completed the four-timer – and the Grade 1 hat-trick – in the Herald Champion Novice Hurdle. Visually not as impressive, it has to be remembered that this was his fourth start in four months and he still readily put Aintree winner Felix Desjy in his place. He will now head down the Champion Hurdle route and he remains open to considerable improvement.

 ACROSS THE SEA

LONGHOUSE POET

5yo Yeats – Moscow Madame (Moscow Society)

Trainer:
Martin Brassil

Owner:
Sean & Bernardine Mulryan

Optimum Conditions:
2m4f on decent ground

Career Form Figures:
1-1

The winner of a maiden Point at Boulta when in the care of Sam Curling, Longhouse Poet made his debut for Martin Brassil in the 2m2f bumper at the Punchestown Festival, where he ran out a taking winner from another winner between the flags, Monkfish.

Having led early, the five-year-old son of Yeats dropped back a little under Derek O'Connor – who also rode him to win his Point – but he could be spotted travelling strongly in behind, and once the opening arrived, he eased through to the lead on the home bend. Asked to win his race, he really stayed on strongly to score in the manner of a horse with a very bright future.

The strength of the form is difficult to evaluate, but it was hard not to be impressed by the manner of success and he represents the powerful connections of last season's Ballymore winner, City Island. The owners actually sponsor that Cheltenham novice contest, so if Longhouse Poet looks like developing into a Graded-class novice, they are likely to have that race in mind.

Both his pedigree and the way he won his bumper suggest that he will want at least 2m4f to be seen at his best over hurdles, and he rates another exciting prospect for his shrewd trainer, who also enjoyed big race success with the likes of Numbersixvalverde, Nickname and Double Seven in recent years.

MINELLA INDO

6yo Beat Hollow – Carrigeen Lily (Supreme Leader)

Trainer:
Henry de Bromhead

Owner:
Barry Maloney

Optimum Conditions:
3m on any ground

Career Form Figures:
13/321-1

Third in a bumper at the 2018 Punchestown Festival (finished just behind City Island) on his first start for current connections, Minella Indo made his debut over hurdles at Limerick during the festive period, finishing third over 2m4f.

Upped in both trip and class for his next start, he was ridden more positively in a Grade 3 at Clonmel over 3m. Partnered for the first time by Rachael Blackmore, the son of Beat Hollow travelled well on the front end and was only collared after the last by Allaho, to whom he was conceding 3lb.

Despite being a maiden, he was allowed to take his chance in the Albert Bartlett, where he appeared to be racing keenly from an early stage. He still appeared to be running away when joining the lead at the top of the hill, but this didn't prevent him from seeing the race out and he shed his maiden tag on the biggest stage.

He confirmed the form with another strong-staying performance at Punchestown and now rates a very exciting prospect for fences. It looks a competitive division in Ireland, but whilst some of those previously mentioned could be effective over shorter, Minella Indo really does look a 3m-chaser and is likely to develop into a leading contender for the RSA Chase. He made a nice shape when winning his Point and is certainly in the right hands to exploit that jumping technique.

SAMS PROFILE

5yo Black Sam Bellamy – Lucylou (Bob Back)

Trainer:
Mouse Morris

Owner:
Michael O'Flynn & John O'Flynn

Optimum Conditions:
2m4f+ on easy ground

Career Form Figures:
13/1225-2

Another of what appears to be a strong-looking crop of staying novice chasers in Ireland this season, Sams Profile won just once over hurdles last term, but he fared well in Graded company thereafter and has the scope to make up into a better chaser.

A maiden Point winner, he went on to finish third in the four-year-old bumper at the 2018 Punchestown Festival, and made a winning hurdling debut over 2m at Cork last November. He stayed on strongly up the home straight to beat Éclair de Beaufeau (won twice before finishing fourth in the Ladbrokes Hurdle) by three lengths.

Upped in trip, he returned to Cork for a Grade 3 over 3m, where he found only the more-experienced Derrinross too strong. Dropped back to 2m4f on quicker ground, he again ran a sound race at Naas, when chasing home Battleoverdoyen, setting up a crack at the Ballymore.

He travelled well at Cheltenham and lost his hind legs when upsides Champ two out. He didn't appear to have the pace of the front four in the closing stages, but again kept on really well and again hinted that he might want 3m this season.

There was still time for one more run, and Sams Profile went down by just half-a-length to Aintree winner Reserve Tank at the Punchestown Festival. It was another fine effort and he is another likely contender for the RSA Chase.

THE VERY MAN

5yo Jeremy – Mill Meadow (Kalanisi)

Trainer:
Gordon Elliott

Owner:
Gigginstown House Stud

Optimum Conditions:
2m–2m4f on decent ground

Career Form Figures:
F/117-

An impressive winner of a maiden Point at Loughanmore last May, The Very Man also created a really good impression on his debut under Rules, in a bumper at Navan.

His Points form reads quite well, with the second, Jasmin des Bordes, shaping with promise for David Pipe, whilst Ash Hill (5th) won a bumper at Leopardstown over Christmas and a maiden hurdle in the summer. He showed plenty of pace to win that day and it was a similar story when beating Neptune (also won at Leopardstown's Christmas fixture) and stablemate Bigbadandbeautiful at Navan. The son of Jeremy clearly wasn't inconvenienced by the lack of pace and quickened up in style, having moved smoothly under Lisa O'Neill.

Off the track for more than four months, he returned at Fairyhouse on Easter Monday, and with stablemate Andy Dufresne a non-runner, he was sent off favourite. Struggling with half-a-mile to run, he quickly dropped away and this clearly wasn't his running.

When he returns, he can hopefully leave this run behind and make up into a smart novice hurdler, as he certainly looked to possess plenty of ability in his earlier races.

The same connections also have **Abacadabras** to look forward to in this division, and given how he travelled in his races last season, I wouldn't be surprised to see some sort of headgear applied at some stage. He clearly has a big engine, too.

 ACROSS THE SEA

BRIAN ELLISON RACING CLUB
◆◆◆◆◆

The Brian Ellison Racing Club is an exclusive membership-only club formed by Brian and Claire in 2017. For a one-off annual payment of £249.99 members can enjoy a taste of ownership and experience the thrills and emotions involved, without having to pay the, sometimes substantial, fees normally associated with racehorse ownership.

Members will become one of the connections of a minimum of five horses – the club currently has 15 horses - trained by Brian, all of which will carry the club's black and white diamond colours.

As Brian trains both flat and national hunt horses, members are guaranteed racing year round. Application for race day owners' badges when the club has a horse running and entitlement to discounted badges when available, the opportunity to meet the trainer, team and horses during exclusive members-only stable visits are just a few of the perks offered with this membership.

Winning Horses

Exceptional Five Star Benefits

Friendly Community

So what are you waiting for?
Sign up today and be a part of the exciting new Brian Ellison Racing Club. Upon completion of a 12 month's membership period, any member wishing to renew will receive a special loyalty discount off their next subscription.
Visit: www.brianellisonracingclub.co.uk or call: 07757 668349 for more information!

Return Ticket - a potentially smart chaser for Ruth Jefferson

AROUND THE YARDS

NICK ALEXANDER

Ebony Jewel

Runner-up to subsequent winner Mr Grey Sky on debut at Haydock, Ebony Jewel was bought for £70,000 and duly made a successful first appearance for his new connections in a bumper at Ayr during March. The son of Westerner raced enthusiastically and stretched clear to score by 12 lengths in soft ground. Well-supported, Ebony Jewel was then sent off just third in the betting for the Grade 2 bumper at Aintree, but always seemed to be doing a bit too much in front, appearing to over-race from the off. With that in mind, he probably did well to keep the lead until the final couple of furlongs, when he began to fade, eventually coming home in sixth place.

If he can learn to relax in the early part of his races, there is every chance that he can develop into a smart novice hurdler in the north. Clearly at home on soft ground, he is likely to start off over the minimum trip and his style of racing will help in small-field events, when he will be able to dominate from the front.

Elvis Mail

Twice a winner over hurdles last season (both wins coming at Kelso), Elvis Mail will begin the season on a mark of 132 and is one to note in handicap company. Following an eye-catching fourth on debut (sent off 66-1 over an extended 2m4f on heavy ground), he appreciated the less demanding test at Kelso over the festive period, as he had the race sewn up a long way from home. Following solid efforts in defeat behind Galvin (who finished 6th in the Ballymore) at Ayr and when third to Rouge Vif in the Premier Kelso Novices' Hurdle, the five-year-old rounded off a very good campaign with another easy victory at Kelso.

The son of Great Pretender is a half-brother to Donald Whillans' Dali Mail and shapes as though he might be best served by a strongly-run race over 2m, with a bit of cut in the ground. He looks capable of adding to his tally and will jump a fence in time.

KIM BAILEY

First Flow

We only got to see First Flow once last season, when fifth on his belated reappearance in the Imperial Cup during March. The seven-year-old shaped as though he would benefit for the outing and was actually declared to make his chase debut at Uttoxeter in early May. Pulled out due to the ground being too quick, he can be expected to embark on a chasing career when he returns, and judged on his novice form from the previous season, will be of interest on soft ground. Twice a winner on heavy ground, it should be remembered that he beat Midnight Shadow by 10 lengths in the Rossington Main at Haydock in January 2018.

Imperial Aura

Having shown plenty of promise in a couple of bumpers the previous season (a winner at the second time of asking at Ludlow), Imperial Aura continued his progression last season, winning both starts in novice hurdle company. Driven out to lead, he won on debut at Carlisle early on in the campaign, before making it two-from-two at Newcastle, some four months later. Having travelled much more smoothly, the six-year-old wasn't hard pressed to concede weight all around, and the form of his Carlisle success worked out well during the spring, with the runner-up winning three times in Ireland, whilst the third home has also won twice over hurdles.

Given the fact that he has raced just the twice over hurdles to date, I would expect Imperial Aura to return in a handicap hurdle, and from a mark of 133 he would certainly warrant plenty of respect. Looking back at his bumper form, he split Beakstown and Getaway Trump at Kempton on debut and appeals as the type who will continue to progress with racing.

Prince Llewelyn

Runner-up at Ascot on debut, Prince Llewelyn made all and showed a fine attitude when winning his bumper at Wetherby in early January. Challenged all the way up the home straight, the five-year-old kept on in determined fashion to fend off several subsequent winners, with the second, fourth and fifth all franking the form by winning later in the season. Runner-up to the exciting Get In The Queue at Newbury on his third and final start (form again franked, with the fourth and sixth winning over hurdles during May), he shapes as though he will improve as he goes up in distance this season. A good-looking chestnut by Schiaparelli, he looks sure to win more races once sent hurdling.

Shantou Express

Sent off favourite for a bumper at Ludlow on debut, Shantou Express finished runner-up in what might have been a decent event. The form has certainly worked out quite well, with the winner finishing runner-up in a mares' event at Cheltenham and the third winning his next three starts, and Shantou Express was attempting to give the winner 7lb. Having initially relinquished his lead before the home bend, he rallied gamely and shaped as though he would appreciate a stiffer test of stamina next time. When he returns, he ought to be capable of winning a bumper before he is sent hurdling.

PETER BOWEN

Equus Dancer

Showed progressive form in bumpers, shaping with promise behind Get In The Queue at Uttoxeter and then when fourth at Catterick (Peter Bowen later stated that the track was on the sharp side for him), Equus Dancer went on to win at Carlisle and Perth during the spring. He stayed on really strongly to win by 12 lengths at the Cumbrian track, before making most to defy a penalty in Scotland. The five-year-old – who was a faller when holding every chance two out in his Point-to-Point – shapes as though he will relish an extra half-mile or further once sent jumping and ought to come into his own when the emphasis is more on stamina.

JENNIE CANDLISH

Cheddleton

The success of Big Time Dancer in the Lanzarote Hurdle was the clear highlight among the 20 winners saddled by Jennie Candlish last season and her sole bumper winner during the campaign was Cheddleton. In fact, the four-year-old is the trainer's only winner in that sphere during the past five seasons and whilst he might have only beaten two horses in a soft-ground contest at Haydock, he travelled through the race like a nice horse and looks to have a bright future. By Shirocco, he is out of the useful mare Over Sixty (won five times from 16 starts for Alan King) and is a half-brother to Spirit Of Kayf, so his pedigree suggests he will get further in time, and he looks to have plenty of scope for jumping.

BEN CASE

Stoner's Choice

Ben Case recorded a first Cheltenham Festival success last season when Croco Bay won the Grand Annual, and of his 14 winners during the campaign, Stoner's Choice was his sole winner in the bumper division. Runner-up (beaten just a neck) on debut at Market Rasen, he showed signs of greenness when first asked to pick up, but ran on really strongly and only just failed. Just three weeks later, he showed the benefit of that initial experience when beating a couple of well-supported debutants to go one better at Warwick. Ridden patiently by the owner's son Max Kendrick, Stoner's Choice made good headway down the side of the course and despite once again showing greenness early in the home straight, he finished strongly inside the final furlong to score by 1¼ lengths. Stoner's Choice appeals as the type who will develop – mentally – for his summer break and the son of Great Pretender should do well in novice hurdles this season.

MICK CHANNON

Glen Forsa

Looked a top-class prospect when winning his first three starts over fences, latterly in the rearranged Kingmaker at Sandown, before unseating in the Arkle and running below par when pulled up at Aintree. Glen Forsa will return to action on somewhat of a recovery mission, but from a mark of 150 has the option of beginning the season in handicap company. The Listed Colin Parker Memorial Intermediate Chase at Carlisle – a race that the same connections won last year with Mister Whitaker – would be another possible early-season target, and he remains lightly-raced enough to continue his progression. His jumping was his key asset in those first three chase starts.

Hold The Note

Likely to reappear in a novices' handicap chase, Hold The Note is another chasing type who showed loads of promise in five starts last term. A bumper winner on debut, he travelled well in Listed company next time and got off the mark at the second time of asking over hurdles, at Doncaster over Christmas. He jumped well and stayed on strongly to score and went on to run a sound race under his penalty at Huntingdon, when a final flight mistake didn't help. He was conceding plenty of weight to a useful winner that day and again gave the impression that he might appreciate a step up in trip before too long. He rates a really nice prospect for fences this season.

REBECCA CURTIS

Cubao

A Fame And Glory five-year-old out of a full-sister to Coral Cup winner Ninetieth Minute, Cubao made a winning debut in a good-ground Ludlow bumper in May. He only beat five horses and it was a newcomers' event, so the form is difficult to evaluate, but he settled well and was sent for home once turning in. He kept on well under Sean Bowen and was going away at the line. It was a promising start to his career.

Drovers Lane

No more than a reasonable novice hurdler the season before last, Drovers Lane flourished over fences last term, winning three of his first four starts. A serious error at Aintree on his second start was the only blot on his copybook during the first half of last season, and his Cheltenham win in November came at the main expense of subsequent National Hunt Chase winner Le Breuil. He then ran well for a long way in a very strong renewal of the RSA Chase and, likewise, only gave best from two out, behind Delta Work at Punchestown. The pick of his form has come on better ground, and dropping back to 2m4f–2m5f might be advantageous, particularly in a strongly-run race. Provided the ground isn't too soft, something like the BetVictor Gold Cup might be a suitable option in the early part of the season, whilst Aintree's Old Roan Chase is another possible starting point. That Aintree mistake aside, his jumping was assured last season and he looks capable of landing a nice handicap off his current mark of 148.

Lisnagar Oscar

A smooth-traveller, Lisnagar Oscar improved with each run during the first half of last season, before winning at Chepstow and in Grade 2 company at Haydock. He then finished fifth in the Albert Bartlett and third in the Sefton at Aintree, and although not the biggest, looks capable of doing well over fences. An ex-Irish Points winner, it is likely that he will head down that route upon his return, although given how well he won at Haydock in February, I would personally consider having a crack at the valuable Betfair Exchange Stayers' Handicap Hurdle in November, from an appealing looking mark (141). Nimble over his hurdles, he is out of a full-sister to Whisper, and although he has form on soft, seems suited by a decent surface.

KEITH DALGLEISH

Sidi Ismael

A bumper winner at the third time of asking, Sidi Ismael had earlier fallen in his first Irish Point-to-Point, before chasing home Bold Conduct, who subsequently joined the Colin Tizzard stable. Fourth on his Rules debut at Carlisle, he ran a good race against the potentially smart Ebony Jewel at Ayr before opening his account at Hexham. Ridden just behind the speed, he eased into the lead on the home bend and readily drew clear, to score in quite taking fashion. He appeared to appreciate the stiff finish and it could be that he improves for a test of stamina, once sent hurdling in the autumn. A five-year-old by Great Pretender, he probably didn't beat a lot and won as his earlier form entitled him to do, but he can make his mark in northern novice hurdles this season.

HENRY DALY

It's Probably Me

Stoney Mountain did well in the novice hurdle division for Henry Daly last season, whilst the mare Atlanta Ablaze won four times over fences for the yard. Daly introduced another potentially nice mare at Southwell in April, in the shape of It's Probably Me, who came from a long way off the pace to score at 16-1. The fourth has won since and the well-bred daughter of Great Pretender backed up her debut success when beating all bar Vegas Blue, under her penalty at Bangor. She finished 10 lengths clear of the remainder and rates a decent prospect for mares-only novice hurdles.

SEAMUS DURACK

The Swagman

A Ballydoyle cast-off, The Swagman finished fourth on his first three starts in bumpers, before being the beneficiary of a fine ride from Aidan Coleman, when scoring at Newton Abbot in mid-May. The pair made all and having kicked clear off the home bend, he fended off the well-supported market leader, to score by a couple of lengths. Ridden more patiently on his previous starts, the five-year-old clearly appreciated the change of tactics, and despite his pedigree (Flat-bred with an all-weather influence), it will be interesting to see how he progresses over hurdles, following a promising start at Uttoxeter during the summer. He was again ridden positively and looked to have the race won when entering the home straight, but after wandering around a little, he was possibly outstayed over 2m4f and could come back in trip.

STUART EDMUNDS

Queenohearts

A winner at Listed level in bumpers, Queenohearts made a pleasing debut over hurdles when runner-up at Chepstow, before winning her next two starts. She might well have made a winning debut had she hurdled more fluently, but her hurdling was better (albeit not completely foot-perfect) when getting off the mark, in a heavy-ground Listed contest at Haydock. She confirmed the form with the runner-up (on 5lb worse terms) in Sandown's Grade 2 Jane Seymour Mares' Novices' Hurdle, staying on strongly from the back of the last. Dropped back to 2m1f for the Dawn Run at Cheltenham, she found the trip on the short side and having dropped away, she was doing her best work late on, although it was later confirmed that she had suffered a nasty over-reach during the race.

A daughter of Flemensfirth with plenty of size about her, Queenohearts looks the type who could improve again for fences and is very much one to note in mares-only novice chases during the winter, when the emphasis is on stamina. To date she has not raced beyond 2m4f, but she promises to be effective over further and relishes testing ground. There ought to be plenty of opportunities for her and there is also the option to remain over hurdles, to head down the handicap route. Off a mark of 135 and on testing ground, she could certainly be competitive, although her long-term future lies over fences.

BRIAN ELLISON

Windsor Avenue

Malton-based trainer Brian Ellison was down in terms of number of winners during the 2018-19 season, but stable star Definitly Red still more than paid his way by winning both the Charlie Hall and Aintree's Many Clouds Chase. Another horse to record a couple of victories was Windsor Avenue, a Winged Love half-brother to the same connections' Ravenhill Road. A dual-bumper winner the season before, the seven-year-old got to within 1¾ lengths of Al Dancer over 2m1f on his hurdles debut and duly got off the mark at short odds next time (2m4f, Hexham). Only fourth in the French Furze, he was beaten less than a length and won for a second time, at Sedgefield in January. He stayed on powerfully to win by 15 lengths and the next three home all won before the season was out. Dropped back in trip, Windsor Avenue's final start of the season came in the Premier Kelso Novices' Hurdle, where he again stayed on strongly to finish a sound second. Rated 134 over hurdles, it is likely that he will now be sent chasing and there should be plenty more races to be won with him.

HARRY FRY

Ishkhara Lady

A half-sister to Zulu Oscar (won five times for the stable), Ishkhara Lady looked a potentially smart mare when winning a Plumpton bumper by 15 lengths on debut in mid-December. Ridden patiently – and confidently – by Noel Fehily, the daughter of Scorpion swept around the outside of the field on the home turn and quickly shot clear inside the final couple of furlongs. We didn't get to see her again, but the runner-up won a bumper next time and the fifth home won over hurdles in May. She looks just one of a nice crop of novice hurdlers that Harry Fry has on his hands for this season.

King Roland

A ten-length winner of a Point-to-Point for Sophie Lacey, King Roland justified odds-on favouritism on his debut under Rules, when running out a 22-length winner of a Uttoxeter bumper. It later became apparent that he probably didn't beat much, but he powered clear up the straight and had little trouble in handling the heavy ground. Again sent off odds-on, the Stowaway gelding had to work harder to get to the front at Ffos Las, but stayed on strongly to score under a penalty. Again, the form wouldn't be anything to get too excited about, but judged on his demolition at Uttoxeter, he remains a nice prospect for novice hurdles this season. Clearly versatile in terms of ground, he is likely to want stepping up in trip in time.

Green Dolphin would be another bumper winner to note over hurdles, although the 11-length Wincanton winner was a shade disappointing when appearing to race too freely in Listed company at Newbury on his final start. He will need to settle better.

Misty Whisky

Harry Fry really did appear to have a nice bunch of bumper horses last year and a couple of his mares clashed twice, with Misty Whisky finishing in front of Whitehotchillifili at both Sandown and Aintree. A winner at the second time of asking at Ludlow, Misty Whisky stayed on really well up the hill to win Sandown's Listed event, before she again kept on really well to finish seventh in a competitive renewal of Aintree's Grade 2. A daughter of Stowaway – who is a half-sister to the stable's smart hurdler Air Force One and Nigel Twiston-Davies' One For Rosie – she is certainly bred to do well once sent jumping, and given her running style she is likely to relish an extra half-mile. She will probably be high up in the pecking order of the Fry novice hurdlers for this winter.

Stablemate **Whitehotchillifili** deserves a mention, having created a good impression on debut at Southwell. Runner-up to a subsequent hurdles winner under her penalty, she went on to finish fourth at Sandown and ninth at Aintree, but given the stamina in her pedigree, she will appreciate a sterner test once sent hurdling.

TOM GEORGE

Doctor Dex

A winner over hurdles at Wetherby and Doncaster last season, Doctor Dex appeals as the type who could do well in novice handicap chase company, beginning the season on a mark of 126. The strong-travelling six-year-old went on to finish seventh in the Martin Pipe and sixth in a valuable handicap at Aintree, but could easily improve for going chasing, given both his physique and how he jumps.

Seddon

A strong-traveller, Seddon had impressed with the way he won his bumper on debut at Musselburgh the season before last, and duly did the same over hurdles at Stratford last November. Held-up in a couple of slowly-run Grade 2 novices, handicaps promised to suit him better, but he didn't really see his race out at Ascot, and similar comments applied when allowed to front-run on his final two starts. A strongly-run 2m could well bring out the best in him, so I wouldn't be surprised if he were given a chance in a big handicap hurdle on his return (especially given his record first time up), although his future probably lies over fences given how he jumps hurdles.

Summerville Boy

The 2018 Supreme Novices' Hurdle winner struggled last term, but returned from injury at Aintree and shaped better at Punchestown on his final start. Not fluent enough over his hurdles at the top level, the seven-year-old is now set to embark on a novice chase campaign and if he shows more respect to fences, he could be a force in the 2m division. He did hold an entry at Uttoxeter in May, and it is nice to hear some positive comments about his schooling from Jonathan Burke in the *A View From The Saddle* section. He remains very lightly-raced, having had just the nine starts over hurdles in his life.

CHRIS GORDON

Mount Windsor

Having bumped into Blazer's Mill on debut at Fontwell, Mount Windsor returned to the same venue to run out a thoroughly convincing winner. Stepped up to 2m1½f at Plumpton, he duly carried his penalty to success, beating four rivals in taking fashion. Strong at the finish on both occasions, he wouldn't have the most fashionable pedigree, but he appears to have an engine and should win more races once sent hurdling.

NICK GIFFORD

Mystic Dreamer

Didtheyleaveuoutto and Glen Rocco did well for the Nick Gifford stable last season, winning a couple of races apiece, but the trainer also saddled a couple of Cheltenham winners during the campaign, and from just four runners at the track throughout the season. The Mighty Don won a 3m handicap hurdle at the October meeting, whilst the promising Mystic Dreamer won a competitive-looking mares' bumper at the April meeting. Having given the more-experienced Silver Forever a fright on debut at Ascot, the five-year-old appeared to struggle in soft ground behind Misty Whisky at Sandown, before bouncing back at Cheltenham. The better ground might well have helped, but she moved well in behind and once the gap appeared on the rail, she ran on strongly, probably outstaying the smooth-travelling runner-up. The third came out and won over hurdles in late May and Mystic Dancer is certainly bred for jumping, with her dam being a half-sister to both Minella Class and Deputy Dan (both Graded novice hurdle winners).

WARREN GREATREX

Kemble's Cascade

A Kalanisi half-brother to three winners – including Dan Skelton's Pumped Up Kicks – Kemble's Cascade finished runner-up in a Warwick bumper on debut and looks more than capable of going one better, before embarking on his hurdling career. Introduced in the same race which Warren Greatrex won 12 months earlier with the exciting Emitom, the four-year-old ran in snatches and was off the bridle when racing wide into the home straight (in fourth), but ran on well to finish a sound second. The winner, Stoner's Choice, had gone close on debut, whilst the third, odds-on favourite Dundrum Wood, had won an Irish Point before changing hands for big money, so it was a highly encouraging racecourse debut.

La Bague Au Roi

A high-class mare who has been a regular feature in *Jumpers To Follow* since her days in bumpers, La Bague Au Roi made the successful transition to fences last season. The winner of her first four starts, her form reads really well, having beaten Mildmay winner Lostintranslation and bet365 Gold Cup winner Talkischeap on her first two starts at Newbury. She then beat the RSA first and second – Topofthegame and Santini – in the Kauto Star (received 7lb from both) before winning a second Grade 1 in Ireland, Leopardstown's Flogas Novice Chase. Having skipped Cheltenham, she was probably beaten by a speedier rival in Kalashnikov at Aintree, when I felt more use could have been made of her. It could be that the spring isn't really her time – as she has yet to perform at her best in March or April – but she remains a very smart prospect and given the ratings of Santini and Topofthegame, actually looks on a fair mark at present (151). Whether or not she is tried in handicaps remains to be seen (Ladbrokes Trophy would stretch her stamina), and it could be that the Charlie Hall is considered as a prep race for the King George, which is presumably her main aim, in the first half of the season.

Young Lieutenant

Fifth on debut, behind Kim Bailey's Prince Llewelyn, Young Lieutenant got off the mark just 16 days later, winning a bumper at Exeter. Handy throughout, he travelled well to lead and stayed on well to fend off the pursuers. A five-year-old by Robin des Champs, there is plenty of stamina on the dam's side of his pedigree, so he can be expected to want a trip once sent jumping and looks a promising individual.

NICKY HENDERSON

Angels Breath

A 12-length winner of his sole Point-to-Point, Angels Breath created a deep impression on his debut under Rules last December. A week after being pulled out due to quick ground at Cheltenham, the grey showed a fine turn of foot to win the Kennel Gate at Ascot, and the mere fact that Nicky Henderson was prepared to pitch him into a Grade 2 first time out suggested that he was held in very high regard. Runner-up to Southfield Stone (conceding 5lb) in the Dovecote, the son of Shantou could finish only seventh in the Supreme, before appreciating the longer trip when third to Reserve Tank at Aintree. Still only five, there is plenty of time for him to develop, and it could be that he heads straight over fences on his return. He could do with relaxing a little in the early part of his races.

Call Me Lord

We only got to see Call Me Lord twice last season, when hampered and only seventh behind Paisley Park in the Long Walk at Ascot, and then when third off a mark of 160 in the Imperial Cup. That was a fine effort from such a lofty rating, and still only six, he remains full of potential. The fact that he has to race right-handed makes him a little more difficult to place, but there are plenty of good races that way around, especially if he heads down the novice chase route. If he takes to fences – and there is no reason why he wouldn't – he could easily develop into a contender for races such as the Feltham, the Scilly Isles, or the Reynoldstown at Ascot, whilst Fairyhouse and, in particular, Punchestown would offer suitable end-of-season targets. Hopefully we get to see him a bit more frequently this season, as he looked a high-class prospect when winning at Sandown on the final day of the 2017-18 season.

Dickie Diver

Another exciting prospect for Nicky Henderson and JP McManus, Dickie Diver is yet another embryonic chaser, although given that they have both Birchdale and Champ for that division, it could be that he remains over hurdles for the time being. Whichever route is chosen, the lightly-raced son of Gold Well looks a bright prospect, judged on his first two runs at Chepstow, which preceded a fine effort when finishing fourth in the Albert Bartlett. He shaped with bags of promise behind subsequent Grade 2 winner Lisnagar Oscar on his hurdles debut and duly went one place better in a weaker race next time. He stayed on from a long way back to reverse earlier form with Lisnagar Oscar and grab fourth at the festival, suggesting that his future certainly lies over staying trips, once sent chasing. From a mark of 141, he could be of interest in something like the Betfair Exchange Stayers' Handicap Hurdle at Haydock, whilst I just wonder if he could be earmarked for the National Hunt Chase if sent over the larger obstacles. A 20-length winner of his sole Irish Point, he remains a fine prospect and one who was on an upward curve when last seen.

Floressa

A full-sister to Polygona (twice a Grade 3 winner over hurdles in France), Floressa made a winning debut in a Ludlow bumper in March, and the third, Shanroe, has since advertised that form by winning his next three starts. The four-year-old then headed to Cheltenham for a mares' event at the April meeting and looked the most likely winner when taking over with a furlong to run. She couldn't put the race to bed, however, and was possibly beaten by a stronger stayer in the shape of Mystic Dreamer. It is worth remembering that this race was over 2m1f on the stiffer New Course and it could be that she proves best when the emphasis is on speed. She looks a nice prospect for mares' novice hurdles, however.

Mister Fisher

Finished mid-division in the Supreme Novices' Hurdle, Mister Fisher was then sent off favourite for the Swinton Hurdle at Haydock, when he probably raced too close to the pace and actually fared better than his finishing position might suggest, especially given the mistake he made down the far side. The good-looking five-year-old had earlier won at Kempton on Boxing Day and in Grade 2 company at Haydock, and it would appear – at this stage – that the pick of his form has come on flat tracks, with his bumper success also coming at Kempton. Given his physique, I would expect him to be sent chasing now, and races such as the Wayward Lad and Pendil at Kempton are likely to be considered, after which he might be an ideal candidate for Aintree.

Pistol Whipped

An eye-catching third behind stablemate Rathhill on his debut under Rules, before getting off the mark at Fakenham. He beat a subsequent winner on that occasion, staying on strongly despite the track probably being tighter than ideal. Pulled up at Sandown on his final run, the ground was very testing on that occasion and the run can be forgiven. He is another nice prospect for fences and whilst he might not be one of the leading lights in that division for the stable, he is very much one to note in a novices' handicap from a mark of 128. By Beneficial, Pistol Whipped jumped well in the main in two Irish Points, slipping up on the home bend when still in the lead on debut and then when just touched off at the same track last October. That form doesn't amount to a great deal, but I still expect him to make his mark over fences this season.

Precious Cargo

Yet another nice prospect for the novice chase division, Precious Cargo was extremely keen in his bumpers when trained by Lucinda Russell and was given a lovely ride by Nico de Boinville when making a winning debut over hurdles at Kempton in January. A strapping son of Yeats, he followed up under a penalty at Sandown, which teed up a crack at the Top Novices' Hurdle at Aintree. He struggled with the rise in class and looked in trouble leaving the back straight, although to his credit he kept on and only tired on the run to the last. A winner at the first time of asking in each of his two seasons, he is probably one to catch on his chase debut in the autumn and has no problem in handling testing ground.

Santini

Partly due to the outbreak of Equine Influenza, we only got to see Santini three times during his first season over fences, and although he won just once, he remains a top-class prospect and could easily develop into a Gold Cup contender as the season unfolds. A winner on debut – in Grade 2 company – at Newbury, he appeared to find the track on the sharp side at Kempton, before running a blinder in what appeared to be a very strong RSA Chase. Delta Work and, to a lesser extent, Mister Malarky franked that form at Punchestown and Aintree, and given his record at the track, the Ladbrokes Trophy appeals as the obvious early-season target for him. Rated 163, it would take a huge effort off that kind of mark, but he is a big horse who wouldn't have a problem with carrying a big weight, and the track is ideal for his long stride. The longer trip would also likely to play to his strengths and he ticks plenty of boxes with that race in mind. If things went to plan in the first half of the season, the Cotswold Chase at Cheltenham on trials day or Newbury's Denman Chase would appeal as possible stepping-stones to the festival.

Vegas Blue

A full-sister to the stable's Newbury winner Rathhill, Vegas Blue made a winning debut in a bumper at Bangor-on-Dee and is another to note in the mares' novice hurdle division. Quite green, she briefly had to be bumped along to go after the leaders leaving the far side, but once she set her sights on the leader, the outcome looked inevitable, and she really quickened up smartly in the closing stages. The runner-up had won on debut and pulled nicely clear of the remainder, so the form might not be too bad at all and she might be one for the Listed mares' bumper at Cheltenham's November meeting, before hurdling is considered.

PHILIP HOBBS

Kalooki

Kruzhlinin was back in the news earlier in the year, with him winning 13 times during the Irish Point-to-Point season, and he was twice a winner for the Philip Hobbs stable earlier in his career, latterly in the valuable fixed brush hurdle at Haydock. Hobbs introduced his half-brother in bumpers last season and whilst he was unable to win in four starts, Kalooki showed enough to suggest he can win races, once upped in trip over hurdles. An imposing grey by Martaline, his best efforts came either side of the New Year at Ascot and Exeter, latterly when going down by just a length to New Age Dawning, who won a Chepstow novice hurdle in March. Below that form when fifth back at Exeter, that race worked out well, with the first three all winning next time out.

Musical Slave

Sixth in a bumper at the 2017 Punchestown Festival – a race in which Grade 1 winner Tower Bridge finished fourth – Musical Slave took a bit of time to get the hang of things over hurdles, but improved once entering handicap company. A well-supported winner on his handicap debut at Market Rasen, he followed up under a 7lb penalty at Ludlow and relished the step up in trip when successful in a 24-runner race at Punchestown. Given a fine ride by Jonjo O'Neill Jnr, he stayed on well to win off a mark of 121 and I suspect that he might now be sent chasing, although he remains unexposed over 2m5f or further and the 0-140 intermediate handicap at Cheltenham's November meeting would be an option, should he remain over hurdles.

Smarty Wild

Rather like Musical Slave, Smarty Wild won his last three starts and looks the type to continue his progression in novice chases. He finished sixth in a couple of bumpers before going hurdling and got off the mark at the second time of asking, when staying on strongly at Ludlow. He won a conditional jockeys' handicap at Exeter a month later, before following up (unpenalised) just six days later at Taunton, where he appeared to relish the step up to 2m3f. A good jumper, the son of Fair Mix looks to possess plenty of size and scope for fences, and will stay even further in time. He starts the season on a mark of 130.

Thyme Hill

A winner at Worcester back in October, Thyme Hill then finished a neck second behind Master Debonair in a falsely-run Listed bumper at Cheltenham's November meeting, before reversing form with the winner in the Champion Bumper in March. He stayed on strongly to finish 2½ lengths off Envoi Allen in third, pulling nicely clear of the fourth and finishing much the best of the British-trained runners. Given that was his first start in four months, it was a fine effort and having won on debut, too, it goes to show that he clearly goes well fresh. The son of Kayf Tara seems versatile in terms of ground conditions, and if he can translate this form to hurdles – and there is no reason why he shouldn't – he looks capable of making up into a smart novice hurdler. Although there is stamina in his pedigree, he doesn't look devoid of speed and I would expect to see him start off over the minimum trip, with the maiden hurdle at Cheltenham in October being a possible starting point.

Umndeni

Despite winning twice, I was a shade disappointed with Umndeni last season, as he began the campaign as one of my *Leading Prospects* and one who I was particularly excited about. He did win at Fontwell (runner-up won his next two) and in emphatic fashion at Taunton in late-April, so he ended the campaign on a high and certainly has the physique of a chaser. A scopey son of Balko, he is a full-brother to Vision des Flos and it is hoped that he can now begin to fulfil his potential. He is another who begins the season on 130, a mark from which he should certainly be capable of winning a novices' handicap chase.

RUTH JEFFERSON

Black Ebony

Nicely bred, Black Ebony is a half-brother to plenty of winners, including Attaglance, and shaped with promise in two runs in bumpers last season. There was certainly promise in his debut seventh at Kelso and he stepped forward to finish runner-up to Shanroe (won another two bumpers subsequently) at Hexham. He clearly possesses the ability to win a bumper, but given his pedigree, he ought to relish an extra half-mile once sent jumping and looks a bright prospect for northern novice hurdles.

Buster Valentine

A winning Irish Pointer, Buster Valentine made the perfect start to life under Rules, winning a 2m maiden hurdle in heavy ground at Ayr in impressive fashion, before following up over an extra half-mile at Newcastle. He jumped well and stayed on strongly on both occasions, suggesting that his long-term future lies in staying chases. Stepped up in class, he finished runner-up behind Birchdale at Cheltenham on trials day, and although he would have been third had Brewin'upastorm not fallen at the last, there was still promise in the run, with him only giving best after the home turn. Back into handicap company, he was sent off favourite back at Ayr, but was pulled up after dropping away towards the end of the back straight. It came to light that he was suffering with a lung infection, so the run can be ignored and he can bounce back in novice chases this winter. Clearly at home on testing ground, the son of Ask jumped well when winning his Point under Derek O'Connor.

Lemon T

A full-brother to Temple Man and a half-brother to Mac Aeda, Lemon T certainly hails from a family which Ruth Jefferson knows well, and he ran out an eight-length winner of a Newcastle bumper on his second start. Fifth of eight at Market Rasen on debut, the grey left that behind when making all in the hands of Jamie Hamilton, and the pair really stretched clear inside the final furlong to score decisively. There ought to be more races to be won with him once sent hurdling in the autumn.

Mega Yeats

Like Black Ebony and Buster Valentine, Mega Yeats carries the yellow and light blue silks of The Mount Fawcus Partnership, and she won three times from five starts last term. After beating Redbridge Gold (won next time) at Carlisle, she finished runner-up in a Listed bumper at Cheltenham in November. That form reads really well now, with the winner The Glancing Queen going on to win the Grade 2 at Aintree, and she duly made a winning debut over hurdles at Wetherby over Christmas. Despite her lack of experience, she was pitched into open Listed company. She ran with great credit in third and returned to winning ways when making all at Market Rasen to beat inferior opposition. A lovely, imposing individual out of a Presenting mare, she will have no problem jumping a fence in time, but is likely to remain over hurdles for the time being and begins the season on a mark of 134. It could be that she is campaigned down the mares-only route, with the Listed races at Wetherby (2m) or Kempton (3m) possible starting points in November.

Return Ticket

A *Leading Prospect* in last year's edition of *Jumpers To Follow*, Return Ticket – who had already made a winning hurdling debut at Ayr during May last year – went on to win once from three more starts over hurdles. He was given a fine front-running ride when scoring under Henry Brooke at Musselburgh in November and returned in late-March, when going down narrowly – under his double-penalty – at Newcastle. Upped from 122 to 130 as a consequence, the winner went on to advertise the form by winning his next two, and this son of Getaway – who relishes decent ground – looks a chaser waiting to happen. He could start off in novice handicap company, but connections will surely be hoping he progresses beyond that grade, and he remains a smart prospect.

MARTIN KEIGHLEY

Big Nasty

An imposing son of Black Sam Bellamy, Big Nasty really filled the eye in the paddock before his debut run at Haydock, where he finished third behind Mr Grey Sky and Ebony Jewel (both won their next start in bumpers). He failed to build on that at Chepstow over Christmas, but returned from three-and-a-half months off to finish runner-up on his hurdles debut, over 3m at Wetherby. Beaten 2½ lengths by the 131-rated Trio For Rio, it was a promising start, and whilst he won't come into his own until going chasing, he can probably win something similar. He could be most interesting once he is handicapped and sent over fences.

ALAN KING

Deyrann de Carjac

It was slightly disappointing that he was unable to add to his maiden hurdle success at Warwick last May during last season, but Deyrann de Carjac made a really pleasing debut over fences at Cartmel before his summer break and, perhaps, chasing will be the making of him. A really good-looking son of Balko, he certainly has the scope for the job, and although a mark of 137 seems a bit harsh on the back of that debut success, there should be plenty of opportunities for him in novice company.

Wynn House

The Glancing Queen might well be top of the pecking order in terms of novice hurdle prospects at Barbury Castle, but Alan King introduced another potentially nice filly at Uttoxeter in late March, in the shape of Wynn House. The daughter of Presenting ran in snatches a little and still had half-a-dozen in front of her, when the pace increased three furlongs out. Once getting to the leaders, she again showed greenness and rolled around a little, but the penny seemed to drop late on. The runner-up, The Milan Girl, won next time at Bangor to give the form a boost, and it is worth noting that King also saddled Outonpatrol in the Uttoxeter race and she was sent off considerably shorter in the market.

NEIL KING

Farne

An imposing daughter of Stowaway, Farne finished runner-up to Shantewe (winner again at Hexham in May) on debut at Wetherby, and filled the same spot at Uttoxeter on New Year's Eve. Ridden a little closer to the pace, she travelled well into the straight and looked all over the winner when taking over. Perhaps she was in front for longer than ideal, and was caught late on. Stepped up in class, Farne finished third behind Misty Whisky and Silver Forever in Listed company at Sandown, despite refusing to settle for Bryony Frost. Having pulled her way to the front, she came wide into the straight and given her early exertions, did well to finish as close as she did. She settled better at Aintree, where she reversed earlier form with both Shantewe and Misty Whisky to finish fourth, staying on well in the closing stages.

Given her running style, her pedigree, and also her physique, Farne promises to make up into a really nice novice hurdler this season, once Neil King steps her up in trip. Her breeding also suggests that she will probably always appreciate an easy surface and it will be disappointing if she can't win races now she goes hurdling.

TOM LACEY

Capac

Whilst most people were focused on the opening day from Aintree's Grand National meeting, Capac was justifying favouritism in the concluding bumper at Taunton. A half-brother to Champion Hurdle winner Brave Inca, the son of Aizavoski always moved well on the wide outside, despite the track looking a little on the sharp side for him. He still readily hit the front in the home straight and drew away from Bergamot (won at Ludlow next time out) to win with a bit to spare. It was a likeable performance and the sustained market support suggested that the victory wasn't unexpected. When he returns, Tom Lacey has the option of running Capac in another bumper under a penalty, or sending him straight over hurdles. He looks a really promising four-year-old.

Glory And Fortune

Pitched straight into Listed company on his racecourse debut, Glory And Fortune made the perfect start when winning at Cheltenham on New Year's Day. Still only fifth when turning for home, the Fame And Glory gelding really found his stride inside the final quarter-mile and stayed on strongly up the hill. The form didn't work out particularly well, but he ran out a clear-cut winner in the end and forms part of a decent-looking novice hurdle team for the Tom Lacey stable.

Kateson

Runner-up in the Aintree bumper the season before last, Kateson made an impressive start to his hurdling career, winning a maiden at Chepstow and a novice at Newbury during November. Third in a slowly-run Challow (form worked out well), the grey then raced too freely and appeared a non-stayer at Haydock. He was again far too keen in the Mersey Novices' Hurdle on his final start, and getting him to settle could be the key to whether or not he can fulfil his potential. It could be that fences help on that score, and if he does learn to relax, he can make up into a smart novice chaser. The six-year-old likes soft ground and boasts a decent record at Chepstow, so don't be surprised to see him start off there.

Lossiemouth

Twice a bumper winner, Lossiemouth was still in contention on debut at Huntingdon when running out and depositing Tommie O'Brien on the turf. Sent north to Newcastle the following month, the son of Makfi came from off the pace to beat Alright Sunshine, who had earlier won at Carlisle. The runner-up advertised the form by winning a couple more bumpers, before switching to the Flat to good effect. Lossiemouth was able to win again himself, under a penalty at Carlisle. Again, it seemed a little unlikely when being pushed along on the home turn, but he kept on really strongly for Richard Johnson, eventually getting to the front inside the final furlong, and was doing his best work late on. He doesn't exactly have a pedigree for jumping, but clearly has an engine and stays well, so it will be interesting to see how he progresses.

EMMA LAVELLE

De Rasher Counter

A useful novice hurdler the season before last, De Rasher Counter improved over fences last season, winning twice from six starts. A winner at Newbury over Christmas, the seven-year-old rounded off his season with an impressive success at Uttoxeter on Midlands Grand National day, and although he will find life tougher off his revised mark (149), appeals as the type who could go well in the Ladbrokes Trophy, back at Newbury. At home on testing ground, the son of Yeats might even get a bit further, and the Welsh National might be another race to feature on his agenda in the first half of the season.

Down The Highway

The winner of an Irish Point-to-Point, Down The Highway made a winning debut for the Emma Lavelle stable at Lingfield in November, appearing to relish the testing ground. Pulled up in the Grade 2 Winter Novices' Hurdle next time, the Duke of Marmalade six-year-old returned to form, when finishing fourth in a competitive novice event at Chepstow, where he conceded weight to the front pair (Lisnagar Oscar and Dickie Diver). For his final start, he entered handicap company for the first time, but could finish only eighth of 13 at Haydock. Dropped just 1lb (to 132), he looks capable of returning to winning ways now he is sent chasing and could develop into a smart handicapper in time. He clearly handles testing ground, and the Uttoxeter race which De Rasher Counter won last season might end up being an option, come next spring.

Killer Clown

A Getaway five-year-old from the family of Watson Lake, Killer Clown finished runner-up in a Warwick bumper during May, having earlier won his sole start in an Irish Point. Not too fluent down the far side, he stayed on strongly to beat Carry On The Magic (now with Paul Nicholls) by a length. Well-positioned throughout at Warwick, he looked all over the winner when grabbing the lead with a furlong to run, only to be collared late on by the fast-finishing Trincomalee. He showed signs of greenness – running about a bit up the straight – so should have done well for his summer break and looks to have a bright future.

CHARLIE LONGSDON

Old Jeroboam

The winner of two good-ground bumpers, Old Jeroboam has plenty of stamina in his pedigree and could develop into a fairly useful staying novice hurdler this season. By Jeremy, out of an Old Vic mare, he is certainly bred to jump and finished really strongly, once the penny dropped, on debut at Wetherby. He was again strong inside the final couple of furlongs, when defying his penalty at Southwell, where he beat Olly The Brave (won next time) by a length, under 7lb claimer Jordan Nailor. He is one to note once going up to 2m4f or beyond.

CHARLIE MANN

Ivilnoble

Third in an Irish Point, Ivilnoble shaped with plenty of promise in three novice hurdles last season, despite not winning. Runner-up to Hold The Note at Doncaster on debut, he again finished just behind that rival when third at Huntingdon on his final start. Ridden prominently on both occasions, he didn't do much wrong in either race, although he could have hurdled more fluently in the closing stages last time. The six-year-old also finished third in a competitive maiden hurdle at Chepstow (form worked out well) and he certainly looks capable of winning races, having been well purchased for just £26,000 (presumably due to his unfashionable pedigree).

DONALD McCAIN

Chuvelo

A full-brother to Double Seven (Munster National winner and third in the 2014 Grand National at Aintree) Chuvelo made an encouraging racecourse debut when runner-up in a valuable sales bumper at Fairyhouse. Trained by Sam Curling at that point, he moved well to lead and was only collared late-on by Uhtred (a Gigginstown purchase prior to that debut). Purchased for £100,000 just five days later, the four-year-old by Milan will sport the silks of Tim Leslie on his return, and there should be plenty of options for him this season.

The Con Man

A winner at Carlisle in early December, we didn't get to see The Con Man again, although he reportedly returned to training later in the season, only for the ground to turn against him. He travelled well – clearly coping with the bad ground – and was too strong for Garrettstown (won next time) from two out, whilst Paper Promises (5th) also won before the season was out. Prior to joining Donald McCain and Tim Leslie, The Con Man won a Monksgrange maiden Point for Colin Bowe, in fine style. Always travelling comfortably, he jumped well and had the race well sewn up before Classic Escape (a handicap hurdle winner for Denis Hogan in May) came down at the last. His future clearly lies over fences, but given his inexperience, I would expect McCain to keep him over hurdles for the time being, although as he hasn't been handed a handicap mark at this stage, it is difficult to pinpoint any specific targets. When the time comes, he ought to make a smart novice chaser in soft ground in the north.

The Some Dance Kid

This six-year-old is probably more likely to head straight over fences in the autumn, after enjoying a fine novice hurdle campaign, which resulted in three wins from four starts. Third behind Good Boy Bobby on his debut at Carlisle, the Shantou gelding then made all and fended off all-comers to score at Bangor. The next five home all won races subsequently and he beat another decent field – under his penalty – back at Bangor a month later. Similar tactics were employed and he had 1¼ lengths to spare over Colonel Custard, who won easily at Ffos Las on his next start. The Some Dance Kid completed the hat-trick at Catterick, when he appreciated the step up in trip and hurdled really well up the home straight. He stayed on well to beat Skidoosh (won a handicap hurdle next time) and although we didn't get to see him again, he rates a nice prospect for the season ahead. Runner-up to Blue Flight (won three times over fences last season) in the second of his Irish Points, he looks sure to win more races and can develop into a smart handicapper. His form stacks up really well and he should get further in time.

GRAEME McPHERSON

Ask Ben

After springing a 50-1 surprise on his debut under Rules at Newcastle – where he beat subsequent Grade 2 winner Beakstown by a head – Ask Ben relished the step up to 3m, when winning by 19 lengths at Ayr in January. He made all under Kielan Woods and galloped on really strongly up the home straight, to tee up a tilt at Haydock's Grade 2 Prestige Novices' Hurdle. He attempted to make all once again and found only Lisnagar Oscar too good. Having looked as though he might get swallowed up on the home bend, he showed a fine attitude, staying on strongly and jumping particularly well up the straight. Ridden with more restraint in the Albert Bartlett, he seemed quite keen in mid-field but ran a really sound race, moving well for a long way before eventually tiring into 10th. When he returns, Ask Ben will be sporting the blue and yellow silks of Liz Prowting, and although he will make a chaser in time (runner-up to Danny Whizzbang in an Irish Point), he is likely to remain over hurdles. From a mark of 133, I would seriously consider a return trip to Haydock, for the valuable Betfair Exchange Stayers' Handicap Hurdle. There is also a 3m Listed handicap at Cheltenham's Open meeting in November to consider, and he looks potentially well-treated.

Calum Gilhooley

A 33-1 winner on debut in a bumper at Bangor-on-Dee, Calum Gilhooley really got going once some pace was injected into the race, and finished strongly up the inside rail to score. The third and fourth both won bumpers during March to advertise that form, by which time Calum Gilhooley had changed ownership and finished unplaced at Ffos Las. Now sporting the colours of Paul and Clare Rooney, the five-year-old – who is a half-brother to the useful Gurkha Brave – never really landed a blow behind King Roland, but remains a nice prospect for novice hurdles this season.

REBECCA MENZIES

Breizh Alko

Dual-purpose trainer Becky Menzies saddled 21 winners during the 2018-19 season, and the fact that she was able to get Im Too Generous – who featured here in *Jumpers To Follow* several years ago – back to winning form paid testament to her talents. He had more than four years off before winning handicap hurdles at Musselburgh (March) and Ayr (May), and Menzies saddled another nice handicap hurdle winner, in the shape of Breizh Alko. Formerly trained in France by Menzies' former boss, Ferdy Murphy, the eight-year-old is another who returned from a lengthy lay-off when sixth at Ayr in February. With that run under his belt, he relished the longer trip and softer ground at Haydock the following month, when winning well off a mark of 105. Upped 6lb for that success, he did hold entries towards the end of the season before the ground dried up, and is now likely to return in a novices' handicap chase in the autumn. Despite being eight, he remains lightly-raced and is unexposed over staying trips.

KELLY MORGAN

Timetochill

Kelly Morgan enjoyed big-race success at Aintree last season, when Top Wood – twice placed in the Foxhunter at Cheltenham – stayed on strongly to win over the Grand National fences, under Tabitha Worsley. No doubt that was a day to remember for all connected, and although Timetochill was unable to land a blow in the Grade 2 bumper later on the card, she remains a nice prospect for mares' novice hurdles this season. An impressive winner on debut at Kelso (2nd and 6th won next time), the daughter of Scorpion was then successful at Listed level at Huntingdon. Silver Forever (3rd) won next time before going close at Listed level at Sandown, whilst Kisseforkatie (4th) finished sixth at Aintree. It could be that the ground was too soft for her at Aintree, as she failed to win in three starts in Irish Points under similar conditions. On better ground, she can bounce back.

LAURA MORGAN

Zakharova

Kelly Morgan's sister, Laura, also has a nice prospect for the mares' novice hurdle division, in the shape of three-time winner Zakharova. The five-year-old daughter of Beat Hollow actually contested the Aintree contest the previous season (12th behind Getaway Katie Mai) and returned to action with a smooth success at Newcastle in January. She was again entered at Aintree, but the ground was presumably deemed too soft and instead headed to Kelso during May, where she put up a fine performance under a double-penalty. Ridden positively, she made most and had her rivals in trouble a good way from home, and although the runner-up reduced the deficit in the closing stages, she won with a bit in hand, completing a double for the trainer. She looks quick enough to win on the Flat, but is also related to some jumpers and her half-sister Balmusette was a Listed novice hurdle winner for Keith Reveley. There should be plenty of options for her, going forward.

HUGHIE MORRISON

Third Wind

Following Third Win's 40-1 win on debut over hurdles at Plumpton, Hughie Morrison – who is predominantly Flat-based, of course – was quick to praise the work done by Henrietta Knight and it seems that Best Mate's former trainer will have a key role to play in the Shirocco gelding's progression. Following that debut success, he bumped into a nice sort under his penalty, before winning at Taunton, teeing up a crack at Sandown's EBF Final. Held up by Tom O'Brien, he made steady progress up the straight and stayed on really strongly to grab One For Rosie on the line. It was a fine performance and one that offers hope that he will stay even further. He begins the season on a mark of 137 and has the option of continuing in handicap hurdles, or embarking on a novice chase campaign.

NEIL MULHOLLAND

Tango Boy

A full-brother to Jessica Harrington's Impact Factor, Tango Boy made a winning racecourse debut in a Market Rasen bumper in March, making all under Robbie Dunne. He might well have been allowed an easy lead, but raced enthusiastically and kept galloping right up the home straight. He should be fine over 2m to begin with and there should be more races to be won with him, once sent hurdling in the autumn.

OLLY MURPHY

Dundrum Wood

Looked a future stayer when winning his Irish Point at the second time of asking for Sam Curling, Dundrum Wood made his debut under Rules in a bumper at Warwick and shaped with promise in third. Well positioned, he seemed to travel comfortably under Aidan Coleman, before running a little green around the home bend. Once he realised what was required, the five-year-old stayed on again and it could be that the front three are quite useful. When he returns, I would expect Dundrum Wood to need further over hurdles, so he will be one to note once going 2m4f or beyond.

Finawn Bawn

A bumper winner at Ayr the season before last, Finawn Bawn won twice from four starts over hurdles last season and rates a nice prospect for staying novice chases. Third in a decent maiden hurdle at Sandown on debut, he appreciated the extra half-mile when getting off the mark at Bangor where he stayed on strongly. He again kept on really well when third in the Grade 2 Leamington Novices' Hurdle at Warwick, before rounding off his campaign with an odds-on success at Huntingdon. He was once again really strong at the finish, leaving the impression that he will appreciate 3m this season, and the way he jumps his hurdles suggests he won't have a problem taking to fences. Currently rated 133, there is also the option of running in a handicap hurdle on his return, although he certainly has the look of a staying chaser.

I K Brunel

A winner on debut, in a bumper at Carlisle during November, I K Brunel was then campaigned at a decent level over hurdles and shouldn't have any trouble in shedding his maiden tag in the early part of this season, once his sights are lowered a little. Third behind Elixir de Nutz on debut at Cheltenham, he dropped out as if something were amiss in the Dovecote on his only subsequent start, and with that experience under his belt he can leave that form behind as a second-season novice this year.

Itchy Feet

Rated 150 (1lb inferior to stablemate Thomas Darby) after a highly productive novice hurdle campaign, Itchy Feet was well placed last year and started his campaign by winning a Stratford bumper in September. After winning his first two starts over hurdles – latterly in Listed company at Kempton – he ran a blinder in the Grade 2 Sharp Novices' Hurdle, when narrowly beaten by Elixir de Nutz, to whom he was conceding 5lb. Given the winter off (likes better ground), he returned to Cheltenham in March without a prep run under his belt and stayed on in tremendous fashion to finish third behind Klassical Dream in the Supreme. Only fourth in the Top Novices' at Aintree, he appeared to run a little flat and is best judged on his earlier Cheltenham form. Given his rating, he might not be the easiest to place, although the Welsh Champion Hurdle has been mentioned as a possible starting point.

Notre Pari

Runner-up to his now-stablemate Dundrum Wood in a maiden Point at Rathcannon, Notre Pari ran a race full of promise in a 2m novice hurdle at Warwick on his debut for Olly Murphy and JP McManus. Given that he will eventually want further and a fence, he travelled with ease in behind and ran right through the line, having jumped big and bold and the final flight. There should be races to be won with him over hurdles this season.

Thomas Darby

Will long be remembered at Olly Murphy's stable for providing the trainer with his very first Cheltenham winner, Thomas Darby ended the campaign with a fine second in the Supreme Novices' Hurdle and rates an exciting prospect for the novice chase division. Having defied greenness to beat Elixir de Nutz (won his three subsequent starts, including the Grade 1 Tolworth) in October, he ran sound races in defeat at both Ascot and Kempton, before returning to winning ways in a minor event at Taunton. Despite the ground being softer than ideal, he ran a career-best in the Supreme, when coming from well of the pace. A strongly-run race really suits the son of Beneficial, who should have no trouble in stepping up to 2m4f if required over fences. He seems at his best on a decent surface, although his half-brother, Muirhead, won the Royal Bond Novice Hurdle on heavy ground for Noel Meade, and connections will no doubt be hopeful that he returns to the festival as a live contender for either the Arkle or the JLT, come next March.

PAUL NICHOLLS

Ask For Glory

Looked an exciting prospect when winning his maiden Point in Ireland and also when making a winning debut for the Paul Nicholls stable, in a Chepstow bumper over Christmas. He raced keenly in the Champion Bumper on his final start and can leave this form behind when stepping up in trip over hurdles this season. He looked a smart stayer in the making at Chepstow and a return to the Welsh track would be suitable over hurdles, as he looks as though he will appreciate a galloping track.

Danny Kirwan

Still a maiden after two starts over hurdles last term, Danny Kirwan will come into his own over fences, but is likely to start off over the smaller obstacles once again. An emphatic bumper winner at Kempton the season before, the imposing son of Scorpion still looked quite immature last term, but his run behind Angels Breath was very promising and he remains a decent prospect. He also looked very good when winning his Point-to-Point in Ireland, when he had the useful Ask Ben 21 lengths back in fifth.

Enrilo

McFabulous looks the pick of the Paul Nicholls-trained novice hurdlers this season, but Enrilo won twice from three starts and could well make up into a nice novice hurdler, too. A winner at Worcester early in the season – where he showed a nice attitude – he went on to finish fourth in Listed company at Ascot – where he stayed on from a long way back – before returning to winning ways at Kempton. He attempted to make all on this occasion and after briefly losing his position on the side of the course, the son of Buck's Boum stayed on in determined fashion to beat House Island (Listed bumper winner next time), to whom he was conceding 7lb. He already looks ready for 2m4f and has been described as a future 3m-chaser by his trainer.

Eritage

Another decent prospect for novice hurdles, Eritage had won an AQPS race over 1m4f before joining Paul Nicholls, and following a third behind Get In The Queue at Exeter, he made all to score at Wincanton. He fought off the attentions of the runner-up in the closing stages, with the pair well clear, and there are more races to be won with him once sent jumping.

Flic Ou Voyou

Fourth in a Fontwell bumper in April 2018, Flic Ou Voyou returned to action at Wincanton in November and made most to score with plenty in hand. Green when first asked to go and win his race, he got the message late on and had clearly learnt plenty for that when looking more the finished article at the same track on Boxing Day. The Kapgarde gelding made all to beat Now Look At Me (won a bumper and a maiden hurdle on his next two starts) by 3¼ lengths, with stablemate and subsequent Fontwell winner Hugos Other Horse back in fourth. This teed up a crack at the Champion Bumper and although he finished only 10th in the end (one place behind Ask For Glory, who carried the same colours), he shaped well for a long way. He possesses plenty of size and scope for jumping, and is another to note in what would appear to be a strong bunch of novice hurdlers at Ditcheat.

Getaway Trump

Unable to win in two bumpers the season before last, Getaway Trump made giant strides after winning a Plumpton novice hurdle, on his second start over timber. Having successfully dropped back to 2m1f to beat Tedham (won a handicap off 125 next time) at Exeter, he ran a blinder in the slowly-run Challow, where he travelled very strongly and only found subsequent Sefton Novices' Hurdle winner Champ too good. A shade disappointing in the rearranged Betfair Hurdle and also when fourth in the Premier Kelso Novices' Hurdle, the six-year-old bounced right back to form in the spring, winning at Ayr and then off a mark of 147 at Sandown, on the final day of the season.

An ex-Irish Pointer, I would like to see him head down the novice chase route – when he could easily develop into an Arkle contender – but it seems that Paul Nicholls is thinking about keeping him over hurdles, with the Fighting Fifth mentioned after Sandown.

Master Tommytucker

Sadly, we only got to see Master Tommytucker once last season, when falling at Chepstow in mid-October. The winner of two novice hurdles the season before, the late-developing eight-year-old went through the Chepstow event – a Listed novices' chase – like a very smart prospect, travelling with zest and jumping proficiently. That was until the second fence in the home straight, when he dived at the open ditch and paid the price. He picked up an injury and his season was over, whilst the eventual winner, Spiritofthegames, gave a strong indication to his level of form, as he went on to finish third in the Plate at the festival off a mark of 147. Expected to return this season, he can make up into a smart novice chaser and despite his age, he remains very lightly raced.

Posh Trish

Only eighth in the Dawn Run at Cheltenham, Posh Trish had earlier made up into a really nice novice hurdler and promises to be even better over fences. I was at Chepstow when she made her debut over hurdles last October and, physically, she was dominant before the race and put up a fine performance to win over 2m3½f. That form was later well advertised by the third home, Annie Mc, and after being beaten for speed by Lust For Glory at Newbury, she reversed that form on revised terms in Listed company. She relished the soft ground that day and went on to win twice more before Cheltenham.

A former winning Irish Pointer, that piece of form reads really well now and she jumped soundly. Still just about in front of Colreevy (Grade 1 bumper winner) who came down at the last, she crossed the line with 14 lengths to spare of Getaway Katie Mai (Grade 2 bumper winner), with Ellie Mac (three times a winner over jumps under Rules) a further seven lengths back in third. Already rated 142, she has the size and scope to improve for fences and she might even be up to taking on the boys, in receipt of the sex-allowance. Going back up to 2m4f on a galloping track will see her to best effect.

Silver Forever

Another potentially smart mare, I wouldn't be at all surprised if Silver Forever begins the season in the same Chepstow event which was won by Posh Trish last season. A good-looking grey, the daughter of Jeremy made a winning debut for the Nicholls stable at the Welsh track last November and won again at Ascot, when defeating subsequent Cheltenham winner Mystic Dreamer. Twice placed at Listed level in bumpers, the former Points winner promises to be even better once sent hurdling over further and it is worth noting that she gave Annie Mc (won the mares' final at Newbury) a ten-length beating in her Point-to-Point. She should do well in the mares' novice hurdle division this season.

Topofthegame

Rather like Santini – who he beat by half a length in the RSA – Topofthegame is likely to be aimed at the Ladbrokes Trophy at Newbury. As things stand, he would need to concede 1lb to Nicky Henderson's runner, but Paul Nicholls stated through the summer that he would like to get a run into him somewhere beforehand, and given that the RSA was his first win over fences, he is actually still a novice until the end of October. With that in mind, this offers his connections the opportunity to gain a little more experience – and put him spot-on for Newbury – without having to pitch him in too deep on his reappearance. After Newbury, he would have the option of the King George (although Nicholls has plenty of options for that event) or heading to Ireland over Christmas, before he is freshened up ahead of the festival, as he was last year. He remains a top-class prospect and the Ladbrokes Trophy should tell us more about his chances of lasting home in the Gold Cup.

Trevelyn's Corn

Another really smart Irish Points winner, Trevelyn's Corn ran a race full of promise on his debut under Rules at Ascot (finished fourth) before getting off the mark with ease at Wincanton. He attempted to make all in the Sefton at Aintree, where it might have been more suitable had he set a stronger gallop, as the race developed into a sprint in the end. The huge six-year-old jumped his hurdles like he was crying out for fences and measured his obstacles well when winning at Borris House, for Colin Bowe and Barry O'Neill. Given a mark of 130, he is one to note in a staying novices' handicap chase to begin with.

FERGAL O'BRIEN

Ask Dillon

After shaping well in a couple of decent early-season bumpers, Ask Dillon won twice from four starts over hurdles, starting at Ascot over 2m5½f on debut. Having bumped into a nice sort over an inadequate trip next time (Umbrigado) and finishing 10th in the Ballymore, he returned to winning ways at Exeter on his final start. Prominent throughout, he stayed on strongly to draw clear of a well-strung-out field. He also stayed on strongly on heavy ground to win his Irish Point, and although he will be of interest in a 3m handicap hurdle, I would be more interested in him as a staying novice chaser, should that route be taken.

Imperial Alcazar

Although Imperial Alcazar failed to win in three starts in bumpers last term, he shaped with plenty of promise and should develop into a nice staying novice once sent hurdling. Fourth on debut at Newbury, he stayed on from a long way off the pace and he had no problem in coping with softer conditions at Ascot during December. Again, shaping like a stayer, he found plenty off the bridle to collar subsequent Aintree winner The Glancing Queen for second. The fourth and fifth both won next time, too, so that form looks strong, and Imperial Alcazar again finished placed in Listed company, back at Newbury in March. Ridden more prominently, he again looked a little outpaced early in the home straight, before staying on stoutly for third. A half-brother to the useful mare Jesber's Dream, he shouldn't have a problem in handling mid-winter ground and already looks to be crying out for a stiffer test of stamina.

Liosduin Bhearna

Ended last season with a couple of handicap hurdle wins – at Ayr and Chepstow – Liosduin Bhearna looked a decent prospect with the manner in which he disposed of his field at Chepstow, and although he has gone up another 12lb (132), he is clearly progressive. A full-brother to Jonjo O'Neill's Cloth Cap, it could be that he appreciated the better ground on his last two starts, having earlier finished runner-up in a Chepstow maiden which worked out well. Both his pedigree and running style suggest that he should get 3m or further in time, although something like the 2m5f intermediate handicap at Cheltenham's November meeting might be a race worth considering in the early part of the season. There is also the option of sending him chasing, and he finished behind some nice horses in his Irish Points.

JONJO O'NEILL

Addici

A Shirocco four-year-old whose dam is a half-sister to Winter Escape and from the family of Black Jack Ketchum, Addici is well-bred and made a promising start to his career, when runner-up in a bumper at Warwick. Beaten by a horse two years older than him, who had run well on debut, he was held-up and forced wide into the straight, and looked a little green when first asked to chase the leaders. However, he ran on really well to finish a clear-cut second, suggesting that there should be plenty of improvement to come. He is one of a number of youngsters from the stable to note in novice hurdles this season.

Annie Mc

Progressed nicely as a novice hurdler last term, winning twice from six starts, latterly in the valuable mares' final at Newbury, where she was eight lengths too good for Sixty's Belle, who franked the form by winning a decent event at Newton Abbot next time. A five-year-old from the family of classy staying hurdler Princeful, the daughter of Mahler bumped into Honeysuckle and Silver Forever in her two Irish Points, and given the comments of Jonjo O'Neill Jnr (in the *A View From The Saddle* section), it would appear as though she has done really well – physically – since arriving at Jackdaws Castle. She is now set to embark on a novice chase campaign and she should be capable of doing well over intermediate trips.

Arrivederci

A junior bumper winner at Hereford in mid-December, Arrivederci finished only fourth behind Get In The Queue at Exeter on his second start. It is difficult to be too dogmatic about that race – given that the visibility was extremely poor – but the form worked out really well, with the front three all winning next time out. By Martaline and out of a Dom Alco mare, he is certainly bred for jumping, and being from the family of Crystal d'Ainay, he should have little trouble in going up in distance as he matures.

Carys' Commodity

Runner-up on his debut at Newton Abbot in mid-May, Carys' Commodity should be capable of winning a bumper on his return, before he goes hurdling. Well-supported in the market, the son of Fame And Glory moved well but could probably have enjoyed a smoother passage. Still going well entering the straight, the eventual winner had already slipped the field and he could only keep on for second. It was still a promising start to his career.

Cloth Cap

Did well as a novice chaser last season, winning twice from his first three starts, before finishing third in the Scottish Grand National. The seven-year-old won at Stratford off a mark of 118 and begins this campaign on 137, highlighting the progress he made. At home on good ground, he ran a blinder at Ayr, travelling well just in behind and staying on strongly in the closing stages. This suggests that there could be a good race in him at some stage, and given his ground preference, he could be out fairly early.

Django Django

Appreciated stepping up to staying trips last season, Django Django won twice from four starts and ended the campaign on a mark of 131. Having looked in need of his reappearance at Stratford, the son of Voix du Nord scored with something to spare at Chepstow, before finishing only seventh at Haydock. Given three months off, he returned to the Merseyside track and bounced back to form, seeing the trip out really well to forge clear late on. Not necessarily the most consistent, he could now head down the novice chase route, although given his proven stamina, the Pertemps route might be an option, and with his liking for Haydock, the Betfair Exchange Stayers' might also be worth considering.

Seaton Carew

Looked a really nice prospect when winning a bumper at Wetherby on her second start, Seaton Carew is a Getaway half-sister to Grade 1 novice chase winner Coney Island and from the family of both Wichita Lineman and Rhinestone Cowboy. She appeared to have learned plenty for her debut run at Warwick and looks to have the size and scope to do well over hurdles. Given her smart pedigree, she might need an extra half-mile once sent jumping and looks a decent prospect for the mares' novice hurdle division.

Tedham

Tedham is another who is likely to head over fences, and if he progresses as I still believe he can, he could also be one for the 0-145 novices' handicap at the festival. He shaped with loads of promise behind some leading novices – including Al Dancer and Getaway Trump – over 2m or thereabouts, before getting off the mark at Wincanton on his handicap debut. He relished the step up to 2m5½f and readily brushed off the opposition in the style of an improving young horse. Four of the next six home franked that form by winning subsequently (two of them won twice) and Tedham was sent off favourite for the competitive 2m4f handicap hurdle at Aintree on his final start. Although briefly looking like he would take a hand approaching three out, his effort levelled out and he came home in seventh. It could have been that the ground was softer than ideal for him, but I still expect him to improve beyond his current mark (131). A strong-traveller, he's still only five and I would be disappointed if he couldn't land a nice prize at some stage.

When You're Ready

Jonjo O'Neill introduced several nice types in bumpers in the spring, and one of them was this grey by Malinas who finished third at Warwick during May. Prior to that, When You're Ready had finished runner-up in a five-year-old maiden Point at Belharbour and that form reads quite well, with the third having won over hurdles for Oliver McKiernan. He showed plenty of pace that day and travelled well to lead, whilst he came from off the pace at Warwick and was forced wide to throw down his challenge. He kept going in a likeable fashion – despite probably being inconvenienced by coming so wide – and looks a decent prospect for novice hurdles.

BEN PAULING

Bright Forecast

Only third in his Irish Point, Bright Forecast caused a 20-1 shock on his debut under Rules, when winning a maiden hurdle at Newbury's Winter Carnival. Held-up in mid-field, it appeared after two out that he was running a sound race to finish behind the main protagonists, only to pick up stoutly, despite an awkward jump at the last. Still fifth with half-a-furlong to run, he flew home to grab Sevarano on the line, with Dashel Drasher (won four times later in the season) back in third. After winning under a penalty at Leicester, he ran a sound race against Mister Fisher in the Grade 2 Rossington Main at Haydock, going down by just 2½ lengths despite losing ground on the stable bend. On to the festival, where he relished the step up in distance and finished third in the Ballymore, staying on all the way to the line. Given that he is completely unexposed over this sort of trip, I had thought that the son of Arcadio might remain over hurdles for the time being, but it instead seems as though he will be sent chasing on his return. Reported to have schooled well at home, he should get 3m in time.

Chess Player

A four-year-old by No Risk At All, Chess Player ran a blinder on his racecourse debut, in the bumper at Ayr on Scottish Grand National day. Well-supported into joint-favourite, the market support looked well placed for most of the home straight, as he travelled with purpose and was still seemingly going very well when taking over. Prominent throughout, he took up the running a couple of furlongs out and having quickened well, he looked to have done enough, only for the fast-finishing December Second to pass him inside the final furlong. It was still a hugely encouraging start and the subsequent exploits of the winner give the form a decent look. Given that his dam is a half-sister to Djakadam, he is certainly bred for jumping and can make an impact in novice hurdles. He looks quick enough to start off over the minimum trip.

One Touch

The winner of a 2m4f maiden Point when trained by Francesca Nimmo, One Touch shaped with plenty of promise on his debut under Rules at Chepstow, finishing fourth behind McFabulous when in the care of Michael Scudamore. The son of Court Cave was then outpaced in a slowly-run Listed bumper at Cheltenham, after which he was switched to the Ben Pauling stable. He made a winning start for his new trainer, when returning to Chepstow in early-April and staying on strongly to score by 2¾ lengths. It was a decent performance and one that offers up hope that he will develop into a nice staying novice hurdler this season. He looks sure to be suited by at least 2m4f over hurdles.

DAVID PIPE

Extra Mag

A winner on the Flat in France, Extra Mag was unlucky on his debut for the David Pipe stable, when stumbling after the final flight at Wetherby with the race at his mercy. He had cruised through that race – in the manner of a potentially smart recruit – and got off the mark at Exeter on New Year's Day. Unable to concede 7lb to Precious Cargo, the five-year-old was then a non-runner in the Imperial Cup, but begins this season on a fair handicap mark (132). A buzzy son of Kapgarde, if he can learn to relax he looks to have a bright future, and strongly-run handicaps might well help him settle.

First Lord de Cuet

Runner-up on debut in a bumper at Taunton – when he conceded both weight and race-fitness to the winner Perfect Predator – First Lord de Cuet made no mistake next time, making most and quickening right away to score in style at Plumpton. It wasn't the strongest of bumpers, but visually he did it really nicely, and he had Thunder Down Under (bumper winner for Gordon Elliott and Gigginstown) back in third, when winning his Point at Tralee. He looks a nice sort for 2m4f novice hurdles this season.

Induno

A five-year-old by Flemensfirth with a stout pedigree, Induno ran a sound race on his racecourse debut, when runner-up to Irish Point winner Overthetop, in a bumper at Warwick. Sent off joint-favourite with the winner, he travelled well to lead on the home bend, having been held up for most of the contest. He picked up well – despite showing signs of inexperience – and it was a good race between the pair up the home straight. He only gave best late on and is another to note once upped in trip over hurdles.

New Age Dawning

Looked a potentially useful long-distance chase prospect when staying on strongly to win a novice hurdle at Chepstow in March, having earlier finished runner-up over half-a-mile shorter at Lingfield. Runner-up to Bold Plan in his Irish Point, New Age Dawning then had the best part of a year off before winning his bumper at Exeter, where he again stayed on really strongly. He should have no problem in handling softer ground and could well be sent chasing, despite just having had the two starts over hurdles. If he remains over the smaller obstacles, he is set to begin the campaign on a mark of 133.

Remastered

Like New Age Dawning, Remastered carries the multicoloured silks of Brocade Racing and he, too, rates a decent prospect for fences. From the family of the smart Le Vent d'Antan, the six-year-old had some decent form to his name in bumpers in Ireland (when trained by Liz Doyle) and beat Kateson on his debut for David Pipe in February of last year. He won once from three starts over hurdles last season – when relishing the heavy ground at Ffos Las on debut – and rounded his campaign off by finishing runner-up to Dashel Drasher at Newbury. Also rated 133, he stayed on strongly at Newbury, suggesting that he shouldn't have problem in going up to 3m.

Umbrigado

Runner-up on his sole start in Irish Points (beaten by Brewers Project – who is now with Paul Nicholls), Umbrigado made an immediate impact under Rules, when running out a stylish bumper winner at Uttoxeter. Despite racing a little keenly, he travelled with real zest and stretched right away from a couple of subsequent winners in fine style. He then beat Khage (won three times subsequently) at Southwell on his hurdles debut, before having too much speed for Ask Dillon (won again later in season) at Exeter, which set up a crack at the Mersey Novices' Hurdle. Ridden patiently and out wide, he never really landed a blow, although he threatened to get involved on the approach to two out. He kept on for sixth in what I think was a strong Grade 1, and in that exalted company he might appreciate softer ground to be at his best. Off a mark of 142, he would certainly be of interest in handicap hurdles, although his long-term future lies over fences and he remains a smart prospect.

KATY PRICE

Éclair des Sablons

An Irish Point winner at the fifth time of asking (jumped well on the front end) for Colin Bowe, Éclair des Sablons showed progressive form in three starts over hurdles for Katy Price in the spring. Having travelled well for a long way at Exeter, he dropped back to an extended 2m3f at Wincanton, where he was booked for third until Storm Arising made a serious error at the last. He kept on to take second behind Hey Bud, then went on to run a sound race over the same distance at Huntingdon. Prominent throughout, he led the field into the straight and saw the race out really well, only being grabbed late on by Skandiburg, and the close-up third won a maiden hurdle during June. Given that he had been on the go for a long time in Ireland, he was probably due for a break and might well improve for his summer at grass. He has the look of a chaser, but there are races to be won with him over hurdles beforehand and he begins the season on a mark of 115.

NICKY RICHARDS

Marown

A five-year-old by Milan, Marown made a winning racecourse debut in a heavy-ground bumper at Newcastle in March, but it didn't seem likely until the final half-furlong. Held up by Brian Hughes, he began to keep on inside the final quarter-mile, but still looked held in third as they passed the furlong marker. The penny dropped late on and he ran on, despite not having to have been given a hard time, so clearly possesses plenty of natural ability. Given how he finished, he looks the type who will appreciate a step up in trip over hurdles and also appeals as the sort to have done really well for his summer break.

Uncle Alastair

A smart novice hurdler the season before last (when a *Leading Prospect* in *Jumpers To Follow*, following his successful bumper campaign), Uncle Alastair made a really pleasing introduction to his chase career at Carlisle, when runner-up to Vinndication. Sadly, we didn't get to see him again after that, but he is expected to return this autumn and, hopefully, can make up for lost time. Provided he returns at the same level, he ought to make up into a very smart novice chaser in the north. The son of Midnight Legend relishes testing ground and is effective between 2m4f and 3m.

LUCINDA RUSSELL

Highland Hunter

Winner of his first two starts over hurdles (both in heavy ground), Highland Hunter – who had earlier won an Irish Point and a bumper at Kelso, before finishing 10th in the Grade 2 at Aintree – went on to run respectably on his handicap debut, then finished fifth in the Grade 2 Prestige Novices' Hurdle. The ground would have been quicker than ideal for him on that occasion and the reason we didn't get to see him thereafter was due to his need for testing conditions. After just the four starts over hurdles, he will remain over the smaller obstacles for the time being and begins the season on a mark of 131. He is one to note in staying handicap hurdles, especially on testing ground – his form on heavy reads 111.

JEREMY SCOTT

Champagne Court

Looked really promising when fourth in a Cheltenham bumper and, even more so, when winning at Lingfield on his hurdling debut. It took a while for him to recapture his form after that, but he might have been over-faced a little, pitched straight into Grade 2 events after his win at Lingfield. Fourth in the Martin Pipe at Cheltenham and third at Sandown on the final day of the season, he should relish going 3m once sent chasing, and should do well in novice handicap company from a mark of 126.

Hey Bud

Relished the step up to 2m4f when shedding his maiden tag at Wincanton in March, Hey Bud looks another nice prospect for staying novice chases, and from a mark of 124 he is very much another to note in a novice handicap. Having shown promise over shorter trips, the son of Fair Mix really saw his race out well when scoring and looks the type to progress further over fences. After just four starts over hurdles, he might start in a handicap hurdle, especially given that the yard have several options for the novice chase division.

Kissesforkatie

A bumper winner on her debut for Jeremy Scott, Kissesforkatie went on to perform with great credit in Listed and Graded company, latterly when sixth behind The Glancing Queen at Aintree, where she led into the straight. Having tired late on in soft ground, it looked as though she might be better served by a less-demanding test and similar comments applied to her hurdling debut at Newton Abbot, where she failed to get home having travelled best. I suspect she will be dropped in distance a little for her reappearance and there should be plenty more races to be won with her in the mares' division this season.

OLIVER SHERWOOD

Brummie Boys

Third behind more experienced rivals on his debut in a bumper at Wincanton, Brummie Boys is a well-bred son of Flemensfirth, being a half-brother to Definitelyanoscar and Towering. Only four, he came from off the pace and the experience won't be lost on him when he returns to action in the autumn. He also looks the type who will improve as he goes up in distance and he could be a useful prospect.

Donladd

Whilst his form figures from bumpers would be a little uninspiring, Donladd shaped with a bit of promise on each of his three starts last term. He appeals as the type who will, hopefully, have matured for his summer break, and given the stamina in his pedigree, he will probably appreciate a stiffer test once sent jumping. Being by Cloudings, he might also appreciate a softer surface than he ran on the last twice.

Sevarano

Failed to win in four starts over hurdles last term – having impressed as a bumper horse the previous season – Sevarano did little wrong on his first two starts and was a little unlucky at Newbury on his second outing, when possibly in front for longer than ideal. Disappointing at Chepstow in January (beaten at odds-on), he finished behind subsequent dual-Grade 1 winner Reserve Tank on his final start, and now looks ready for a stiffer test of stamina. A future chaser, he can surely win races over hurdles beforehand and the handicapper has dropped him to a mark of 130.

Shaughnessy

Another who failed to win in novice hurdles last season, Shaughnessy had earlier beaten Ask Dillon (won twice over hurdles) in his bumper at Towcester. Third on debut at Exeter, he finished the season with another third-placing on his handicap debut at Ffos Las and that form now reads really well, thanks to the subsequent exploits of the front two. Upped 3lb to a mark of 115, there should be races to be won with him – probably once going back up in trip to 3m – and he is a staying chaser of the future.

DAN SKELTON

Ardlethen

Twice a winner over an extended 2m7f at Uttoxeter last season, Ardlethen looks a thorough stayer and appeals as the type to do well in the staying novice chase division. The Arakan six-year-old – who possesses plenty of size for fences – went on to take his chance in the Grade 1 Sefton at Aintree, but the lack of pace wouldn't have helped him there. He showed a fine attitude when winning his Irish Point, and the Listed novices' chase at Warwick in January might well be something that Dan Skelton has in mind for him.

Beakstown

Twice a winner from four starts over hurdles last season, Beakstown is another who will be going down the novice chase route, and the strapping son of Stowaway looks every inch a chaser. Runner-up in a strong Kempton bumper the season before (had Imperial Aura and Getaway Trump directly in behind), he made a winning debut at Uttoxeter before finishing a head second in the French Furze at Newcastle just a fortnight later. Being a big, green horse, that race might well have come too soon for him and he bounced back by impressively winning the Grade 2 Leamington Novices' Hurdle at Warwick. Pulled-up in the Ballymore on his final start, he struggled from three out, but may not have been ready for a race of that nature. It wouldn't, therefore, surprise me if he ended up at Aintree rather than Cheltenham in the spring, should things go to plan earlier in the campaign. He jumped really well when winning his Point and remains full of potential.

Montego Grey

Got off the mark at the third time of asking in bumpers, bringing up his trainer's 200th win of last season in the process. The grey made his debut in a slowly-run race at Aintree, before staying on strongly in a competitive Listed event at Ascot. He travelled really well on that occasion and had little trouble in beating much weaker opposition at Market Rasen, where he made all and quickened clear up the straight. He clearly isn't short of speed and I would expect him to start off over the minimum trip over hurdles.

Shan Blue

Third on his debut for the Skelton stable in a bumper at Warwick, Shan Blue had earlier won a maiden Point for Andrew Slattery. Having taken up the running four out, he quickened up well over the last two fences to score decisively. Held-up at Warwick, he made stealthy headway into the home straight and ran a sound race to finish third behind the exciting Chantry House. He was probably unlucky to lose second to a more-experienced rival and looks a nice type for novice hurdles this season. Given the pace he showed in Ireland, trips ranging between 2m – 2m4f might prove ideal.

Tokay Dokey

Another who won twice at Uttoxeter last season, Tokay Dokey – a bumper winner at Market Rasen the season before – showed plenty of speed to win on debut and readily gave Speed Company (a winner on the Flat during June) 7lb and a beating under his penalty. Given three months off, he was pitched into the Grade 2 Dovecote, where he fell before the race had really got going. A non-runner in the Supreme Novices, the five-year-old is certainly one to note when returning in a handicap, off his current mark of 130. The son of Gold Well looks to be fairly speedy, so a track like Aintree might be suitable.

Touching upon Uttoxeter again, Dan Skelton boasts a 30% strike rate at the track, which is the highest of any course where he has saddled more than just one runner. During the 2018-19 season, the stable had 44 winners from 111 runners at the Midlands track (40%) and it seems apparent that he likes to run his novice hurdlers there.

SUE SMITH

Hill Sixteen

Won just once from six starts over hurdles last term, Hill Sixteen really ought to come into his own over fences this season. Having shaped with promise behind One For Rosie and Glen Forsa on his debut for Sue Smith and Trevor Hemmings, the strapping son of Court Cave finally got off the mark, back at Carlisle in February. He stayed on really strongly that day, before finishing fourth in a competitive handicap hurdle at Uttoxeter, on Midlands Grand National day. He stayed on strongly – and jumped well – when winning his Point-to-Point in Ireland and looks capable of developing into a smart staying handicap chaser in time. He begins the season on a mark of 123 and his best form has come on decent ground.

Midnight Shadow

Another exciting prospect for the novice chase division, the former Scottish Champion Hurdle winner progressed as he went up in distance last season. After winning a 2m4f handicap at Aintree, the six-year-old won the Grade 2 Relkeel Hurdle on New Year's Day, and although he disappointed on his final start in the Cleeve, he can bounce back upon his return in the autumn. He travelled well at Aintree – where he fended off County Hurdle winner Ch'tibello – as he did when winning the Relkeel, and there won't be many higher-rated hurdlers going chasing this winter. Rated 155, he has the physique for chasing, and should things go to plan earlier in the campaign, races such as the JLT and Aintree's Manifesto Novices' Chase could prove ideal spring targets. Haydock's Grade 2 Altcar Novices' Chase – a race Sue Smith won in 2015 with Wakanda – would be another possible target for the likeable son of Midnight Legend.

Rare Clouds

Being a full-brother to Vintage Clouds and a half-brother to Vintage Stage, Rare Clouds hails from a family that Sue Smith and Trevor Hemmings know very well, and he made a really pleasing introduction, when sixth in a bumper at Wetherby in January. Eventually beaten 11½ lengths, the five-year-old travelled really well in the hands of Danny Cook and only faded inside the final quarter-mile. Three of those who finished in front of him won a bumper before the end of last season, and although his future lies over further once going jumping, there is a chance that Rare Clouds could himself reappear in another bumper. Once sent hurdling, he is very much one to note when there is more emphasis on stamina.

JAMIE SNOWDEN

Early Morning Rain

A winner of one of her four starts in bumpers, Early Morning Rain progressed with each run and got off the mark at Plumpton on her third outing. Having shown promise at both Ludlow and Taunton – where she finished runner-up to Miss Honey Ryder (won again next time before finishing fourth at Punchestown) – the daughter of Martaline won at Plumpton, form which was advertised when the third won next time. She went on to finish fifth at Cheltenham and can win again once sent hurdling, perhaps when reverting to a sharper track, as she's not short of pace.

Kiltealy Briggs

A five-year-old by Fame And Glory, Kiltealy Briggs has yet to race for Jamie Snowden, but spent the whole of last season in his Lambourn yard and his Point-to-Point form has since been well advertised by Shishkin, who finished third. From the family of Ballabriggs, Kiltealy Briggs is now in the ownership of the McNeill Family and very much one to note in a bumper – or a novice hurdle – in the early part of the season. I expect that Snowden will want to crack on with him after missing last season, and given the speed he showed when second in his Point (travelled really well), he rates a smart prospect for his new connections.

Minella Beat

Another who has yet to race for the burgeoning Snowden stable, Minella Beat was purchased last December (£140,000) on the back of a maiden Point success (left clear to score) and two solid runs in bumpers. On the second of those runs, he chased home subsequent Grade 1 winner Battleoverdoyen on good ground at Punchestown, and that form has been further enhanced by Active Force (won a bumper) and Ash Hill (won a bumper and maiden hurdle). He was due to run before the snow arrived, followed by the outbreak of Equine Flu, before the ground turned against him. I would, therefore, expect that Snowden will be keen to get him out fairly early in the season, too.

Shantewe

A nice prospect for mares-only novice hurdles, Shantewe won twice from four starts in bumpers and her form is very solid. She defeated Farne on debut at Wetherby and finished just one place behind that rival when fifth in the Grade 2 at Aintree. The daughter of Shantou probably would have appreciated a stronger gallop at Market Rasen on her second start and rounded off her campaign with a smooth win under Page Fuller at Hexham in May. She showed plenty of pace in her bumpers, so shouldn't have a problem starting off over the minimum trip, and although she isn't the biggest, she is a nice prospect.

Thebannerkingrebel

Jamie Snowden began the 2019-20 season in red-hot form, saddling no fewer than 18 winners from 53 runners (34% strike rate) from May through July. Thebannerkingrebel provided him with two of those victories, when winning a shade cosily on his debut over hurdles at Warwick, after which he scored by 14 lengths under a penalty at Newton Abbot. Thought good enough to take his chance in the 2018 Champion Bumper, the son of Arakan returned from almost 13 months off to run an absolute blinder, when runner-up to McFabulous in the Grade 2 at Aintree. The six-year-old was handed a mark of 132 after those two victories, and with that experience under his belt, he could be one to side with in the early part of the new season proper. The Listed event at Kempton in October – won last season by Itchy Feet – would be a possible starting point, after which Cheltenham's Grade 2 Sharp Novices' Hurdle might be worth thinking about.

I wouldn't actually mind seeing him in a handicap off his current rating, but I suspect that Snowden will treat him like a high-class prospect and Graded races probably await.

COLIN TIZZARD

Bold Conduct

Purchased at the Tattersalls Cheltenham sale back in November of last year, Bold Conduct had impressed with the way he travelled en route to beating Sidi Ismael (bumper winner for Keith Dalgleish at Hexham in March) at Loughanmore. A five-year-old by Stowaway and out of an Old Vic mare, he hails from the family of Maljimar, and although we have yet to see him race for the Tizzard stable, he remains one to really look forward to. He showed enough pace to suggest that he would be more than capable of winning a bumper, although having missed last season, connections might want to head straight over hurdles.

Elixir de Nutz

Sadly forced to miss the Supreme Novices' Hurdle due to being lame on the eve of the race, Elixir de Nutz had earlier made up into a very smart novice, winning his last three starts. Having beaten subsequent Supreme third, Itchy Feet, in the Sharp, he returned to Cheltenham to beat Jarveys Plate (conceding 10lb), before winning the Tolworth at Sandown. Gutsy on that occasion, he appeared to relish front-running tactics, and having originally been handed a mark of 145 after the Tolworth, he found his rating increased twice due to collateral form lines. The second and third – Grand Sancy and Southfield Stone – won Grade 2s on successive Saturdays during February, meaning Elixir de Nutz is now rated 153. He appeals more as a future chaser than a Champion Hurdle contender to me, and considering the same connections have Eldorado Allen to factor in, it will be interesting to see which direction they take. A really slick jumper, the grey was on a sharp upward curve when last seen.

Fiddlerontheroof

Showed a fine attitude when winning a bumper at Navan in March, Fiddlerontheroof was then purchased for £200,000 at the Goffs UK sale at Aintree and is now in training with Colin Tizzard. The Stowaway five-year-old had earlier shown a decent level of form when placed in bumpers either side of the New Year, and the placed horses from Navan went on to perform with credit at the Punchestown Festival. Like stablemates Faustinovick and Lostintranslation, Fiddlerontheroof will sport the colours of Taylor & O'Dwyer and is likely to appreciate at least 2m4f once sent hurdling.

Master Debonair

Twice a winner in bumpers, Master Debonair showed good form on decent ground early on last season, before seemingly finding the ground too soft at both Cheltenham and Aintree. The five-year-old still finished fifth at Liverpool, having travelled well into the straight, and given it came at the end of a long season, his effort can probably be marked up a little. He earlier had the Aintree winner, McFabulous, and the Champion Bumper third, Thyme Hill, in behind when winning a Listed event at Cheltenham and can make his mark over hurdles, when the ground is more in his favour. He is one to catch early on in the campaign.

Russian Hawk

A winner on debut over hurdles at Exeter last season, Russian Hawk's best effort came when narrowly denied by the progressive Dashel Drasher at Ascot, where a mistake at the last didn't help his chance. Sent off favourite for the EBF Final on the back of this, he failed to get involved at Sandown, but that could easily be put down to the bad ground. Judged on his earlier form, he looks a nice type to go chasing with, and given that he still appeared quite immature at times last season, he ought to have done well for his summer break.

NIGEL TWISTON-DAVIES

Earlofthecotswolds

A horse who clearly has a good constitution, Earlofthecotswolds had eight runs in all last season and the progressive five-year-old won four times. A bumper winner on his reappearance, he got off the mark at the second time of asking over hurdles, and having caught the eye in fifth on his handicap debut, he was well-supported when running out a convincing winner at Market Rasen. He looked a shade unlucky when caught for speed in a slowly-run race at Ludlow, before returning to winning ways – back at Market Rasen – when making all and jumping well. His hurdling improved with racing last year and the imposing son of Axxos (sire of stablemate Calett Mad) has the stamp of a chaser. Now rated 133, he could form part of what appears to be a strong-looking novice chase team for the stable.

Good Boy Bobby

Three-from-four in bumpers, Good Boy Bobby repeated the feat in novice hurdle company last season and is another who could be heading over fences this autumn. A highly-strung individual, I think the fact that he has been kept away from the spring festivals in each of his two seasons to date could pay dividends as he matures. He will need to learn to settle, but he proved at Ffos Las in April that he gets 2m4f, so is learning to relax and clearly possesses a high-class engine. Rated 139 over hurdles, the six-year-old has worn a hood on six of his eight career starts to date.

One For Rosie

Like Good Boy Bobby, One For Rosie carries the yellow and navy silks of owners Paul and Clare Rooney, and the grey – who had won a bumper at Bangor the previous season – won twice from five starts over hurdles last season. After beating smart novice chaser Glen Forsa on debut, he returned to Carlisle and appeared to find the ground too testing, having raced a shade keenly early on. The son of Getaway – who is a half-brother to Air Horse One and Misty Whisky – returned to winning ways with a smooth success at Warwick. He then shouldered top-weight and ran an absolute blinder – on what I thought would be unsuitably soft ground – in the EBF Final, sweeping around the field in the manner of a very smart prospect. He jumped to the front at the last and was only collared in the dying strides by Third Wind, despite being called the winner – incorrectly – on course. On to Aintree, One For Rosie was upped in class to take his chance in the Mersey and he again shaped well, finishing dead-heated for third with Angels Breath.

Rather like the pair who finished in front of him, he looks an exciting prospect for fences and should develop into a Graded-class novice, if taking that route. Given the ammunition the stable seems to have for that division, it could be that they consider trying him in a handicap hurdle (currently rated 145) and a step up in trip could open up more options.

The Hollow Ginge

Another for the novice chase division, The Hollow Ginge looks an out-and-out stayer, who relished the heavy ground when scoring at Haydock in December. He galloped on strongly on that occasion, and although he failed to back it up when upped in grade at Sandown, he looks one to keep onside in deep ground during the winter. Eventually, he could develop into a decent handicapper for those marathon chases.

Torn And Frayed

Only fifth on his debut in a Southwell bumper during March, Torn And Frayed certainly shaped with a deal of promise and should come on plenty for that initial experience. The Califet five-year-old travelled with ease at the head of affairs and only gave best inside the final quarter-mile, shaping as though he might have needed the run. He looks to possess plenty of size for jumping, but also looks capable of winning a bumper beforehand.

TIM VAUGHAN

Tippingituptonancy

We sadly didn't get to see this daughter of Stowaway run last season, but Tim Vaughan told me during the summer that she is back in training and it is hoped that she can make up for lost time. Purchased for £185,000 on the back of her second in an Irish Point, that form now reads really well, given that she was beaten by Grade 2 bumper winner The Glancing Queen. Having made most of the running, the five-year-old – who is a half-sister to Mr Whipped – came back strongly after the last and looks to possess plenty of size and scope. With that in mind, it could be that she heads straight over hurdles and remains a very interesting prospect for the mares' division.

HARRY WHITTINGTON

Khage

A winner at Taunton after the turn of the year, Khage twice made all to score at Chepstow in the spring and rates a nice prospect for novice chases. Whilst they might not have been the strongest of races, he won impressively and appeals as the type who will do well when able to dictate the pace in small fields. Progressive when last seen, he likes a decent surface and should continue to do well once sent over fences in the autumn.

Rouge Vif

Proved to be a star for the Harry Whittington stable last season, winning three times, including the Grade 2 Premier Kelso Novices' Hurdle in March. Having made all under a well-judged ride by Gavin Sheehan at Kelso, he headed to Aintree for the Grade 1 Top Novices' Hurdle, where he finished third, having chased the front-running Felix Desjy throughout. At his best when allowed to dominate, he is still only five and given his mark of 142 seems more than fair, I would expect him to be campaigned in the top handicap hurdles this season, as opposed to heading over fences, although that decision has yet to be made.

Stick With Bill

Made all to win what was just an ordinary bumper at Ffos Las on debut, Stick With Bill then made a bold bid to follow up under a penalty, finding only the unbeaten and well-regarded King Roland too good, with the pair drawing nicely clear. An Oscar five-year-old from the family of Made In Taipan and Made In Time, he should have no trouble in staying further once sent jumping and seems versatile in terms of ground conditions.

Young Bull

Having shaped with promise in a Ffos Las bumper, Young Bull – who ran twice in Points in Ireland – got off the mark in determined fashion at Chepstow. The imposing son of Dubai Destination appeared to appreciate the heavy ground, and although he was a shade disappointing on better ground at Carlisle on his final start, he is still one to note once going up in distance over hurdles. A half-brother to Shanroe Santos (plenty of winning form over 3m+), he boasts a stamina-laden pedigree and ought to relish a thorough test in time. Given his physique, his long-term future lies over fences.

CHRISTIAN WILLIAMS

Win My Wings

Looked a potentially smart mare when bolting up by 19 lengths at Ffos Las, Win My Wings went on to finish third in what looked a strong mares' novices' hurdle at Newton Abbot, conceding weight to the pair who finished in front of her. Still a novice until the end of October, the daughter of Gold Well went on to twice finish runner-up during July, appearing to appreciate the step back up in trip at Stratford. She stayed on really strongly when winning her Point, so it probably isn't a coincidence that her best form has come over staying trips, and she also has the option of switching to fences, given that she won that maiden Point at Lingstown.

EVAN WILLIAMS

Esprit du Large

Twice a winner from four starts over hurdles last term, Esprit du Large is open to plenty of improvement after just one season with racing under his belt. Having finished seventh in a Chepstow bumper on debut, he won a maiden hurdle at Uttoxeter by 12 lengths and with any amount in hand. It could be that the Grade 2 at Haydock came too soon for him (still green at Uttoxeter) and he bounced back once upped in trip and dropped in grade at Hereford. He again travelled really well and jumped like a horse who will come into his own once sent chasing.

That could well be on the cards this season, and although he again struggled once upped in class at Aintree, I think the son of No Risk At All will have grown up a lot for his summer break and could be a different proposition this season. He remains a nice prospect for fences and similar comments apply to several of his stablemates.

Present Value

Very closely related to Paisley Park (out of the same mare and both sired by sons of Sadler's Wells), Present Value made an encouraging debut when runner-up to Al Dancer over 2m at Ffos Las and readily got off the mark once upped in trip at Chepstow. Purchased by leading owners Mr & Mrs Rucker ahead of that maiden hurdle, he stayed on strongly to beat Hill Sixteen (won subsequently at Carlisle), with another subsequent winner back in fourth. Well-beaten into third at Exeter on his third and final start, I'm fairly sure that he didn't give his true running on this occasion and is another who might well have appreciated his summer break. Given his lack of experience, he might start off in handicap hurdles.

Quoi de Neuf

Flagged up in the *Under The Hammer* section of last year's publication, Quoi de Neuf duly made a winning debut under Rules, at Aintree in November. Despite showing signs of greenness, he stayed on well to score and three of his five opponents won subsequently. Upped sharply in grade to contest the Winter Novices' Hurdle at Sandown, he travelled really well for a long way, but struggled to pick up from the back of two out and appeared tired. Given four months off, he returned with a sound second at Ffos Las, behind the potentially smart Good Boy Bobby. Another lightly-raced and unexposed five-year-old, he begins the season on a mark of 127.

IAN WILLIAMS

King of Realms

Bookended last season with wins over fences, King of Realms remains unexposed as a chaser (had just four starts) and is clearly talented on his day. The good-looking son of King's Theatre was impressive on his chase debut at Ascot, where he jumped particularly fluently and looked as though he would have the pace to drop in distance. He flopped next time when upped in grade, but ended his season on a winning note and begins the season on a revised mark of 140. Twice a winner on his reappearance, he is one to take seriously first time out and interestingly has started all three seasons at Ascot, recording form figures of 121. There could be a nice handicap in him at some point.

Seven de Baune

Ian Williams sent out three runners on 18th June. The Grand Visir and Time To Study finished first and third respectively in the Ascot Stakes, while Seven de Baune – a *Leading Prospect* in last year's publication – finished runner-up in a hurdle race at Dieppe in France. It was an encouraging return to action from the six-year-old, who hadn't been seen since disappointing at Doncaster over Christmas, having earlier won a weak novice hurdle at Ludlow. The son of Tiger Groom showed plenty of pace when winning his bumper and when runner-up in an Irish Point, so I suspect 2m4f (or thereabouts) will remain his optimum, and he remains an unexposed horse of some potential. He was actually declared to make his debut over fences at Uttoxeter in late-July and although he was pulled out due to the ground (meeting was actually lost to the rain shortly after), it shows the intent to head down the novice chase route when he does reappear.

The Grand Visir

As stated above, The Grand Visir was a game winner of this year's Ascot Stakes (off a mark of 100) and his trainer hinted after the race that he could return to hurdling later in the year. The five-year-old got off to an inauspicious start when unseating Tom Scudamore at the first flight at Aintree (forcing Eldorado Allen to do likewise) and then finished only fourth at Doncaster. His jumping needs to improve, but Ian Williams is very adept with these dual-purpose stayers and there is every chance – given his latent talent – that he could still make an impact under National Hunt rules. It could be that he needs 2m4f once returning to the winter code.

AROUND THE YARDS

JANE WILLIAMS

Erick Le Rouge

Between them, Nick and Jane Williams look to have some lovely prospects for the upcoming season, with Moonlighter (Jane) and Siruh du Lac (Nick) the standout pairing. Jane has another couple of smart types in her name, the first being Erick le Rouge, who completed a four-timer in handicaps last season and saw his handicap mark rise from 112 to 137 in the process. His latest two wins came on big days at Kempton and although he was pulled up in the Coral Cup when last sighted, he remains a bright prospect for fences. Being by Gentlewave, he hasn't exactly got a chasing pedigree, but has the size and scope and jumped hurdles like a staying chaser in the making. He showed a fine attitude when winning at Kempton in February and is at his best on a decent surface.

Monsieur Lecoq

Another relatively lightly-raced five-year-old, Monsieur Lecoq is another who made giant strides over hurdles last season, winning at Ffos Las (maiden) and Sandown (handicap), before finishing runner-up in the Imperial Cup. Held up in the County Hurdle, he failed to get involved, but ended the campaign on a mark of 138 and remains another nice long-term prospect. Given that he looks to possess the scope to jump fences, it could be that he also heads down that route, although there is probably further progression to be made over hurdles, as he could be worth a try over further and has no problem handling testing ground.

NICK WILLIAMS

Le Cameleon

Sixth on debut in what I believe to be a very good bumper at Newbury, Le Cameleon shaped really well for a long way, racing prominently throughout and looking as though he might play a hand in the finish until fading inside the final quarter-mile. Given that Nick Williams' runners – over the years – have tended to progress a fair bit with each run in the early part of their careers, it was a hugely encouraging start, and being only four, there is probably a chance that he could return in a bumper. A good-looking son of Great Pretender, he hails from a family that Williams knows well (a half-brother to *Leading Prospect* Moonlighter) and is one to look forward to in the autumn.

Prudhomme

Having unshipped Lizzie Kelly at the start on debut at Wincanton, Prudhomme got off on terms at Newbury on his second start. Having tracked the pace, the four-year-old hit the front going best, but was alone for a long time and that probably proved costly in the end. Kelly did her best to hold him together, but in the end he was worn down in the shadow of the post. He again travelled really well when going one better at Ffos Las, this time only hitting the front on the run to the final furlong. The son of Martaline – who is a half-brother to Pont Alexandre – saw his race out to record a taking success, and looks another nice prospect for the novice hurdle division.

Siruh du Lac

Still only six, Siruh du Lac did nothing but improve throughout last season, winning all four starts and rising 27lb in the handicap (he's actually now 38lb higher than when winning his first chase in November 2017). Victories at Newbury and Exeter preceded a tenacious win at Cheltenham on trials day, before he completed the four-timer in the 'Plate' at the Festival. His jumping really is a key asset and I would love to see him tackle the big fences at Aintree – in the Topham – one day. If he continues his ascendancy when he returns, that is unlikely to become a spring target and he seems an obvious type for the BetVictor Gold Cup in the first part of the season. From a mark of 150, his performance there will probably tell connections which way they need to go for the remainder of the campaign.

NOEL WILLIAMS

Breaking Waves

An extraordinary winner of a Huntingdon bumper the season before last (form worked out well), Breaking Waves ran a sound race under his penalty at Cheltenham on his reappearance, before finishing third to EBF Final winner Third Wind – who had finished behind him in his bumper – and undergoing wind surgery. He returned to action in a competitive novice hurdle at Chepstow, then stayed on well to get off the mark at Huntingdon, making the most of the weight he received from Hold The Note. Fourth behind Dashel Drasher on his final start, he kept good company over hurdles last term and will start the season in a handicap hurdle off a mark of 131. He also has the option of going chasing, but I would be disappointed if he can't prove competitive in handicap hurdles beforehand.

Kalinihta

Sadly, we didn't get to see Kalinihta in action last season, but the five-year-old is expected to return in the autumn and the form of his bumper win at Fontwell now reads very well.

Despite running around in the closing stages, he stayed on well to beat the 150-rated hurdler Itchy Feet by 3¼ lengths. The runner-up, of course, won three times last season before finishing third in the Supreme, whilst Shut The Box (3rd) won over hurdles in March, and Flic Ou Voyou (4th) won twice before contesting the Champion Bumper. It is, therefore, sincerely hoped that the son of Kalanisi retains all of his ability, as he is clearly very talented and could easily make up into a decent novice hurdler.

VENETIA WILLIAMS

Cloudy Glen

Won three times from four starts last term, Cloudy Glen won handicaps at Haydock and Chepstow either side of the turn of the year, then bounced back to win a weak novice event at Carlisle following his only disappointing run, at Ascot. Clearly at home on testing ground, the son of Cloudings looks to possess plenty of scope, so can continue his progress over fences this winter. He appeared to have tons in hand when winning his first two last season, and his front-running style will stand him in good stead in small fields over fences.

Geordie B

The winner of his last two starts in novice hurdles last season, Geordie B is another who likes soft ground and should do well in the staying novice chase division. A heavy-ground bumper winner, the grey looks a strong stayer and galloped on strongly when shedding his maiden tag at Lingfield in January. The form worked out well, with three of the next four home winning next time out (runner-up Samburu Shujaa won his next two), and he again stayed on really well when scoring at Exeter, where he came right away from the second in the closing stages.

That form was again advertised when the fourth home, No Hidden Charges, won a couple of times during May, and despite being kept to a low-level, Geordie B ended the campaign with an official rating of 140. He looks to have plenty of size for fences and is one to note when the emphasis is on stamina.

Steven Keating
Equestrian Art

View the complete Steven Keating collection
available from Rowles Fine Art
53 Mill Street, Ludlow, SY8 1BB

CLOSELY BUNCHED!

Oil on Canvas

36" x 48" | Signed

CLOSE FINISH!

Oil on Canvas

36" x 48" | Signed

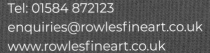

Jonathan Burke

Jamie Codd

Aidan Coleman

Brian Hughes

Jeremiah McGrath

Jonjo O'Neill jnr

Nick Scholfield

Harry Skelton

A VIEW FROM THE SADDLE

Jonathan Burke – *The first of this year's three new additions, Jonathan enjoyed a first Cheltenham winner in April when successful aboard Mister Whitaker and formed a fine partnership with Glen Forsa – for the same connections – last season. He will also be riding plenty of Tom George's horses this season.*

Jamie Codd – *Again successful at all three spring festivals – and from limited numbers of rides – Jamie needs no introduction and his insight into the Irish Point-to-Point scene is once again an invaluable tool.*

Aidan Coleman – *Another of this year's newcomers, Aidan enjoyed Grade 1 success for the first time last winter when Paisley Park won at Ascot and the pair, of course, went on to win the Stayers' Hurdle. His horses to follow hail from seven different stables.*

Brian Hughes – *The leading National Hunt rider in the north, Brian has again started the 2019-20 season in fine form and has also selected horses from various stables.*

Jeremiah McGrath – *An important part of the team at Nicky Henderson's stable, Jerry enjoyed big-race success aboard Verdana Blue (Elite Hurdle) and Beware The Bear (Ultima Handicap Chase) last season and again selects his pick of the squad from Seven Barrows.*

Jonjo O'Neill Jnr – *The third new name on the teamsheet this year, Jonjo Jnr has quickly developed into a very accomplished young rider. Having ridden his first Cheltenham winner aboard Palmers Hill last November, he secured festival success when partnering Early Doors to win the Martin Pipe.*

Nick Scholfield – *A Jumpers To Follow stalwart, Nick has been a regular since the introduction of this section and again came up with the goods for readers last year, by selecting Paisley Park amongst his 10 to follow.*

Harry Skelton – *2018-19 was another stellar season for team Skelton and 172 of Harry's 178 winners were trained by his brother, Dan. Roksana and Ch'tibello provided festival success in March and his 10 once again include a couple of horses who have yet to race for the stable, one being unraced.*

BLUE SARI *Willie Mullins*

This wouldn't be one who I have ridden, or even ridden against, but I was very impressed with him in Gowran Park on Thyestes day; I have never seen a horse quicken up like him in a bumper – he came up the straight at some speed. He went on to finish second in the Champion Bumper and it wouldn't surprise me if he reversed the form with Envoi Allen over hurdles. Visually, I was just taken aback by him in Gowran and he showed battling qualities at Cheltenham, so I think we will be seeing big things of him when he goes over hurdles.

I rode a few for Willie in the spring, including **Acapella Bourgeois**, who I wanted to give a mention to, as I think he will be aimed at Aintree's Grand National. I actually rode him when Sandra Hughes had him and thought the world of him when he won a Grade 2 novice hurdle, and he took a while to find his feet at Willie's. He won in Clonmel, then I finished third on him in the Irish Grand National, after which France just didn't suit him. If he comes back into form after his summer break, I think they will have Aintree in mind for him, along with Burrows Saint, and there wouldn't be much between them. He jumps very well.

BOYHOOD *Tom George*

A horse who ran in the Pertemps Final and I won a beginners' chase on him in Newton Abbot in May, when he jumped well and beat a couple of nice horses. He ran to a good level over hurdles and improved for fences; he was kept going to get a run into him for experience before the summer, and that should stand him in good stead when he goes to war, plus he is experienced over hurdles. He jumped very, very well and I would be happy to see him pitched into handicap company. He stays forever, so something like the Welsh National could be a possible target for him.

CITY ISLAND *Martin Brassil*

Another who I didn't ride, but he is a horse who really impressed me and I hope they go chasing with him. He travelled supremely well in the Ballymore, was very comfortable, and Mark (Walsh) could go wherever he wanted to in the race. He stuck his head down once taking up the running and I loved the way he ran all the way to the line. I rode against him in Punchestown and he probably didn't perform that day, with his whole season geared towards the festival, after winning in Galway in August. He was trained supremely for that day and you could see it with the manner in which he won the race, as he went through it with such ease. I love a horse who travels like him, but can also battle and find plenty. Hopefully, they will go chasing with him and it can bring about more improvement.

DOCTOR DEX *Tom George*

I won a couple of novice hurdles on him in Wetherby and Doncaster, and he's rated 126 over hurdles. It took a while for the penny to drop with him; he was always a very good work horse and you would have thought he could win a bumper, so it was a disappointment to everyone that he couldn't. He's a nice horse who has a likeable way of going; he just gets the job done, without being a flashy horse who will go and win by 10 lengths. He's schooled nicely over fences and I think he can materialise into a decent chaser; he could actually be one for that Kempton race which I won last Christmas on Glen Forsa and there could be a couple of nice races in him over fences.

ENEMY COAST AHEAD Tom George

I didn't actually ride him, but have ridden him at home and he is a flashy, gorgeous-looking horse, who was very impressive when winning his bumper in Stratford. He had done some bits of work with a couple of good horses and we were hopeful that he would go and win. He schooled last winter and jumps well, and he was showing all the right attributes at home, so it was nice to see him go and win like he did. He should be winning plenty of races.

EXOD'ELA Jamie Snowden

He won a Point-to-Point for my father and is one to keep an eye out for in a bumper. He is by a good sire in Saddler Maker, who is sadly no longer with us, as they all have great attitudes and this lad is no exception. He probably isn't the biggest of horses but is a tough and smart horse, who showed plenty of gears to win, coming from last of 14 under a typical Derek O'Connor ride. He missed the last that day, but really stuck his head down to win and he is in good hands now.

GLEN FORSA Mick Channon

I had to include him as he is the horse who helped propel my career in England. The way he won in Chepstow, then Kempton and Sandown, I've never come across one quite like him and I still have plenty of belief in him.

He was foot-perfect in them first three runs, Kempton especially where he never missed a beat, and the way he jumped around Sandown – which is one of the best chase tracks in the country – is one of the greatest thrills I've ever had. Sadly, it never happened at Cheltenham and then Aintree wasn't his form, as he usually takes you into a fence, whereas I was chasing him along and it was probably the end of a long season, having been on the go since October. He is still relatively lightly-raced and when he comes back as a fresher and stronger horse, you would like to think that we could target some of those big Cheltenham handicaps, then see if he can develop into a Grade 1 horse. I believe he can.

Another who deserves a mention for the same connections is **Hold The Note**, who is going chasing and was a big, light-framed horse last season, who was forced to miss the Albert Bartlett, which could end up being the best thing that happened to him. He starts the season on 133 and he's an exciting horse, who, physically, should have benefited for the break.

OLD JEROBOAM Charlie Longsdon

I won a bumper on him in Wetherby on debut, when he took a long time to get going as he was quite green, but when he realised a furlong down what I wanted him to do, he really quickened up and hit the line well. It was good to see him back it up with his second bumper win, when connections were clever to claim the penalty off him. He again showed that he has an engine, a good attitude, and is another by a good sire (Jeremy), whose horses seem to improve with time and just get better and better. If things go right for him, he should win races and there could be a nice handicap in him along the way. He will want a trip once sent hurdling and he's a nice relaxed horse, who should improve with the further he goes.

RESERVE TANK *Colin Tizzard*

Another who impressed me when riding against him, he won the Grade 1 in Punchestown in which I finished third aboard Eglantine du Seuil. They went a decent gallop that day and there was no let-up, so I think the winner is a fair horse, and I think over fences, he could be the real deal. He is in good hands and given his size (he is a big, massive horse) I think once they put a fence in front of him, he will improve again. He got better as last season progressed and I remember Robbie Power saying after the Punchestown race that not only has he progressed, but he has gotten quicker with each run and really found his gears. Obviously, he was a healthier horse at Aintree and Punchestown, but he has the stamp of a chaser and resembles Lostintranslation in many ways.

SUMMERVILLE BOY *Tom George*

Rather like Boyhood, the plan was to get a run into him over fences in the spring, but the ground wasn't suitable and he was ready for a break, having been in since the Fighting Fifth, so we put him away. He has schooled very well; I schooled him on grass and he was very good, and he regularly schools over baby fences. Not the best jumper of a hurdle, he actually respects fences a lot more and has been a much more relaxed horse since Punchestown, where he actually ran really well and was beaten only six-and-a-quarter lengths. If he can translate his hurdles form to chasing, he should be a force to be reckoned with and he isn't confined to 2m, as he is relaxing more now so could go up in trip. You could say he is on the comeback trail, but if things go right, he could be a JLT horse come the spring and will, hopefully, be out early to gain some chasing experience.

Glen Forsa

BIGBADANDBEAUTIFUL *Gordon Elliott*

The first of two mares trained by Gordon who I have included. She went under the radar a little last season, winning just once from three starts. Third on debut, it was a funny race in Navan, but she improved no end when finishing second in a Grade 2 in Leopardstown, behind Dermot McLoughlin's smart filly (Santa Rossa) who went on and run well in Aintree. She had a little break after that and absolutely hosed in, winning by nine lengths in Clonmel. There are plenty of options for her going forward – she could probably win on the Flat – but she could end up being a very good filly and I wouldn't be at all surprised to see her ending up in the mares' novice hurdle in Cheltenham.

CHANTRY HOUSE *Nicky Henderson*

I won a Point-to-Point on him in Fairyhouse and he has since gone on to Nicky Henderson's, winning a bumper on his debut for JP McManus in Warwick. He's a lovely horse by Yeats, who they think very highly of in Seven Barrows, and I would imagine that he could make up into a very smart novice hurdler this season. He's a great jumper that won't have a problem in handling a bit of soft ground and will stay well, too.

ENVOI ALLEN *Gordon Elliott*

The most obvious horse on my list, having ridden him to win four bumpers, including the Champion Bumper in Cheltenham. He had won his Point-to-Point for Colin Bowe, then progressed to win a bumper in Fairyhouse, then on to Navan, where he beat a nice horse of Joseph O'Brien's (Midnight Run) in a Listed race. He then went on to win the Grade 2 in Leopardstown when he handled good ground, and had no problem coping with the easier ground in Cheltenham. He is a 3m chaser-in-the-making, but hopefully he can develop into a leading contender for the Ballymore this season, having strengthened up nicely over the summer. He looks great at the moment and is very exciting.

GENERATION TEXT *Dan Skelton*

A nice Getaway horse who was beaten in his Point-to-Point by Sporting John – who was purchased by JP McManus – and it was certainly an above-average maiden in Borris, with no fewer than four horses from in behind coming out and winning subsequently. The front pair could be very nice, and Generation Text gave me a nice feel, although he probably did a bit too much in the early part of the race. He was quite keen and his effort just levelled out once I let him down, whereas the winner seemed to relax a little better and saw out the race really well. Out of a King's Theatre mare, he showed lots of pace, so I wouldn't be surprised to see him develop into a nice bumper horse this season for Dan Skelton.

GIANT'S TABLE *TBC*

This is a horse who I actually bought at the Tattersalls Cheltenham Festival sale on behalf of Lady Bamford, and I know Colin Bowe thought the world of him. He only just won his Point-to-Point, but the ground turned very heavy throughout the day and after travelling very well, he got a little bit lost in the last couple of furlongs. Being by Great Pretender, he should have no bother in dropping back in trip and could start off in a bumper.

L'AIR DU VENT Colin Tizzard

A Coastal Path horse who fell at the third-last in his Point-to-Point, a race won by **Shishkin** who is another who deserves a mention. I was very impressed with the winner, who went on and won his bumper in Kempton for Nicky Henderson. L'Air du Vent was also travelling well at the time he came down in Lingstown and went on to win his bumper in Bangor for Colin Tizzard. I think they are two very nice horses and you could be hearing a lot more of both in the coming months, as they are another pair of potentially smart novice hurdlers.

MALONE ROAD Gordon Elliott

A Point-to-Point winner for Stuart Crawford, I won two bumpers on him, starting off in an ordinary race in Down Royal. He was impressive there, then stepped up to win a winners' bumper in Punchestown, beating Mt Leinster very easily. He picked up a little injury after that and, in fact, they probably could have brought him back at the end of last season, but Gordon and the owners decided to give him more time, and hopefully their patience will be rewarded. I would imagine that he will start off over hurdles and, hopefully, progress into being a graded novice. A sharp horse, he has the pace to start off over 2m, but his pedigree – being a half-brother to both Ravenhill Road and Windsor Avenue – suggests that he will want a trip and will have no trouble in staying further. Like the same owners' Envoi Allen, it actually wouldn't surprise me if he turned into a Ballymore horse, too.

MOUNT IDA Gordon Elliott

A Yeats mare, who is a half-sister to Sizing Tennessee, she won her Point-to-Point last December in Fairyhouse and after having a run over hurdles (finished runner-up in a Punchestown maiden hurdle over 2m6f), absolutely hosed up in a bumper for me in Wexford. The mare she beat came out and won two bumpers for Declan Queally and I think she will end up being a Graded filly. She should give her owners a lot of fun this season.

MY WHIRLWIND Nicky Henderson

This is one who I haven't ridden, but she is a lovely Stowaway filly who won her Point-to-Point very well, and was well talked up by handler Paddy Turley. The top-priced filly to go through the sales (cost £400,000 at the Tattersalls Cheltenham Festival sale), she looks to have a lot of class given the way she travelled in her Point-to-Point and never really came out of second gear. The sky is the limit for her and she has joined the powerful team of JP McManus and Nicky Henderson.

OVERTHETOP Olly Murphy

A big, fine Flemensfirth who I rode to win a Point-to-Point in Ballindenisk in December, he subsequently went on to win a bumper for Olly in Warwick. He's got a lovely pedigree and was an expensive store horse, so is yet another who I would be hopeful could develop into a very nice novice hurdler. He didn't enjoy the clearest of runs in his Point and we came from a long way back, but he picked up really well and Ballindenisk is a stiff track, so he proved he has plenty of stamina. He's a winter horse who will want a bit of dig in the ground, so the fact that he could win a good-ground bumper was a bonus.

Envoi Allen

A VIEW FROM THE SADDLE - JAMIE CODD

DICKIE DIVER *Nicky Henderson*

I like him a lot and his run in the Albert Bartlett was very good for such an inexperienced horse. His first run was also very good, as Lisnagar Oscar won a Grade 2 on his next start, then I won on him back at Chepstow – in a race which he was entitled to win – and we didn't really learn a lot there. Then he was pitched into the Albert Bartlett and was quite green; he was a bit further back than I wanted to be, he was learning on the job, and he did remarkably well to overcome that inexperience to run such a respectable race. Going forward, he gave me the feel of a chaser, but whatever path he goes down, I think he is one to follow.

I also won on **Champ** for the same connections last season and he is another very, very good horse. He has a high cruising speed and it surprises me a little that he can be keen in his races, as he isn't like that at home. He is every inch a chaser, so I would expect him to head down that route.

DUNDRUM WOOD *Olly Murphy*

He finished third in a bumper at Warwick, but I remain confident that he will develop into a nice horse. At home, he's very straightforward and does everything you ask so easily. When I let him down, he was very green and this is where these horses learn most, on a racecourse. He had won a Point-to-Point, but would have learned more on this occasion and he stayed at it very well, so there was still a lot to like about the run. I expect him to improve a lot for that experience.

FARNE *Neil King*

I rode her to finish fourth in the mares' bumper at Aintree and she's a nice, big, strong mare, who should do well over hurdles. Watching her Sandown run back, she looked very keen that day, but was relaxed at Aintree and went through the race very professionally. Her form is very good and looking at her, she's not really a bumper mare, but her form is right up there, having run in the two strongest races. Physically she is very imposing, and with the mares' programme the way it is, you would be disappointed if she didn't have a successful season.

FONTSANTA *Emma Lavelle*

Emma and Barry (Fenton) have done a great job with this horse, as they realised that he would be too keen if we rode him handy, and I was told to relax him on debut at Newbury and teach him on the job. He ran really well that day and that is one of the best things about riding for Barry and Emma – and having an owner like Tim Syder – who have the patience to do the job right. He still needed to relax when we went to Chepstow and having learned as he did on those first two runs, he put it all together at Hereford where he was very impressive. He is still very much on a learning curve and there should be plenty more improvement to come. Rated 134, he is a chasing type.

GEORDIE B *Venetia Williams*

He's a funny horse, in that he's got a bit of a streak in him. He would test the boundaries a bit and did just that when almost refusing at Ascot on debut, despite us doing plenty of schooling beforehand. I couldn't ride him that day, or at Hereford, where James Bowen gave him a great ride, even though he got beat. I then won on him at Lingfield – in a race which worked out well – and he won very well that day, before we pulled him out due to the ground at Haydock. He instead went to Exeter and was very impressive, after which the plan was to run in the Listed novice hurdle at Perth, but unfortunately the ground was too dry.

He's a smashing horse who wants soft ground. He will go chasing, but he might just have one run over hurdles beforehand, given that he is a bit of a character and having done what he did at Ascot. Despite being a strong stayer, I've no doubt that he has more class than it looks, it is just the way he races.

MINELLA BOBO *Rebecca Curtis*

A nice horse who I first rode at Doncaster, which was a very good run and the winner franked that form by winning a Grade 2, then I won on him at Stratford in April. Once Ferrobin fell, he probably didn't have too much to beat, but he went round in a common canter and won by 18 lengths. He's a very good jumper, a very straightforward horse, and an opening handicap mark of 126 looks attractive.

OVERTHETOP *Olly Murphy*

He won the first division of the Warwick bumper in which Dundrum Wood finished third and a lot went wrong for him that day, yet he was still able to win. The start was a bit messy and they didn't go that quick, so we weren't in the best position and to do something about it, we had to go wide to make up ground. I didn't want to give away first run, but it was the lesser of two evils, and in going wide, we basically gave away ground everywhere, but still won. He did very well to overcome what he did and win. I have ridden him plenty at home as well and he is a very powerful horse, who is all quality through and through.

PAISLEY PARK *Emma Lavelle*

An obvious choice, but I couldn't really leave him out after the season he had last year. He came out and won a competitive handicap under top-weight really nicely at Aintree and after that I thought he would take a lot of beating at Haydock. I hadn't really thought beyond that and that was a good race to win in its own right, although the sharp track nearly got him beat. Then Ascot was huge for everyone and every run – even after Ascot – was another step forward. The Cleeve was a Grade 2 but was arguably a stronger field and he carried a penalty, then we also had the best of the Irish to beat in the Stayers'.

The path he is likely to take is there for everyone to see and although we haven't spoken in detail, I would imagine that we will substitute Aintree and Haydock with Newbury, and it would be nice, if everything went to plan, to fit in Aintree or Punchestown in the spring.

TARADA *Oliver Sherwood*

I rode him at Chepstow on his hurdles debut when he finished second and I loved him. He was very green, very babyish, but the way he jumped and travelled through the race – albeit a bit behind the bridle – suggested that he had to be a nice horse. Leighton (Aspell) was back from injury when he won at Fontwell by 10 lengths. He's got nice, staying chaser written all over him – very straightforward, very likeable, travels well, and probably did well to win around a sharp track like Fontwell.

THOMAS DARBY *Olly Murphy*

Runner-up in the Supreme Novices' Hurdle, he's a sharp horse with a high cruising speed and I won on him at Taunton before Cheltenham. He is a very good jumper and has a very good attitude, but was just a little keen early, so they rode him quietly at Cheltenham on debut to educate him to do it the right way, and he still went and won. He stayed on well in the Supreme and his best form has come at both Cheltenham and Ascot, which suggests the stiffer tracks suit, so he should get further, although I would think he will start off over 2m over fences. He's a stereotypical Beneficial, in that they can be quite racy, but they all tend to be very good jumpers.

I could have included **Brewin'upastorm**, as I did plenty with him at home although have yet to ride him in a race. Another very strong traveller, I was convinced he would have won at Cheltenham on trials day when falling at the last and he is another exciting novice chase prospect, as his novice hurdle form is rock-solid.

Paisley Park

GLINGER FLAME *Nicky Richards*

He will make a lovely novice chaser when the time comes, but I don't think he has finished winning over hurdles just yet, as his form is strong. He was long odds-on the last day when he completed the hat-trick, despite the fact that he would have appreciated a stronger gallop. A big horse, he took a couple of runs to realise what was required of him – which is why Nicky put the cheek-pieces on him – but he is a nice horse with plenty of ability. Whether he goes for a nice handicap hurdle or a novice handicap chase I don't know at this stage, but either way he should win more races.

I'M TO BLAME *Keith Dalgleish*

Won three times over hurdles last year and is one to note in handicaps, as he was still raw and should improve. He has a lot of ability and always wants to please you, every stride he takes, so he can be a bit keen. We just need to get him to drop his head and race properly. It was a funny race when beaten the last day, I got hampered a bit and the ground was probably a bit sticky for him. A year older and a year stronger, I think he can improve again, and he's a big horse so should jump a fence in time.

MAROWN *Nicky Richards*

A lovely, big chasing type by Milan, who I won a bumper on at Newcastle, despite the fact that he would have appreciated a bit of nicer ground. He'd always shown plenty at home, so it wasn't a massive surprise that he could win his bumper, but I went very wide on him to try and find a bit better ground, and he finished really strongly, in the style of a stayer. He schooled well before he went out in the field and is a typical Trevor Hemmings horse, in that he will be a 3m chaser in time. A big frame of a horse last year, he is a good mover, so the plan was to only give him just the one run.

RIBBLE VALLEY *Nicky Richards*

He's a really nice horse and whatever he did in bumpers was a bonus, as he's a lovely, big horse who jumps well, and I schooled him before his break. He won his bumper first time very well and then I rode him at Cheltenham, where he was a bit green in a falsely-run race. A horse hampered me after four or five furlongs and he almost came down, so he would have learned a lot that day, and then he won nicely again back at Ayr. At that point, Nicky thought he had done enough for the season and it is all about this year with him. He has a lot of pace and a high cruising speed, so he will probably start over 2m and I'm really excited about him. He is a horse with a lot of ability, so granted a bit of luck and he stays healthy, I think he could be quite smart.

SIDI ISMAEL *Keith Dalgleish*

Another lovely, big horse and probably not a bumper horse, despite winning one at Hexham. He'll be a lovely hurdler and, hopefully, chaser during the next couple of seasons and although his bare form might not look particularly strong, he is a lovely-looking horse, who jumps well. By Great Pretender, he has loads of scope and would be one that I am looking forward to, both this season and beyond. A big unfurnished horse, last year was only ever about preparing him for this season, as he is a proper jumps horse.

I would certainly have included his stablemate **Alright Sunshine** if I knew he was going hurdling. Any four-year-old who can win three bumpers is a good horse and he is probably unlucky not to be unbeaten. He won nicely on debut despite being green, then was beaten next time on soft ground, and won his next two, very well, on better ground at Musselburgh. He's a lovely big, scopey horse, but he could be a very good Flat horse, so time will tell as to which route they take. He has plenty of ability and I would love to see him entered in a maiden hurdle.

STREETS OF DOYEN *John C McConnell*

He's a real smart horse, who I won a bumper on for Stuart Crawford and has subsequently joined John McConnell, finishing fourth for his new connections at Bellewstown in July. He's a nice type and is a nice size, but he should have learned plenty as he was green on debut. Despite this, he knuckled down and won well in the end, beating another potentially nice horse from the same stable. Although that race was run in May, I think it was a decent bumper and one that can throw up a fair few winners.

THE SOME DANCE KID *Donald McCain*

He did nothing wrong last year, finishing in behind Good Boy Bobby on debut, before winning his next three. He beat Colonel Custard at Bangor, before beating Skidoosh – who won a handicap next time – under his double-penalty at Catterick. A grand horse, he's very consistent and could easily jump fences, if that is the route they chose, having finished second in a Point-to-Point. He's tough and should get 3m in time.

Another of Donald's which I like is **The Con Man**, who picked up a little injury after winning a novice hurdle at Carlisle. He did come back into training, but then the ground went against him, so he should be back this season. He beat Garrettstown – who franked the form by winning next time – and given his lack of experience, I would think that he might have a couple of runs over hurdles. I think he is quite a nice horse and unusually for an Oscar, he likes soft ground. Hopefully, we get a clear run with him this time around.

UNCLE ALASTAIR *Nicky Richards*

Unfortunately, he picked up a slight knock after a really encouraging debut over fences at Carlisle and had to have the rest of the season off. That novice chase rode like a very good race and he gave Vinndication a real fright. I was very happy with the way he jumped, and having finished placed on him over 3m over hurdles, we know he gets further.

Because he is such a nice horse, they rightly decided to give him all the time he needed and, hopefully, he will be back this season, when he should be a very exciting novice chaser. Given that he picked up that injury, it was kind of a blessing that he finished second as he still has his novice status for this season. He is another to really look forward to.

WAITING PATIENTLY *Ruth Jefferson*

An obvious horse to include, but one who I couldn't really leave out. Despite the fact that things didn't go to plan last season, I still retain plenty of belief in him and there are still plenty of races to be won with him. He felt great in the King George, but after that he just didn't give me the same feel in the second half of last season, at either Ascot or Aintree; for whatever reason, he just didn't feel himself. He also never really got his ground last season and if he returns fit and well, I think that he can get back to winning ways; I certainly haven't lost any faith in him and he remains lightly-raced for his age.

WINDSOR AVENUE *Brian Ellison*

He never ran a bad race last year, winning two for me and he was placed in a couple of decent novice hurdles. He won at Hexham and Sedgefield, then ran very well in the Grade 2 at Kelso, when dropping back a couple of furlongs probably caught him out on decent ground. That was a strong race and he was put away, presumably with novice chasing in mind – I'm not sure – but he is a smart horse, with a nice pedigree, being a half-brother to Malone Road and Ravenhill Road. I've won four times on him in all now, he's a good jumper who won a Point-to-Point, so I would imagine he will go novice chasing. His form is rock-solid and Brian has taken his time with him, and he would be another nice horse for fences.

Ribble Valley

BIRCHDALE *Nicky Henderson*

I like this horse a lot. He won his novice hurdle at Warwick on debut for us – having won his Point-to-Point in Ireland – then went to Cheltenham on trials day, when winning the Grade 2, a race I thought he still would have won, even if Brewin'upastorm had stood up. He travelled really well in the Albert Bartlett, and once he was beaten, Barry (Geraghty) looked after him. You can put a line through that and he is a horse to really look forward to, now he goes chasing. A very straightforward horse, he will have no problem in getting 3m.

CHAMP *Nicky Henderson*

One of the more obvious selections, I couldn't leave him out, as I think he could be even better over fences; out of a half-sister to Best Mate, he is certainly bred to be a chaser. It helped him last year having a full season as a novice, as he was hard on himself and was still learning all of the time. He was very keen when bolting up in a handicap at Newbury on his reappearance and would have appreciated a stronger gallop when winning the Challow, as he settles off a better pace. He did nothing wrong in the Ballymore, then went on to win the Sefton at Aintree, and I think he could be very good over fences this year. It is difficult to say for certain what his ideal trip will be and I don't even think Nicky would at this stage, as he could even start off over 2m before going up in trip, once he relaxes and drops the bit.

Another novice chaser who I wanted to touch on – albeit at a lower level – is **Pistol Whipped**, who won at Fakenham and is rated 128 over hurdles. He's a good-actioned horse – he skips along the ground – so you can put a line through his last run on account of the ground, and he can bounce back over fences.

CHANTRY HOUSE *Nicky Henderson*

The first of three of last season's bumper horses which I have included, he won easily on debut at Warwick and we have always liked him at home. A non-runner on a couple of occasions before he actually ran, they wanted to find the perfect ground for him, which tells you the regard in which he is held. An Irish Point-to-Point winner before joining us, Barry (Geraghty) only had to shake the reins at him at Warwick to win smoothly. I've done plenty with him at home and he could have easily gone hurdling last year, as he jumps for fun. He has the speed to start off over 2m, but all being well, you would be hoping to see him end up in something like the Ballymore in the spring. He's exciting.

ELUSIVE BELLE *Nicky Henderson*

A nice mare owned by Robert Waley-Cohen who was very impressive on her debut for the stable around Wincanton. She was very keen at Sandown on her next start – when pulling Sam (Waley-Cohen) to the front – and in the circumstances, ran a decent race. That form was strong as she was beaten by Reserve Tank, who went on to win at Aintree and Punchestown, and after running in the mares' race at Cheltenham, she gained a confidence-boosting win at Warwick. We only got her part way through last season – she had finished runner-up in a Listed bumper in Ireland – and probably had a busy enough campaign in the end. With a break behind her, she can progress now, especially with the mares' series, and I would be hopeful that she could gain some valuable black type. She will jump fences when the time comes, too, as she's a lovely, big scopey mare.

FUSIL RAFFLES *Nicky Henderson*

He is a very interesting horse, as he shows nothing at home. Therefore, it was a pleasant surprise when he bolted up at Kempton in the Adonis on his debut for the stable, when he struck into himself, forcing him to miss Cheltenham. I worked him again shortly before Punchestown and he still didn't show much, but he went over there and won very well, so is clearly very talented and saves his best for the track. He remains very unexposed and is National Hunt-bred, so will make a chaser in time, and he will stay beyond 2m, too.

MARIE'S ROCK *Nicky Henderson*

Owned by Middleham Park, she was only bought at the Land Rover Sale last June, so ran within a year and was very impressive on debut in a Ffos Las bumper. I loved the way she travelled through the race and she put the race to bed quite smartly. A racy type of filly, she is one who we can crack on with, and there is probably a chance that she could start off in another bumper, but she will be hurdling sooner rather than later.

She looks to have plenty of speed, as does **Floressa**, who won her bumper impressively at Ludlow and also deserves a mention. She was probably just outstayed at Cheltenham on her second start and is one who should have strengthened up over the summer.

PENTLAND HILLS *Nicky Henderson*

Bought privately by Owners Group, he was only rated in the low 70s on the Flat and took to jumping from day one. The first day we schooled him, he was a natural, and he won three races in the space of five weeks, two of them being Grade 1s. Nicky will probably think about the four-year-old hurdle at Cheltenham early in the season, and even though he will get further in time, he has the Flat speed to remain over the minimum trip. He needs to go and keep improving now, but he's unexposed and versatile, as it was quick ground at Plumpton, then much softer at Cheltenham and Aintree.

PRECIOUS CARGO *Nicky Henderson*

Disappointing on his final start at Aintree, but he's fairly hard on himself in his races and it could be that Kempton and Sandown left a mark on him. He was very impressive on his debut for us and is – like Chantry House – another by Yeats. A gorgeous big horse, we were probably still getting to know him properly last year, having arrived from Lucinda Russell's, and he can be headstrong in his races. He's not far off 17 hands and could be a smart chaser this season. Versatile in terms of ground, he's rated 140 over hurdles, and given that he is a brilliant jumper, you would like to think that he will improve for a fence, and might just settle a bit better by backing off his fences.

SANTINI *Nicky Henderson*

Another rather obvious inclusion, but I still think he can go to the top and certainly reverse form with Topofthegame. Not to take anything away from the winner, but Santini didn't have the best of preparations – as was well-documented – ahead of the festival and he will be a stronger horse again this year. He's still a big baby, who is learning the whole time, and he could go down the Ladbrokes Trophy route, or there is the option to go for the Future Stars Intermediate Chase at Sandown, which comes up 20 days before Newbury.

SHISHKIN *Nicky Henderson*

Very impressive in his Point-to-Point, he won very easily at Kempton the day after the Gold Cup and although we got that run into him, we could have easily turned him away as he came up a bit light and he's another who will have done well for his summer at grass. If you look back at the Kempton form, it wasn't a particularly strong race, but it was the way he did it which was impressive. A big 16' 2" son of Sholokhov, he took off in the closing stages and is likely to head straight over hurdles, starting off over 2m, then stepping up when necessary.

ANNIE MC *Jonjo O'Neill*

Winner of the Mares' Final at Newbury, she is likely to go chasing now, as she has been crying out for a fence – she has loads of size and scope. She could do with filling out a bit more and, hopefully, she has done that over the summer. I certainly think there will be more improvement to come from her now she goes chasing and her form is rock-solid. She had two very good runs in Point-to-Points, and given that she was very tall and leggy when arriving with us, she did well to do so much in Ireland as a four-year-old. She is pretty versatile in terms of ground and is one I am particularly looking forward to.

ARRIVEDERCI *Jonjo O'Neill*

A bumper winner at Hereford in December, I then rode him at Exeter in what was a very hot bumper. That form is very strong, with Get In The Queue winning again at Newbury, while the second (Sheshoon Sonny) and third (Eritage) both won next time, too, and our horse was still a bit weak last year. With another summer break behind, he should be a nice prospect for novice hurdles this season and soft ground won't be a problem.

CLOTH CAP *Jonjo O'Neill*

All being well, he could turn out to be our Grand National horse this season. He will need to improve a good bit to get in, but he did nothing wrong last year, winning twice and then running a cracker in the Scottish National. After just four starts, I would like to think there is a good bit of improvement there, and Dad deliberately gave him a light campaign last season, with the future in mind. With the right campaign, he could just sneak in at the bottom and would be a great spin around Aintree. He definitely prefers good ground, so I think we might get him out early and then give him a mid-winter break ahead of the spring.

GET IN THE QUEUE *Harry Fry*

I've put this one in, as he really impressed me when I rode against him and I wouldn't be at all surprised if he were to develop into a top novice hurdler. He won at Uttoxeter on debut before I rode against him at Exeter and then he followed up in the sales race at Newbury. He looks a very smart prospect.

L'AIR DU VENT *Colin Tizzard*

I won a bumper on him at Bangor and although it might not have been a strong race, he gave me a really nice feel and couldn't have done it any more impressively. A faller when favourite to win his Point-to-Point, the race was eventually won by Shishkin, who won easily at Kempton for Nicky Henderson, so that form is strong, and I will be surprised if he didn't develop into a nice novice hurdler. He has plenty of pace, so I would expect him to start off over 2m, and given that he has plenty of size about him, he will make a chaser in time.

LOSTINTRANSLATION *Colin Tizzard*

I've yet to ride him and not even sat on him, but he is a horse who has always impressed me when riding out at Colin's, and the step up to 3m at Aintree looked to be the making of him. To be able to do as well as he did against Defi du Seuil over 2m4f earlier in the season shows the amount of class he has, but over 3m he could be top-class. Races such as the King George and Bowl at Aintree would seem suitable, and he could even develop into a Gold Cup horse.

MISTER MALARKY *Colin Tizzard*

I rode him in the handicap chase at Aintree on Grand National day and he could easily be a 'Hennessy' horse. He has won around Newbury and that race tends to suit second-season chasers, and he has a touch of class, having won the Grade 2 Reynoldstown. He just got a little outpaced at Aintree, so the longer trip would suit and there could be a big handicap in him off 150.

PAPA TANGO CHARLY *Jonjo O'Neill*

A Point-to-Point winner who cost a lot of money when we bought him at Aintree. He won his Point really well and the placed horses were well thought of and also fetched big money at the sales. We actually bought the third **Meyer Lansky** as well, as we thought it was a strong race. When Papa Tango Charly arrived, we didn't do a lot with him, just rode him out for a week and then we put him out in the field. A nice, athletic son of No Risk At All, there is probably a chance that Dad will run him in one bumper, but it won't be long before he is hurdling and he is an exciting recruit to the yard.

RESERVE TANK *Colin Tizzard*

He's another who I have yet to ride in a race, but I have schooled him once at Colin's and all he did was improve throughout last season. I thought his victory at Punchestown solidified him as one of the leading novice hurdlers, and both that race and the Mersey at Aintree were strong pieces of form. I'm not sure what they will do with him now, but he's a big horse who could be a JLT type, if they decide to go down the novice chase route.

SEATON CAREW *Jonjo O'Neill*

A half-sister to Coney Island, she won a bumper at Wetherby, after being pretty green on debut at Warwick. She took a big step forward and put up a nice performance at Wetherby. We've always liked her at home and she should do well over hurdles. She has plenty of size about her and could make up into a smart mare, especially when stepping up in trip.

ARRIVEDERCI *Jonjo O'Neill*

I won a three-year-old bumper on him at Hereford, beating Logan Rocks, who ran well in a Listed race at Newbury. He then finished behind Get In The Queue – who obviously won the big sales bumper at Newbury and I think was probably one of the best bumper horses in England last season – but he was only a weak horse last year and I expect that he will have improved for a summer at grass. A nice grey by Martaline, he won on horrible ground at Hereford, which wouldn't be ideal, and he should only improve.

CHAMPAGNE COURT *Jeremy Scott*

Fourth in a Cheltenham bumper, just behind the likes of Master Debonair and Breaking Waves, he then went novice hurdling and beat Nordic Combined over 2m at Lingfield, before running in a couple of Grade 2s, behind Angels Breath and Beakstown. I didn't feel he got his conditions in either race, however, as I feel he needs 3m and he went on to run well in the boys' race at Cheltenham, then when third on quick ground at Sandown. He's quite a big horse, a super jumper, and it might be that he wants good ground over a trip, but I can see him picking up some nice staying novice chases. Even though he's only rated 126, the December Novices' Chase at Doncaster springs to mind, and I'm sure he can win a novices' handicap before going on to better things.

DASHEL DRASHER *Jeremy Scott*

Another novice chaser of Jeremy's, he is one that I've not actually ridden in a race, but he is a very nice horse. A six-year-old whom Jeremy bred himself, he's now rated 145 after winning four novice hurdles around the bigger tracks - Chepstow, Ascot, Newbury and Cheltenham. He's always been big and weak, but he developed in the second half of last season and any horse who can win four novice hurdles has to be smart. He has a high cruising speed, jumps well, and should do well over fences, and it is nice for Jeremy to have a good one, particularly a homebred.

HEY BUD *Jeremy Scott*

A six-year-old by Fair Mix, who was big and weak last year. He ran over 2m a few times, and then as soon as he stepped up in trip, he fairly dotted up at Wincanton, beating Storm Arising and Chef d'Equipe, who are rated 130 and 129 respectively. This horse was just crying out for a trip and as soon as he got it, he bolted up. He's very unfurnished and was put away after that win, and going forward over anything from 2m3f and beyond, he could be a force to be reckoned with. He could be sent over fences, but Jeremy has plenty of similar chasing types and he has never run in a handicap, so it would be interesting to see if that option is considered, from a mark of 124. Wincanton was the first time that his form really reflected his ability.

KISSESFORKATIE *Jeremy Scott*

She's a nice mare by Jeremy, a sire that Jeremy has done well with – Unison has won nine times for the stable over hurdles. She won her bumper at Fontwell and then took on the geldings at Cheltenham, beaten less than two lengths by Master Debonair. She then finished fourth in a Listed race at Huntingdon, which has worked out well, before finishing sixth in the Grade 2 at Aintree, so her bumper form is very solid. She was beaten on her hurdles debut at Newton Abbot in May, but she ran too freely that day and didn't get home. I would imagine that she will come back in trip, as she's a super jumper and that can be put to better use. You might not see her in the depths of winter on really deep ground, but she can pick up some more black type at some stage.

PAPA TANGO CHARLY *Jonjo O'Neill*

A horse now owned by Mr Tedham, he's a four-year-old by No Risk At All, who won a maiden Point in March at Liscarroll, beating a horse called Big Bresil, who was bought by Roger Brookhouse. He was trained by Colin Bowe, who always produces nice young horses, including Samcro, and although they didn't go quickly in the race, he quickened up well. He was green around the home bend and slightly missed the last fence, but still went away and won well. A light-framed horse, he seems sure to improve and to do what he did as a four-year-old was very impressive. He was purchased at the Aintree Goffs Sale for £440,000, so there was obviously a lot of interest in him and he's spent the summer in a field at Jonjo's. I've not sat on him yet, but I have had a good look at him and he ticks all the right boxes to develop into a proper horse.

TEDHAM *Jonjo O'Neill*

I included Tedham last year and still really like him. He ended his novice hurdle season with a mark of 131, despite being beaten on his first three starts, but all by good horses, finishing behind Al Dancer, The Big Bite and Getaway Trump. After that, the handicapper gave him a mark of 125 and he went and won well at Wincanton, where he appreciated the step up in trip. He went to Aintree and finished seventh, but didn't give me the same feel that he did at Wincanton, so I'm hoping there is still plenty of improvement in him. He has the option of going chasing as he is a good jumper, but whatever route they go, he is only five and is far from the finished article. He's maturing with age and is another who will have benefited from his summer at grass.

UMBRIGADO *David Pipe*

I won a bumper on him at Uttoxeter last November and the race worked out well, with The Macon Lunatic (2nd) going on to win a Newbury bumper and Liosduin Bhearna (3rd) winning a couple of handicap hurdles and now rated 132. He then went on to win two novice hurdles, beating Ask Dillon at Exeter, and is the type of horse who only does enough, only does what he has to. He was slightly disappointing in a Grade 1 at Aintree finishing sixth, but he's a young horse who could fulfil his potential this year. He finished second in a Point-to-Point to a horse called **Brewers Project**, who is a horse that I know Paul Nicholls thinks a lot of. He is probably one to note when he runs for Paul, but I think Umbrigado is a proper horse and chasing should be the making of him.

WASDELL DUNDALK *Jonjo O'Neill*

He had been working nicely before finishing fourth in a bumper at Huntingdon. He's a four-year-old by Spirit One and whose dam is closely-related to Hinterland, a Grade 1 winner for Paul Nicholls. He's a nice, big individual, and another who should have strengthened up over the summer. He's a proper National Hunt type, so I suspect he will go hurdling now.

WIN MY WINGS *Christian Williams*

She finished third in the race won by Sixty's Belle at Newton Abbot, just behind Kissesforkatie, having earlier won at Ffos Las. She's an Irish Point winner and found 2m too sharp, before appreciating the longer trip at Ffos Las. She won well that day, beating a good yardstick, and ran quite flat when trying to concede weight to the front two at Newton Abbot. I don't think she was quite herself that day and the lack of pace proved against her at Market Rasen, where she probably bumped into another nice mare. She is a serious jumper, so could be another for some black type, and as she only won her maiden in April, she can run in novice hurdles until the end of October, although as she made her handicap debut at Stratford in July, there are plenty of options.

BEAKSTOWN *Dan Skelton*

I included him last year and he didn't really do anything wrong. He won at Uttoxeter on debut, then went up to Newcastle and finished second in what was a bit of a messy race. The race probably came soon enough for him – being just a fortnight after Uttoxeter – and he made a mistake three out, which put him on the back foot, before he stayed on strongly. He was impressive when he won the Leamington at Warwick, beating a really good field in what was a proper test. Again, he was still a bit green in the finish but was learning all the time and probably wasn't ready for Cheltenham; the track – at that stage of his career – wasn't really suitable and he couldn't pick up when I asked.

We're going to go chasing now, as he's a big horse and wants a fence, but I still think he will improve with another season under his belt and it could be that he is better again in 12 months' time. That said, we hold him in high regard and we hope that he will take high rank in the novice chase division.

DESTRIER *Dan Skelton*

Another who I included last year, he has always shown us an awful lot at home and is now beginning to show it on the track. He ran well over hurdles in proper heavy ground on his reappearance, then went to Southwell for a novices' handicap chase – which he won – and the next four home came out and won seven times between them, including Castafiore who won a Grade 2 at Haydock. He then went and won a small novice chase up at Ayr, before going to Aintree, as he really wants a big, open, galloping track, and ran a really good race to finish third in a Grade 1 on just his third start, against more experienced rivals. I'm not quite sure where we will start, but, hopefully, the time we have given him will benefit him now. I still have plenty of belief in him.

MAIRE BANRIGH *Dan Skelton*

A mare who went through the sales ring and cost plenty of money a couple of years ago, she came good last season after a wind operation, winning a maiden hurdle at Market Rasen and a handicap at Carlisle. Unfortunately, she picked up a little niggle and lost the rest of the season, but the time off won't have done her any harm – as she's a big mare – and we will go chasing with her sooner rather than later, and that will be her game. An Irish Point-to-Point winner, we're looking forward to getting her back and getting her going over fences. She's a good jumper who likes to bowl along, so we are likely to start off over 2m on a galloping track.

MONTEGO GREY *Dan Skelton*

He is the horse who provided us with our 200th winner last season and he had some good bumper form, before winning at Market Rasen. He matured with each run and was quite a nervous horse when he first started, but the penny is now dropping and if he continues to go in the right direction, he could be a smart novice hurdler. A beautiful mover, he jumps really well and hopefully with another summer break behind him, he has grown up again. He has always had the ability, but inexperience just caught him out early on last season, and we hope that he can reach quite a high level as a novice hurdler. Given the way he moves, he appreciates nice ground.

OLLY THE BRAVE _Dan Skelton_

A little bit older than our other bumper horses, being six, he was weak as a baby, and the owners have given him plenty of time. He's a really nice, big horse and finished second at Southwell on debut, then went one better at Warwick, where he did it really well. The race was run at a strong pace and he picked up to win like we hoped he would. By Black Sam Bellamy, there is plenty of stamina in his pedigree and he is a chaser-in-the-making as he's a good jumper, but can do well in novice hurdles beforehand. He's a really likeable horse.

PERCY'S WORD _Dan Skelton_

Rated in the 90s on the Flat, he had just one run for us last season, when very free in an introductory hurdle at Newbury. Bridget rode him that day and she dropped him in, but he carted the whole way, so we were all very surprised how he kept going to finish second. He was held up with a little niggling injury after that, which kept him off, but he is definitely one to have on side as a second-season novice. He will start off in a 2m novice hurdle and will appreciate a bit of nice ground. We will probably see the best of him in the spring.

SHAN BLUE _Dan Skelton_

He won his Point-to-Point impressively in Ireland, and finished third on his debut for us, in a bumper at Warwick. We were really pleased with the run as I always think that it is difficult for these horses to run in the same season as they have contested a Point-to-Point in Ireland. They have to travel over and change their entire routine, which I never think is ideal. If you can, it can sometimes be better to start off a fresh the following season.

He's a strapping big horse, a proper chaser-in-the-making, but we are very hopeful that he will develop into a decent novice hurdler this season. In time, he will want stepping up in trip and it could be that 2m4f ends up as his optimum.

VISION DU PUY _Dan Skelton_

A winner in France at Auteuil, she came over to us and won in the last week of the season up at Perth. I would hope that there is a lot more to come from her, as she has a very willing attitude and might progress into a mare who can contend some of the better races later in the season. We will probably keep her to 2m for now, but she will have no problem going up in trip and she's a very honest filly.

WEST CORK _Dan Skelton_

A Midnight Legend five-year-old who was an impressive winner of an Irish Point-to-Point. We really liked what we saw at home during the spring, but just ran out of time to run him. Typical of the sire, he's got a great mind and he's a full-brother to several winners, including Alan King's William H Bonney. He jumps really well and we are looking forward to running him in a bumper in the autumn.

WILDE ABOUT OSCAR _Dan Skelton_

I'll finish with an unraced horse, who also showed us plenty in the spring, after which we just ran out of time to get a run into him – we did that with a lot of the four-year-olds, thinking another summer wouldn't do them any harm. He is a horse we like a lot and is another who we are really looking forward to running in a bumper somewhere in the autumn. He jumps really well and has a great attitude being by Oscar.

Wessex Racing Club

Experience the thrill of National Hunt Racing with horses in training with Jack Barber and Anthony Honeyball. The Wessex Racing Club have three horses in training – two-mile chaser Le Coeur Net, staying chaser Three in One and Novice Hurdler Lamanver Bel Ami.

Membership includes stable visits to both yards, gallop watching, regular communications about the progress and plans for the horses, days out with other members at the races to see your horses run and a share of the prize money at the end of the season.

**Contact Jeremy Barber (07778937581)
or Jeremy Blackburn (07540755261) to find out more.
or email: jeremyblackburn10@gmail.com
Visit: www.wessexracingclub.com for more information**

Ramillies - the Bishops Court winner is now in the care of trainer Willie Mullins
picture courtesy of Tim Holt

POINT-TO-POINT GRADUATES

BIG BRESIL *Tom George*

Given that he hails from the same family as Cheltenian (dam being a full-sister) – who won the Champion Bumper for the owner in 2011 – it isn't surprising that Roger Brookhouse was keen to secure Big Bresil and he did that at the Goffs sale at Aintree in April. Runner-up to the exciting Papa Tango Charly on his sole start, the son of Blue Bresil was the only horse who could go with the winner from two out and he finished a clear-cut second. He looks to possess plenty of size and will probably come into his own over 2m4f over hurdles and, in time, has the look of a stayer. He hailed from the Donnchadh Doyle stable, and as you will read shortly, he was responsible for plenty of this year's more exciting Irish recruits. As with many of the Brookhouse-owned horses, Big Bresil has been sent to Tom George.

BLOSSOMING FORTH *Ruth Jefferson*

Ruth Jefferson did extremely well with Mega Yeats last year and has bought another interesting mare in the shape of Blossoming Forth, who won a maiden at Eyton-on-Severn for trainer Philip Rowley. Ridden by Alex Edwards, the Flemensfirth filly might have only beaten two opponents, but she cruised around, jumped well, and ran out a very easy winner. It was a case of visual impression over form substance with Blossoming Forth, who also boasts a nice pedigree, being a full-sister to Beg To Differ (a four-time winner for Jonjo O'Neill). Bred to get a trip, she didn't look devoid of pace when winning her Point and I would expect Jefferson to start her off in a bumper, perhaps attempting to follow a similar path to that taken 12 months ago with the aforementioned Mega Yeats.

BRAVEMANSGAME *Paul Nicholls*

An eight-length winner at Lingstown for Donnchadh Doyle, Bravemansgame was the most expensive gelding to be sold at this year's Cheltenham Festival (Tattersalls) sale. A four-year-old by a relatively unknown sire in Brave Mansonnien, he is out of a Nickname mare and had the race sewn up two fences from home. He kept up the gallop to collect, but should be more than capable of coming back in trip once sent hurdling. He has joined the Paul Nicholls stable and is expected to start off in a bumper.

CALTHOR *TBC*

A faller five fences from home on debut, Calthor made no mistake at the second time of asking, bolting up under Derek O'Connor at Ballysteen. Having travelled stylishly, the four-year-old strode right away and was eased right down to score by 10 lengths for Ellmarie Holden. An athletic-looking half-brother to Black Kalanisi (winner of a bumper and a maiden hurdle for trainer Joseph Tuite), he has been bought privately by JP McManus and looks to have plenty of speed, so most certainly appeals as the type to land a bumper before being sent hurdling. There is a suspicion that the race might have fallen into his lap a little, but there was no denying that the performance was impressive on the eye.

DEPLOY THE GETAWAY *Willie Mullins*

Despite making a mess of the final fence, Deploy The Getaway ran out a 20-length winner of a four-year-old maiden at Tallow for Donnchadh Doyle and was subsequently purchased by Willie Mullins (£200,000 at Tattersalls Cheltenham, February). The form wouldn't appear to be anything out of the ordinary – although The Hotelier (pulled up) did come out and finish third behind the exciting Lets Go Champ – and Deploy The Getaway looked in a completely different league to the opposition. He moved very well, which bodes well as there is tons of stamina on the dam's side of the pedigree, so he will no doubt want a trip in time. He will sport the colours of Cheveley Park Stud.

FADO DES BROSSES *Evan Williams*

As I have alluded to elsewhere in this year's publication, Evan Williams and his long-standing leading owners, The Ruckers, have a strong team of a young horses for the season ahead, and they paid £200,000 for the acquisition of Fado des Brosses at Cheltenham (Tattersalls sale) in February. A four-year-old by Balko with a stamina-laden pedigree, he stayed on really strongly to win a Belharbour maiden by 15 lengths for Pat Doyle. The winning margin would have been much reduced had Goaheadwiththeplan not come down at the last, but he had just appeared to take his measure at the time and is one to note over a trip once sent hurdling. He didn't jump particularly well and found himself outpaced when the tempo increased, so it is to his credit that he was still able to win.

FAROUK D'ALENE *Gordon Elliott*

Donnchadh Doyle sold two horses for big money at the Tattersalls Cheltenham Festival sale in March, with Bravemansgame joining Paul Nicholls for £370,000, whilst the hammer came down on Farouk d'Alene at £260,000 and the Racinger gelding was picked up by Mags O'Toole on behalf of Gordon Elliott. A wide-margin winner at Belclare, he really opened up inside the final half-mile and was eased down in the end, with those in behind well strung out. Racinger seems to put a speed influence into his offspring and this four-year-old looks to possess the pace to win a bumper before going hurdling.

FERNY HOLLOW *Willie Mullins*

From a family that Willie Mullins knows well (trained his half-sisters Chiltern Hills and Vittorio, who both won a bumper), Ferny Hollow showed loads of speed to win on debut at Knockanard (over 2m4f on soft ground), where he readily drew 15 lengths clear of Bloodstone. The runner-up was an expensive store horse and went on to go close next time, whilst the winner – who looks a racy type – went on to fetch £300,000 (Tattersalls Cheltenham, February) just four days after his taking success. Mullins resisted the temptation of running him in a bumper in the spring and he is very much one to note in that sphere on his debut for the stable. In fact, if he makes a successful debut under Rules, I wouldn't be surprised if he were saved for the better bumpers later in the season, and, like Deploy The Getaway, will be representing the powerful Cheveley Park Stud. Incidentally, the son of Westerner was the 300th Point-to-Point success of Wexford trainer Colin Bowe and is a horse who I cannot wait to see in action under Rules. He could be very exciting.

picture courtesy of Tattersalls Ireland - www.tattersalls.ie

GABBYS CROSS *Henry de Bromhead*

A winner on debut at Monksgrange for Bernadette Murphy, Gabbys Cross was bought by leading owner Roger Brookhouse at Punchestown (Goffs) in early-May. By a sire I wouldn't be too familiar with (Frammassone), the four-year-old was sent for home at an early stage by Tom Hamilton and it proved to be a decisive move, as he wasn't for catching, seeing the race out really well. A sound jumper, his dam is related to several jumps winners including Mister Banjo (won the Grade 1 Finale Juvenile Hurdle at Chepstow for Paul Nicholls and John Hales), and whilst the form wouldn't appear to amount to much, he did it well and rates a decent prospect for his new connections.

GENERATION TEXT *Dan Skelton*

Runner-up to the potentially smart Sporting John on debut at Borris House, Generation Text ran a race full of promise and would have certainly been capable of winning something similar, had Denis Paul Murphy run him again during the spring. A four-year-old by Getaway, he finished in front of four subsequent winners, and given how he travelled, looks more than capable of making his mark over shorter distances under Rules. There is plenty of speed on the dam's side of his pedigree, so he appeals as the type who will be up to winning a bumper, should his new connections opt to head down that route to begin with.

GET IN ROBIN *Donald McCain*

Another winner for Donnchadh Doyle, Get In Robin won a mares' maiden at the second time of asking in late-April, having tipped up on debut when in the process of running a sound race. The Robin des Champs filly appeared to appreciate being ridden more positively on her second start, and although she might not have beaten a great deal, it was a pleasing performance on the eye. She crossed the line with a couple of lengths to spare, but was value for a good bit more than the official margin and is one to note in a mares' only bumper or a mares' novices' hurdle in the autumn. At £55,000 she could prove to be well bought and will carry the yellow and blue silks of Tim Leslie.

GIANT'S TABLE *TBC*

A winner in atrocious conditions (heavy rain/sleet) at Ballycahane in early-March, Giant's Table travelled notably well throughout for Barry O'Neill and also impressed with how he jumped. Out to his left a little at the last, he was about to be challenged by Jeremy Pass (joined Paul Nicholls for £100,000) when that rival came down, leaving him clear to score, eased down. The son of Great Pretender looked to have the measure of Jeremy Pass at the time and might well have run out a more convincing winner under less testing conditions. Despite the fact that those in behind didn't really do much to advertise the form (the exception being earlier faller Fantasio d'Alene, who did run well in a valuable sales bumper for Mouse Morris at Fairyhouse), Giant's Table looks capable of making an impact for his new connections and is another who could easily drop back in trip.

GOAHEADWITHTHEPLAN *Noel Meade*

It could be that two smart four-year-olds came out of the Belharbour maiden won by Fado des Brosses in early-February, as Goaheadwiththeplan really impressed with how he moved through the contest. In fact, I would go as far as saying that he travelled like the best horse in the race for a long way and it could be that he was just about to be outstayed by the eventual winner when coming down at the last. The son of Stowaway travelled sweetly and jumped well, showing good pace to get to the lead on the run to the final fence. Despite coming down, both him and the eventual winner had drawn readily clear of the well-supported favourite Minella Lightning, marking themselves down as potentially useful performers. Like the winner, Goaheadwiththeplan also headed to the Cheltenham (Tattersalls) sale just 18 days later, where he was purchased for £140,000 to join the stable of Noel Meade. I would expect him to start off in a bumper.

GRANDADS COTTAGE *Olly Murphy*

A four-year-old by Shantou, Grandads Cottage is a full-brother of Super Duty (five-time winner for Donald McCain and runner-up in the Grade 1 Mersey Novices' Hurdle) and made a winning debut for – yes, you guessed it – Donnchadh Doyle. Prominent throughout, he wound things up on the run to two out under Rob James and from the back of the penultimate fence galloped all the way to the line. He clocked a time around four seconds quicker to the same connections' Vandemere – who won division one of the same Portrush maiden – and has joined Olly Murphy's stable, for whom he will run in the colours of leading owner John Hales.

GUNSIGHT RIDGE *Olly Murphy*

A four-year-old by Midnight Legend, Gunsight Ridge looked an extremely exciting prospect when winning his maiden Point at Loughrea in mid-May. Just 11 days later, he was withdrawn from the Tattersalls sale at Cheltenham, but has since been bought privately and is now in the ownership of Mrs Diana Whateley. In training with Olly Murphy – who, of course, trains Thomas Darby for the Whateleys – Gunsight Ridge made all and jumped well en route to making a hugely promising winning debut. Yet another from the Doyle academy, he also showed a fine turn of foot once challenged and appeared to take some pulling up after the line. He looks a smart prospect.

HEARTBREAK KID *Donald McCain*

A wide-margin winner at Kirkistown for Colin Bowe and Barry O'Neill, Heartbreak Kid was prominent throughout and took control of the contest when left in front due to a serious error by long-time leader Flying Garry down the far side. Following a good jump two out, the four-year-old really began to open up and was a long way clear by the time he reached the final obstacle. He again met the last on a nice stride and cruised over the line with 30 lengths to spare over his nearest pursuer. The well-beaten runner-up was upsides Dancewiththewind and held every chance at Taylorstown in late-April, suggesting that the form might not be too bad and, visually, Heartbreak Kid was extremely impressive. By Getaway, he is a half-brother to Donald McCain's Sonic and, interestingly, McCain actually bought him – along with Derek O'Connor – as a store at last year's Goffs Land Rover sale. Given that link, it didn't come as a surprise when learning that Heartbreak Kid is now in training at Bankhouse stables.

ISRAEL CHAMP *David Pipe*

An impressive 12-length winner for Mary Doyle at Monksgrange in late-March, Israel Champ was prominent throughout and was eased down to beat On The Bandwagon (joined Jonjo O'Neill for £160,000) with any amount in hand. An imposing four-year-old by Milan, he is a distant relative of both Hollywoodien and Stellar Notion, and looks to have a really bright future under Rules. He has joined David Pipe, who enjoyed success with ex-Irish Pointers Eden de Houx and Umbrigado last season. That pair both won a bumper on debut for the stable, and given the speed on the dam's side of the pedigree, Israel Champ certainly looks to have the pace to start off in that sphere and is another who I am particularly looking forward to seeing this autumn.

KAKAMORA *Tom George*

Another graduate from the Donnchadh Doyle academy, Kakamora made a winning debut at Loughanmore in May, staying on strongly having made most under Rob James. A four-year-old by Great Pretender, his dam is an un-raced sister of the Grade 1-winning mare Bitofapuzzle, and he jumped really well at times (particularly three out when taking a length or more out of his field). Picked up for £105,000 by Gerry Hogan at Tattersalls Cheltenham sale in May, he is now in training with Tom George and will carry the red and white chequered silks of Tim Syder. Whilst he looks a stayer in the making, there is pace in his pedigree so there is a chance that he could start off in a bumper, should his new connections opt to head down that route.

LETS GO CHAMP *Tom George*

A full-brother to Scarlet And Dove (bumper winner for Joseph O'Brien and Gigginstown at Limerick last November), Lets Go Champ won a four-year-old maiden at Bartlemy in May, where he was probably value for more than the official winning distance. The most impressive part of the performance was the way in which he made smooth headway down the far side to join the leaders, and he clearly isn't short of speed. A good-looking son of Jeremy, out of a half-sister to the ill-fated Our Conor, he was also sold out of the Donnchadh Doyle stable and was purchased by leading owner Roger Brookhouse for £375,000 (Goffs UK Spring sale, May). As with Big Bresil – who will carry the same pale silks – Lets Go Champ is now in training with Tom George.

LINELEE KING *Olly Murphy*

Although he only beat three horses – in a four-year-old maiden at Tattersalls in May – Linelee King created a deep impression, with the ease with which he moved through the race. A lovely-looking grey son of Martaline, he breezed through the contest, so clearly possesses a high-cruising speed, and he jumped well en route to running out a very easy winner. The form isn't easy to assess (not really tested, with the second and third not running subsequently), but he was very easy on the eye and clearly has a bright future. Purchased from Colin Bowe for £180,000 at the Cheltenham Festival (Tattersalls) sale, he is now in training with Olly Murphy – for leading owner Mrs Diana Whateley – and looks to have the requisite pace to win a bumper before going hurdling.

MEYER LANSKY *Jonjo O'Neill*

A half-brother to Dramatic Approach (Point-to-Point winner for Denis Paul Murphy before finishing third in a Chepstow bumper for Neil Mulholland), Meyer Lansky finished third behind Papa Tango Charly and Big Bresil in what appeared to be a strong maiden at Liscarroll. The front three all fetched six figures when going through the ring at Aintree (Goffs UK sale) and this son of Mahler impressed with the way he travelled, albeit in snatches at times. He moved up menacingly on a couple of occasions, but also looked really green and could be one who improves considerably for that initial experience. Given the stamina on the dam's side, it probably shouldn't be a surprise that he finished strongly, coming home in third and clear of the remainder of the field. Like the winner, he is now in training with Jonjo O'Neill, and given that he might not have had the pace of the front two, he could well come into his own over 2m4f or beyond over hurdles.

MUSTANG ALPHA *Jamie Snowden*

A Stowaway four-year-old, Mustang Alpha displayed a smart turn of foot when making a winning debut at Bartlemy for Mick Goff and was bought just 10 days later by Lambourn trainer Jamie Snowden. Having travelled well just in behind the pace, he cruised into the lead under Shane Fitzgerald and really did show a smart injection of pace approaching the last, quickening right away from the back of the final fence. His dam hails from a really nice family, and given how he moved through that good-ground contest, he should have little trouble in making an impact over the minimum trip under Rules. He wouldn't appear to be the biggest, so it could be that he develops into a useful hurdler for his new connections, although he will be worth noting in a bumper beforehand should Snowden – who appears to have a lovely bunch of young horses to go to war with this season – opt to start off down that path.

MY WHIRLWIND *Nicky Henderson*

Top-lot at this year's Tattersalls Cheltenham Festival sale, My Whirlwind is a four-year-old by Stowaway, whose dam is a full-sister to Sizing Coal. She made most of the running and jumped really well to win a mares' maiden at Ballycahane in March, coping well with the soft ground and horrid conditions to score with plenty in hand. The fourth home, Calle Malva, went close at Fairyhouse in late-April, whilst the second and third were purchased by Jamie Codd and Mouse Morris respectively. Nicky Henderson secured My Whirlwind, who looks a smart prospect for the mares' division.

PAPA TANGO CHARLY *Jonjo O'Neill*

A four-year-old by No Risk At All, Papa Tango Charly proved hugely popular when going through the sales ring at Aintree in April (Goffs UK sale) and the hammer eventually came down at £440,000, with the successful bid being made on behalf of Jonjo O'Neill and owner Martin Tedham. The chestnut had made a successful debut a couple of weeks earlier, when winning by four lengths at Liscarroll, striking for Colin Bowe and Barry O'Neill. Having travelled sweetly, he jumped his way to the front three out, and although he wasn't quite as fluent two out, he pulled clear on the run to the last. Again not foot-perfect, he opened up nicely on the approach to the final fence, whilst leaving the impression that he would relish a more expansive and galloping track. Whilst I am sure he would be good enough to win a bumper, his pedigree on the dam's side is all about jumping, so I wouldn't be at all surprised if he were to head straight over hurdles. Both Jonjo O'Neill Jnr and Nick Scholfield (who rides the owner's horses) were positive about him when I interviewed them for the *A View From The Saddle* section of this year's publication, and he rates a hugely exciting addition to the team at Jackdaws Castle.

POWER OF PAUSE *Willie Mullins*

Another of the Harold Kirk/Willie Mullins purchases, Power Of Pause won on good ground over 2m4f on the Point-to-Point track on the inside of Punchestown in February. A four-year-old chestnut by Doyen, he was ridden patiently and showed a smart turn to foot to quicken away up the home straight. Given both the distance of the race and the nature of the track (very tight/sharp), Power Of Pause clearly possesses plenty of speed, so I would certainly expect him to form part of Mullins' bumper team this season.

RAMILLIES *Willie Mullins*

Sent off favourite for a 14-runner maiden at Bishops Court, Ramillies made no mistake, scoring in comfortable fashion for Sophie Lacey and Tommie O'Brien. Despite being a little untidy two out, the grey took control of the race and quickened up well on the run to the final fence. Better there, he ran out a relatively easy winner and was subsequently purchased by Willie Mullins at the Festival sale (Tattersalls, Cheltenham). The Shantou four-year-old will run in the colours of Joe Donnelly, owner of last season's Gold Cup winner Al Boum Photo, and is another to note in the bumper division.

SPORTING JOHN *TBC*

A four-year-old by Getaway, Sporting John won what turned out to be a competitive maiden at Borris House in early-March. Having travelled smoothly, he made good headway inside the final mile and jumped well, before going on to beat Generation Text by 2½ lengths. Vandemere (3rd), Direct Fire (4th) and Dancewiththewind (5th) all won next time – as did the pulled-up Hacksaw Ridge – to advertise the form, with the first-named impressing when scoring by seven lengths at Portrush. Purchased for £160,000 at the Cheltenham Festival sale (Tattersalls), he is now in the ownership of JP McManus.

THE BIG BREAKAWAY *Colin Tizzard*

Yet another impressive winner for Donnchadh Doyle and Rob James, The Big Breakaway looked aptly-named as he broke clear of his field on the run to two out at Quakerstown. Having jumped upsides at the third last, the four-year-old really began to pour it on from the back of the penultimate fence and ran out a wide-margin winner despite looking quite green. Purchased by Colin Tizzard at the Punchestown Goffs sale (€360,000), the son of Getaway will carry the red, white and yellow silks of owners Jones, Nicholas and Romans, who paid big money for Slate House two years ago. A half-brother to the 156-rated Kildisart, The Big Breakaway looks to possess plenty of size and scope, and it wouldn't be a surprise if he were to start off in the National Hunt novices' hurdle at Chepstow in October, a race in which Tizzard has introduced both Lostintranslation and Reserve Tank in the past two seasons.

WEST CORK *Dan Skelton*

A well-bred son of Midnight Legend, West Cork joined the Dan Skelton stable following a four-length win at Lisronagh last November, and it was pleasing that Harry Skelton was happy to include him amongst his horses to follow for the season in the *A View From The Saddle* section, suggesting he has been showing all the right signs at home. Sent off 5-4 favourite for Timmy Hyde, West Cork was happy to track the pace, and once asked to pick up the leaders he quickly got to the front on the run to two out. He jumped the final two fences really well, and despite looking distinctly green quickened up nicely to score under Derek O'Connor. The third home, Éclair Surf, advertised the form when winning by 30 lengths before being purchased by Gerry Hogan (now in training with Emma Lavelle), and West Cork – who is a full-brother to William H Bonney and Tiqris among others – looks a nice prospect for owners Mike and Eileen Newbould.

WIDE RECEIVER *Gordon Elliott*

2016 Gold Cup winner Don Cossack was the highest-profile son of Sholokhov to date, and Gordon Elliott has bought another very expensive son of that stallion in the shape of Cragmore winner Wide Receiver. The four-year-old cost his new connections £410,000 when going through the ring at Cheltenham in February (Tattersalls sale) and he looked to have the race sewn up from a good way out. Having taken up the running, he had his opposition in trouble in behind and pulled right away on the run to two out. Despite getting in tight, he was quickly away from the fence and met the last on a much better stride. He crossed the line with eight lengths to spare in the end and could well prove to be an exciting addition to what is already a very strong young team at Cullentra.

Altior - could be set to step up in distance this season

TOP-CLASS PERFORMERS

This year, I decided that I would take a look at the proven Grade 1 performers, as well as touching on several of the up-and-comers. Initially, I thought I would break it down by division, but given that **Altior** is finally likely to go up in trip this season, I thought starting with Nicky Henderson's nine-year-old was the obvious way to go. Now 19-from-19 over obstacles, the High Chaparral gelding again took all before him last season, although arguably his best performances came in the first half of the campaign. Having toughed it out on unsuitable ground in the Tingle Creek, he was faultless in the Desert Orchid. He won a second Queen Mother Champion Chase, and in doing so, won at a fourth successive Cheltenham Festival, where he again left the impression that he would relish going a bit further.

The King George has been mooted as a possible target – as it was last year, in fairness – and he heads the antepost market for the Christmas showpiece. If he is to head down that route, it is likely that he will be stepping up a full mile in distance, as I would struggle to find a suitable prep race for him in the early months of the season, other than the Shloer at Cheltenham or the Tingle Creek. Kauto Star (2006) proved that the Tingle Creek and King George can be won in the same season, although he had earlier won the Old Roan at Aintree and the Betfair Chase at Haydock, both over longer distances. Ideally – and this is not me being bias towards my local track – I would have loved to have seen Altior tackle the Melling Chase in April, as I have always felt that 2m4f around Aintree could prove absolutely ideal. That would have been a nice stepping-stone – over an intermediate trip – into this season, but he again skipped the Grand National meeting, so it really is likely to be a case of entering unknown territory in terms of stamina reserves. Personally, I have never been one for campaigning for him to go up in distance just for the sake of it (I see nothing wrong in racking up victories over 2m), but he definitely looked ready for it last season and whether he can stay the King George trip will be one of the more fascinating questions in the first half of the season.

Should he go and win at Kempton – or even run well for a long way – it is hard to envisage him dropping back for the Queen Mother Champion Chase, so it could be that he ends up in the Ryanair Chase, or, finally, the Melling at Aintree. His second half of the season is likely to be determined by the result of the King George.

Altior is currently rated 175, and much to the annoyance of many National Hunt enthusiasts, the Paul Nicholls-trained **Cyrname** has a slightly superior official rating of 176. Having won a handicap at Ascot off 150 in January, the seven-year-old put up an incredible performance to win the Ascot Chase by 17 lengths. A literal reading of that form – with stablemate Politologue well-beaten in fourth – entitles him to such a lofty mark and it was slightly disappointing that we didn't get to see if he could back this up away from the Berkshire track. The potential clash between Cyrname and Altior didn't materialise at Aintree in April, but there is every chance that it will happen at Kempton on Boxing Day, as the King George looked the obvious race for the former, when running away with the Ascot Chase.

Cyrname

Again, where he will run beforehand is open to conjecture, especially given that he seemingly has a strong preference to race right-handed. He, too, could be a possible for the Tingle Creek – and it should be remembered that he was quick enough to win a Wayward Lad and a Pendil as a novice, albeit against weaker opposition – whilst the Peterborough Chase at Huntingdon would appeal as the obvious race, the problem there being it comes just 18 days before the King George. He would need to relax if he is to get home over 3m, but he is getting better in that respect and certainly wasn't stopping at Ascot last time. It would make for a fascinating race, should this pair both end up lining up.

Staying with the King George, last year's winner **Clan des Obeaux** is likely to be aimed at the race again, too. A stablemate of Cyrname, he was impressive in staying on strongly up the home straight last term, but this season's race – at this stage, anyway – promises to be a stronger renewal and he might need to improve again. Seemingly put in his place in the Gold Cup and also at Aintree, he will appreciate a more strongly-run race at this trip, and it could be that the King George offers him the best chance of landing another Grade 1.

Clan des Obeaux

I've already covered second-season chasers **Topofthegame** (another for Paul Nicholls) and **La Bague Au Roi** (see *Around The Yards* for both), but another of last year's novices to take seriously would have to be Aintree winner **Lostintranslation**. He appears to relish a flat track and appreciated the step up in distance when winning the Mildmay Novices' Chase, in which Topofthegame didn't appear to give his true running. I covered him and Santini earlier, as they are likely to head down the Ladbrokes Trophy route before entering open Grade 1 company, whereas I feel that Colin Tizzard might well consider pitching his imposing seven-year-old into the Betfair Chase at Haydock, en route to Kempton. Given his form over 2m4f with Defi du Seuil, he would certainly have the pace to cope with the sharp track and it could end up being a small-field event in Merseyside. I would give that race some serious consideration if Lostintranslation were mine, with Wetherby's Charlie Hall another early-season option, and the fact that Tizzard used to be happy to aim Cue Card at these races, it is likely that both will be to the forefront of his mind.

Nicholls will have a job on his hands in keeping all of his staying chasers apart and it could be that Ryanair Chase winner **Frodon** ends up being his number one contender for the Betfair this season, although I actually think that Topofthegame has the pace to cope with the tight track, too. The likeable seven-year-old proved himself over this sort of trip when winning the Cotswold Chase on trials day in January and was successful on his reappearance last season, when winning the Old Roan at Aintree.

Whilst focusing on the Betfair, it would be rude not to mention Haydock specialist **Bristol de Mai**, who has, of course, won the past two renewals. Still only eight, Nigel Twiston-Davies' grey ran a cracker in the Gold Cup, and the Betfair Chase would again appear to be his best chance of winning for a fifth time at the top level. He proved last year that he doesn't need the ground to be deep – although it certainly favours him, by means of inconveniencing some of the opposition – and he has to be on any pre-season Haydock shortlist. Mine for the race would certainly be topped by him and Lostintranslation, under the assumption that Topofthegame is aimed at Newbury.

Looking ahead to the Cheltenham Gold Cup, it could be that **Santini** (again already covered in the *Around The Yards* section) develops into the leading contender from England. Very lightly-raced, he only had the three starts last season and his preparation for the Cheltenham Festival was far from straightforward, partly due to the Equine Influenza outbreak. He still only went down by half-a-length to Topofthegame, but I think the extra couple of furlongs – on the stiffer New Course – will be right up his street. His two earlier runs at the track had both come on the New Course, and the Cotswolds Chase on trials day – or Newbury's Denman Chase – appeal as obvious targets in the build-up to the festival. As stated previously, the first half of his season is likely to be geared around the Ladbrokes Trophy, and should he go and win that off a mark of 163, he would probably halve in price (currently 12-1) for the blue riband event.

The Irish could have a big say in the Gold Cup once again, however. Willie Mullins is responsible for the top two in the antepost market, courtesy of Kemboy and last year's winner **Al Boum Photo**. The latter was having just his eighth start over fences when running out an impressive winner under Paul Townend. Still only seven, he jumped and travelled sweetly throughout and backed it up with a sound second – behind his stablemate – at Punchestown.

Having unseated David Mullins at the first in the Gold Cup, it is a case of what might have been for **Kemboy**, who had earlier won the Clonmel Oil Chase over 2m4f and the Savills Chase at Leopardstown, where the rider made a race-winning move with a circuit to run. I must admit that I had stamina doubts about him ahead of the Gold Cup, and he bounced back with a really smart performance at Aintree. Ruby Walsh gave him a fine front-running ride on this occasion, dictating matters and easily drawing clear in atrocious conditions. It was, of course, Walsh's farewell ride when Kemboy beat the Gold Cup winner in the Punchestown equivalent, with the pair pulling a long way clear. Again ridden positively, neither horse jumped the second last well, but Kemboy had more in reserve from the back of the last. It was a fantastic race.

Kemboy

In terms of this season, you would think that Mullins would like to keep the pair apart – at least in the first half of the campaign – so it could be that one is considered for the King George, whilst the other remains on home soil for the Savills. Both horses have the requisite pace to cope with the track at Kempton, although I still see Kemboy as more of a speed horse at the trip. In terms of the Gold Cup – for which he is favourite – I would still have a slight reservation about him lasting home at this stage, and his rather unique way of jumping might also be more suited to a flat track. Time will tell, but both horses remain lightly-raced and were clearly improving rapidly last term.

This time last year, all the talk was of **Presenting Percy** and he certainly shouldn't be forgotten. Clearly nowhere near his best when only eighth in the Gold Cup in March (finished lame), his rather unorthodox approach to Cheltenham was well-documented and it will be interesting to see if he is more aggressively campaigned this time around. He appeared to thrive on racing as a novice the season before, when it should be remembered that he had Al Boum Photo in behind (when falling) in the RSA. He clearly has questions to answer on his return, but he certainly has the ability – and time on his side – to still make an impact in the division.

Presenting Percy

Of last season's novices, **Delta Work** was the clear pick in terms of Irish stayers. The winner of four of his five chases – three of which came in Grade 1 company – the 2018 Pertemps Final winner had no problem in handling decent ground in the first half of last season, and despite things not exactly going his way, he relished the step up to 3m (over fences) when winning the Neville Hotels at Leopardstown over Christmas. Only third in the RSA – perhaps the lack of a prep run played against him – he went on to run out a most impressive winner at Punchestown, where he cruised to an easy 12-length success. Le Richebourg franked his earlier form and he is probably capable of winning over 2m4f, although I wouldn't be surprised if Gordon Elliott had him ready for the JNwine.com Champion Chase at Down Royal, a meeting which he invariably targets. Elliott has saddled three winners of that race in the past six years, and those past six winners all sported the silks of Gigginstown House Stud. With Willie Mullins never really up and running by the first weekend in November, Delta Work is likely to take some beating there and can make a real impact, despite the obvious depth to the division over in Ireland.

One race that Mullins has done well in during recent seasons is the 2m4f John Durkan Memorial Chase at Punchestown in mid-December, having won it four times in the past six years. All four carried the silks of Rich Ricci and last year's winner **Min** is likely to be aimed here once again. After finishing only fifth in the Champion Chase, he was given another Aintree masterclass by Ruby Walsh, as the pair made all and totally dominated the opposition in the Melling Chase. Beaten at Punchestown for a second successive season in April, I think that 2m4f is his ideal trip now, and with that in mind he could be aimed at the Ryanair Chase this season in an attempt to land an elusive festival success. His connections will certainly be hoping that Altior doesn't end up down this route, having finished behind him on three previous visits to Cheltenham.

Over shorter trips, last season's antepost Arkle favourite **Le Richebourg** is another who shouldn't be forgotten. Fifth in the 2018 Galway Hurdle, Jospeh O'Brien's son of Network really took well to fences, winning twice in the early part of the season, before probably just being outstayed by Delta Work in the Drinmore. He gained Grade 1 compensation (twice) at Leopardstown, when winning the Racing Post Novice Chase and the Irish Arkle, and was one horse who certainly benefitted from the dry winter, as he relishes a decent surface. With that in mind, he would be one to tread carefully with should we endure a wet winter, but he was improving rapidly when last seen and his jumping was assured. He is currently 20-1 for the Queen Mother

Champion Chase, and assuming Altior does go up in trip, that price could well look quite big come next March. Assuming all goes well in the build-up to the season, the Paddy Power Dial-A-Bet Chase at Leopardstown over Christmas will be his first major target, and he could well clash there with impressive Punchestown winner **Chacun Pour Soi** (already covered in the *Across The Sea* section).

Domestically, JP McManus has **Defi du Seuil** for intermediate distance races and is another who is likely to be aimed at the Ryanair Chase. The former Triumph Hurdle winner left behind a disappointing second season over hurdles, by winning three times over fences last term, with his brace of Grade 1s – the Scilly Isles and the JLT – the obvious highlights. Huntingdon's Peterborough Chase would appeal as a likely mid-season target for Philip Hobbs' six-year-old, after which Aintree's Melling Chase would be another likely spring objective.

In terms of two-milers, should Altior go up in trip, the division looks a little thin on the ground (**Sceau Royal** – another good-ground specialist – is next-best in England), although another forgotten horse could be **Dynamite Dollars**, who was also forced to miss the Arkle through injury. He was only rated in the low-130s as a hurdler, but really took to chasing and won four of his five starts, only suffering defeat at the hands of **Lalor** (who was very impressive on the day but failed to back it up) at Cheltenham in November. He won his three subsequent starts – including the Grade 1 Henry VIII Novices' Chase – and given that he hails from the Paul Nicholls stable, he is likely to be campaigned with the Queen Mother in mind. Rated 157, he needs to take another step forward (has 7lb to find with Sceau Royal), but given that the division could be quite thin on the ground, there is a good chance that his current odds of 50-1 could contract throughout the season. If he is ready, he is likely to be aimed at the Tingle Creek, otherwise the Desert Orchid over Christmas might be considered as a starting point.

Moving onto the hurdlers, and starting with the two-milers. Of the British-trained horses, the only three who are currently priced shorter than 33-1 for the Champion Hurdle are all trained by Nicky Henderson. Dual-Champion **Buveur d'Air** is the obvious place to start, following his victory at Punchestown. Imperious in the Fighting Fifth – a race in which he is again likely to make his reappearance – he made an uncharacteristic mistake when beaten in the Christmas Hurdle and, of course, came down in the Champion Hurdle itself. Hampered at a crucial stage in the Aintree Hurdle, he was probably outstayed on soft ground over 2m4f and bounced right back to reverse form with Supasundae at Punchestown. He remains very much the hurdler to beat over the minimum trip in England.

Buveur d'Air

Stablemates **Pentland Hills** (Triumph Hurdle and Anniversary 4-Y-O Hurdle at Aintree) and **Fusil Raffles** (AES Champion Four Year Old Hurdle) won all three spring Grade 1s between them in the juvenile division and are both open to considerable improvement, after just three and four starts respectively. It has proven difficult for such horses to make an impact in open company the following season, but Espoir d'Allen proved that it can be done last season, and they are sure to be kept away from Buveur d'Air. I would expect one to reappear in the Masterton Holdings Hurdle at Cheltenham in October, but both have plenty to find with their stable-companion on official ratings, with Pentland Hills rated 153 and Fusil Raffles 152; Buveur d'Air is currently rated 167, which highlights the bridge they must gap.

If the staying chase division in Ireland appears to be deep, it looks quite the opposite in the 2m-hurdle division, especially after the desperate news broke in late-August that last season's Champion Hurdle winner Espoir d'Allen had passed away. A huge blow for the Gavin Cromwell stable and leading owner JP McManus, he leaves a void in what already appeared to be a relatively weak (in terms of strength-in-depth) division. For those who like to follow trends – and this really applies more to the aforementioned pairing of Pentland Hills and Fusil Raffles, and is sure to be covered in next year's *Cheltenham Festival Betting Guide* – the ill-fated Espoir d'Allen became just the second five-year-old winner of the Champion Hurdle in the past 33 runnings.

Klassical Dream has already been covered in more detail elsewhere (see *Across The Sea*) and following the initial news about Espoir d'Allen – who was ruled out for the season a week or so before the sad news broke about his death – he is now clear favourite for the Champion Hurdle in March (best price 7-2, at the time of writing). The Morgiana Hurdle (Punchestown, 17th November) would appeal as the obvious starting point for the son of Dream Well, followed by the Ryanair Hurdle over Christmas, and the Irish Champion Hurdle in February (both at Leopardstown).

Remaining in Ireland briefly – before we move on to the staying hurdle division – I would like to touch upon **Laurina** and Samcro. The former was one of the biggest disappointments of the whole week for me at Cheltenham. Despite the fact that she clearly needed to take a huge step forward on her first start against the boys, I really did think she was up to going very close, and the fact that we didn't see her again suggests that all was not right after the Champion Hurdle. Given her build, I would expect her to head over fences upon her return, and I still think the six-year-old has the ability to mix it at the highest level. She could easily be Arkle or JLT material, if returning with a clean bill of health, and that comment certainly also applies to **Samcro** who endured a difficult first season out of novice company. Following his fifth of six over Christmas, it was announced that he had been suffering from a lung infection, and although he held an entry in the Aintree Hurdle and at Punchestown, he wasn't seen in the second half of the season. Going back to his Point-to-Point form, the son of Germany – who is another with the physique for chasing – beat last season's Welsh Grand National winner Elegant Escape in a four-year-old maiden at Monksgrange. It really is hoped that Gordon Elliott has managed to get to the bottom of those issues, as he is another who still has the time on his side to reach the very top.

Laurina

TOP-CLASS PERFORMERS

Moving onto the staying hurdles – again in Ireland, to begin with – and **Benie des Dieux** would once again appear to have any amount of options. A final-flight faller when looking to have the David Nicholson at her mercy in March, she returned to winning ways at Punchestown, before proving she stays 3m+ in the Grande Course de Hais d'Auteuil in May. In lowering the colours of the brilliant French mare De Bon Coeur, the versatile daughter of Great Pretender opened up even more avenues. The Mares' Hurdle at Cheltenham is once again the most obvious end-of-season target, but the Stayers' Hurdle is probably now an option and races such as the 3m Christmas Hurdle can also now be considered. The Hatton's Grace would seem the logical starting point, although it is worth remembering that she is three-from-three over fences, and being rated much lower as a chaser, the Ladbrokes Trophy at Newbury had been mooted as a possible option. The Irish handicapper has her on a mark of 157 over hurdles, but only 147 over fences, so even allowing for the British handicapper upping her a couple of pounds, she would still receive a fair chunk of weight from the likes of Santini and Topofthegame, should a trip to Berkshire become a possibility. She would be an intriguing runner there.

Last season's leading stayer **Paisley Park** remains very much the one to beat in the division, however. As we have seen in recent years, this is a division which can be dominated by an outstanding performer, and being only seven and having had only four starts over 3m, Emma Lavelle's stable-star looks to have outstanding claims of joining recent multiple winners of the Stayers' Hurdle, such as Baracouda, Inglis Drever and Big Buck's. Likely to reappear in the Long Distance Hurdle at Newbury, he will then probably follow a similar path back to the festival, via Ascot and Cheltenham on trials day. He sets a high bar for the like of *Leading Prospect* **Emitom** and the 7-2 (bet365) about a repeat success seems more than fair. A strong stayer with a turn of foot, he has the ideal way of going through his races, in that he tends to race behind the bridle and like those aforementioned former staying stars (certainly at least the last-named pairing), he appears to hit a flat spot before finishing really strongly. Versatile in terms of track and ground – although he does prefer a decent surface – Paisley Park doesn't appear to have too many chinks in his armour.

Paisley Park

Fellow seven-year-old **If The Cap Fits** is the other likely – and more obvious – British-trained challenger. Having proven his stamina at Aintree, Harry Fry's Milan gelding is likely to be aimed at the Long Distance Hurdle (Newbury) and Long Walk (Ascot) in the first half of the season. Yet to race at Cheltenham, the Cleeve on trials day would, therefore, make the ideal stepping-stone to the festival, by which point we should have a better idea of whether he is to become a serious threat to Paisley Park's crown. Officially rated 9lb inferior to the reigning champion, he does need to take another step forward when he returns.

Al Boum Photo - would be a fascinating contender in the King George on Boxing Day

BIG-RACE TRENDS

BetVictor Gold Cup
(Grade 3) 2m 4f 44y – Cheltenham (Old)
Saturday 16th November 2019

OVERVIEW

The November meeting at Cheltenham is often recognised by many as the first major fixture in the National Hunt calendar, and the BetVictor Gold Cup is the highlight of the three-day meeting. In recent years, it has proven wise to follow a relatively unexposed young chaser who sat just behind the market leader, and previous form at the track is almost essential. Plenty of recent winners had already contested at least one race at the top-level, and many would go on to win at a much higher level, so look for a Graded class performer-in-waiting.

WEIGHT AND OFFICIAL RATINGS

Six of the past 10 winners were rated in the 140s, and during the past 20 years only four horses have successfully defied a mark of 150 or higher. That quartet were *Cyfor Malta*, *Fondmort*, *Al Ferof* and *Taquin du Seuil*, which gives you an indication of the calibre of horse who is required to succeed from a lofty rating.

Exotic Dancer and *Imperial Commander* managed to sneak into this off a mark of 139 (something that we probably won't see again), whilst eight of the past 14 winners were rated in the 140s.

Similarly, only half-a-dozen winners in the past 20 years have carried more than 11st.

PREP RUN OR FRESH?

With 10 of the past 20 winners having had a prep run earlier in the campaign, there is clearly no standout pattern as to whether or not it can pay to arrive at Cheltenham first time up. The past three winners had all been out in the early weeks of the season, with *Taquin du Seuil* and *Baron Alco* having shaped really well at Chepstow's October Jumps Festival, and given how that two-day fixture is continuing to grow, it could be something to pay attention to going forward.

Looking further back, both *The Outback Way* and *Shooting Light* – either side of the turn of the century – won over course-and-distance at the October meeting on their previous outing, something *Johns Spirit* would emulate in 2013. A further three winners – *Exotic Dancer*, *L'Antartique* and *Little Josh* – all contested Carlisle's **Colin Parker Memorial Intermediate Chase** prior to winning this.

Paul Nicholls' *Caid du Berlais* was another winner who had officially run earlier in the campaign, although this race was his first start since finishing seventh in the Galway Plate during the summer.

SECOND-SEASON/LIGHTLY-RACED CHASERS

Following a run of three more-experienced horses winning the BetVictor Gold Cup, *Baron Alco* struck for the lightly-raced types again last year and, in doing so, became the 12th winner in the past 15 years to have run nine times or less over fences. Several of that dozen were second-season chasers, with *Imperial Commander* and *Caid du Berlais* defying considerable inexperience, in winning this on just their fourth chase start.

This race can often be used as a stepping-stone to bigger and better things over fences, so the lightly-raced sorts often get the chance to run in a valuable handicap, before they head into (or back into, in many a case) Graded company.

Although not a second-season chaser, this could be the ideal starting point for **Siruh du Lac**, who was having just his eighth start over fences when winning the Plate at the festival. Last year's winner *Baron Alco* had finished runner-up in the Plate 12 months earlier, and Nick Williams' six-year-old clearly relishes the track, having won here on trials day in January, too. Clearly on an upward curve when last seen, he is now rated 150 but has the potential to develop into a Graded-class chaser, so could attempt to complete a Cheltenham handicap hat-trick on reappearance.

COURSE FORM

Previous course form has proven almost essential in the BetVictor Gold Cup of late – something else which points to a big run from Siruh du Lac, should he turn up – with no fewer than 14 of the past 20 winners having previously won over fences at Cheltenham.

In addition to that, *Baron Alco* became the third winner in the past 15 years (the others coming in 2004 and 2005, in the shape of *Celestial Gold* and *Our Vic*) to have finished placed at a Cheltenham Festival when a novice chaser. As stated above, last year's winner had finished second in the Plate, whilst the David Johnson-owned pairing had hit the frame in the National Hunt Chase and the RSA Chase respectively.

One of last year's novices to have shown decent form at the course is the Rebecca Curtis-trained **Drovers Lane**, who won here last December before shaping well for a long way in the RSA Chase. Whilst Siruh du Lac begins the season on a mark of 150, Drovers Lane has been dropped a couple of pounds to 148 which is more in keeping with several recent winners.

Of the other trio, *Tranquil Sea* (Close Brothers Novices' Handicap Chase) and *Little Josh* (RSA Chase) had finished sixth at the previous season's festival, whilst *Caid du Berlais* is the only winner in the past 20 years to have not previously run over fences at the track. However, he had finished placed at two festivals over hurdles – in the Fred Winter and the Martin Pipe – so course form seems a must.

MARKET FORCES

It is 10 years since a winning favourite has obliged in this race, but five favourites in all have been successful in the past 20 years, and *Baron Alco* became the 13th winner during this period to be sent off at single figures. It has, therefore, been profitable to follow those just in behind the market leader of late and we haven't had too many shocks in this event, with a further three winners during the past 20 years starting between 10/1 and 12/1. Focus on the top end of the market.

GRADE 1 CLASS

As touched upon already, several winners of this race have subsequently gone on to perform at a higher level, but more notably 14 of the 19 winners this century had already contested at least one Grade 1 race earlier in their career. Four of the 14 had won a Grade 1 – three over fences and *Tranquil Sea* had won a Grade 1 novice hurdle at Punchestown – whilst last year's winner *Baron Alco* continued the trend, as he had finished second behind Top Notch in the Scilly Isles Novices' Chase just nine months earlier. He had also contested the Grade 1 Future Champions Finale Juvenile Hurdle (finished fourth behind Bristol de Mai) much earlier in his career and was the fifth winner of this race in a row – and the 9th in 11 years – to have run at the highest level. That touch of class clearly helps.

TRAINERS TO NOTE

Jonjo O'Neill might not have had the ammunition of old in the past couple of seasons and, as a consequence, he hasn't saddled a runner in this race for the past two years, but he won three of the 11 runnings prior to that from just 14 runners.

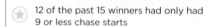
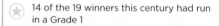
His runners, therefore, warrant utmost respect, and backing his horses blindly since 2006, when *Exotic Dancer* won for the yard would have yielded a level-stakes profit of £20 (to a £1 stake).

Another trainer to have saddled a couple of winners during the past decade is **Paul Nicholls**, who has also seen a further eight of his runners finish in the first five. Frodon went close for Nicholls last year, who has saddled 22 runners during the past 10 years.

Going back to the late nineties and early this century, Martin Pipe was the first name to turn to when looking at this race. He saddled no fewer than six winners in a remarkable eight year spell between 1998 and 2005, after which he handed over the reins to his son, **David Pipe**. The yard still clearly likes to target this race, albeit without the same level of success, as Pipe Junior has since saddled 18 runners (including several well-fancied, none more so than 7/4 favourite Grands Crus in 2012), but has only seen *Great Endeavour* win thus far.

Another leading trainer with a poor recent record in the race is **Nicky Henderson**, who won it for the only time to date in 2003 with *Fondmort*. Since then, the master of Seven Barrows has

 BIG-RACE TRENDS

saddled no fewer than 25 runners without success. He has had a few hit the frame – including 2/1 market leader Long Run – but Rather Be being brought down when seemingly travelling well last year rather summed up his fortune in this race. Henderson only really gets his string going around this time each season, and it could be that other yards have their horses further forward and indeed primed for this particular race, whereas Henderson invariably takes a steadier approach with a long season in mind.

ROLL OF HONOUR

Year	Season Form	Winner	Age	Weight	OR	SP	Trainer	Runners	Last race (No. of days)
2018	2	Baron Alco	7	10-11	146	8/1	G Moore	18	2nd Chepstow Chase (34)
2017	4	Splash of Ginge	9	10-6	134	25/1	N Twiston-Davies	17	4th Listed Wetherby Chase (15)
2016	6	Taquin du Seuil	9	11-11	155	8/1	J O'Neill	17	6th Gr.3 Chepstow Hurdle (35)
2015		Annacotty	7	11-0	147	12/1	A King	20	fell Gr.3 Topham (218)
2014	7	Caid du Berlais	5	10-13	143	10/1	P Nicholls	18	7th Galway Plate (108)
2013	1	Johns Spirit	6	10-2	139	7/1	J O'Neill	20	1st Cheltenham Chase (28)
2012		Al Ferof	7	11-8	159	8/1	P Nicholls	18	3rd Gr.1 Manifesto (219)
2011		Great Endeavour	7	10-3	147	8/1	D Pipe	20	6th Listed Aintree Chase (217)
2010	1	Little Josh	8	10-5	146	20/1	N Twiston-Davies	19	1st Carlisle Chase (13)
2009	21	Tranquil Sea	7	10-13	148	11/2F	E O'Grady (IRE)	17	1st Gr.3 Naas Chase (14)

Siruh du Lac - a likely candidate for this season's BetVictor Gold Cup

BIG-RACE TRENDS

Greatwood Hurdle
(Grade 3) 2m 87y – Cheltenham (Old)
Sunday 17th November 2019

OVERVIEW

It is 17 years since *Rooster Booster* won the Greatwood and went on to win the Champion Hurdle some four months later, and whilst it might not be the trial for the blue-riband that it was once perceived to be, it remains one of the most competitive two-mile handicap hurdles in the calendar. It is another race in which it can pay to focus on the unexposed types, with second-season hurdlers boasting a fine record.

WEIGHTS AND OFFICIAL RATINGS

We have seen lightly-weighted horses succeed in each of the past two seasons, but there has been a real mixed bag in terms of results in recent years. Several horses have carried big weights to victory, notably *Rooster Booster, Rigmarole, Detroit City* and *Menorah*, who all shouldered top-weight and carried 11-12.

Again, there is no real consistency in terms of official BHA Ratings, although 10 of the last 16 winners were rated in the 140s. Subsequent Champion Hurdle winner *Rooster Booster* is the only horse to defy a mark higher than 151 (155).

LIGHTLY-RACED HURDLERS

Last year's winner *Nietzsche* didn't really fit the mould of many a recent Greatwood winner, with no fewer than 16 of the past 20 winners having had nine hurdles runs or less. Thirteen of those had run no more than six times over hurdles, including the novice pairing of *Rodock* and *Westender*.

Thirteen of the past 20 winners – and 12 of the past 15 – were second-season hurdlers and, as with many of the early-season feature handicaps, looking at such horses is as good a starting point as any.

PREVIOUS COURSE FORM

Only two of the past 13 winners hadn't previously run at Cheltenham – *Sizing Europe*, who is the only Irish-trained winner during this period, and *Dell' Arca*, who was having his first start since arriving from France.

Of the 11 recent winners with course form in the book, six had been successful, as had *Rooster Booster* when going back to 2002, with Philip Hobbs' grey having won the County Hurdle earlier

in the year. The same connections' *Detroit City* had won the Triumph Hurdle during the same calendar year, whilst another from the same stable – *Menorah* – had won the Supreme the previous March. *Olofi, Garde la Victoire* and *North Hill Harvey* had all won either juvenile or novice hurdles at the track, and *Old Guard* had won a handicap at the October meeting on his previous start.

Last year's winner *Nietzsche* had finished third in the Fred Winter as a juvenile and had also finished sixth behind *Elgin* in the previous season's renewal. However, the most common Cheltenham race to crop up as a 'key guide' to the Greatwood is the previous season's **Supreme Novices' Hurdle**. Three successive winners between 2008-2010 had all run in the festival-opener some eight months earlier, whilst *North Hill Harvey* had finished ninth in the previous season's Supreme, following a mistake two out. *Elgin* had also contested the Supreme as a novice, albeit two seasons prior to his Greatwood success.

OTHER 'KEY RACES'

During the past eight years, both *Brampour* and *Elgin* won the Listed **Bet With Ascot Handicap Hurdle** just a couple of weeks before the Greatwood.

The previous season's **Top Novices' Hurdle** from Aintree is another reasonable indicator in terms of the second-season hurdlers, with both *Menorah* (2nd) and *North Hill Harvey* (4th) running well at the Grand National meeting. *Brampour* also took his chance in the Top Novices', although with less promise, coming home in ninth as a four-year-old.

FRESH VS FIRST TIME OUT (AND CURRENT FORM)

Rather like the BetVictor Gold Cup the previous day, there is a fairly even mix – during the past 20 winners – between horses arriving at the Greatwood on the back of a recent run or those who were having their first start of the season. Since 2001, nine of the 18 winners had run over hurdles earlier in the campaign, whilst another duo – *Detroit City* and *Nietzsche* – had warmed up for this by running on the Flat during October or November. The former won the Cesarewitch and the latter had finished runner-up in a 1m4f handicap, also at Newmarket.

Since 2011, when *Brampour* won the aforementioned Listed handicap hurdle at Ascot en route to

  BIG-RACE TRENDS

Cheltenham (a feat repeated by *Elgin* in 2017), another two Greatwood winners had already run during the current season. One was *Old Guard*, who scored over course-and-distance at the October meeting, and the other was *Garde la Victoire*, who finished third under top-weight at Aintree.

Of the other winners during the past 20 years who had already had a run earlier in the season, the first three – *Rodock*, *Westender* and *Rooster Booster* – had all won during October. *Accordion Etoile* had finished runner-up in the then-Grade 1 McManus Hurdle, so being in form is clearly advantageous. In total (including the two winners who had run on the Flat), of the 12 winners who had run recently, 10 had won or finished second, so we should focus on in-form horses if looking at those with a run under their belts.

TRAINERS TO NOTE

With four winners since 2002, **Philip Hobbs** is obviously a good place to start. *Rooster Booster*, *Detroit City* and *Menorah* all shouldered top-weight to success, whilst *Garde la Victoire* also carried 11-9 and won from a mark of 144, so it is clear that Hobbs isn't afraid to run a high-class Graded performer in this. In total during the century, Hobbs has saddled 24 horses in the Greatwood, and backing them all blindly would have yielded a small profit of £4.20 to a level-stake of £1. During the past six years, Hobbs has only saddled two horses (not had a runner in either of the past two runnings) and one was successful, so he is clearly being more selective of late.

It could be that **Crooks Peak** represents the Hobbs stable this season. A lightly-raced second-season hurdler, the six-year-old has failed to shine in a couple of runs at the festival – including in the County Hurdle in March – but did win the Listed bumper at this meeting two years ago.

Paul Nicholls is another trainer to respect, having saddled three winners since 2003. He has saddled another six horses to finish in the first three – including a second and two thirds in the past three years from just three runners – and his winners were sent off at 33/1, 12/1 and 12/1. Backing all runners from Ditcheat would have yielded a very healthy profit of £42 to a level-stake £1.

It will be interesting to see if Nicholls considers running **Getaway Trump**, who would have to attempt to match the effort of *Rooster Booster* by defying a mark of 155. The Fighting Fifth was mentioned as a possible starting point last spring, but the six-year-old would relish the likely strong pace of this big-field handicap and would delay a potential clash with the likes of Buveur d'Air.

KEY TRENDS

 16 of the past 20 winners had run 9 times or less over hurdles (13 of that 16 had run 6 times or less over hurdles)

 13 of the past 20 winners – and 12 of the last 15 – were second-season hurdlers

 10 of the past 16 winners were rated in the 140s

 6 of the past 13 winners had previously won at Cheltenham

 2 winners since 2006 ran on the Flat in October/November

 Look for a 1st or 2nd finish if having had a recent run

 Respect Philip Hobbs' runners

 Respect Paul Nicholls' runners

 Rooster Booster is the only winner to defy a mark higher than 151

 Only 2 of the past 13 winners had not run at Cheltenham previously

Nicholls' former assistant **Dan Skelton** won this race with *North Hill Harvey* three years ago and his record in valuable 2m handicap hurdles has been highlighted further on in this section, when dissecting Ascot's Betfair Exchange Hurdle, a race he has won twice in the past six years. He saddled three horses without success last year, but Superb Story finished runner-up for the stable in 2015 and Blue Heron finished fourth 12 months earlier. Skelton clearly likes to target these events.

ROLL OF HONOUR

Year	Season Form	Winner	Age	Weight	OR	SP	Trainer	Runners	Last race (No. of days)
2018	6	Nietzsche	5	9-7 (3oh)	126	20/1	B Ellison	18	6th Warwick Hurdle (179)*
2017	41	Elgin	5	10-8	145	10/1	A King	13	1st Listed Ascot Hurdle (15)
2016		North Hill Harvey	5	11-0	141	6/1	D Skelton	16	4th Aintree Nov. Hurdle (219)
2015	1	Old Guard	4	10-10	145	12/1	P Nicholls	17	1st Cheltenham Hurdle (23)
2014	3	Garde La Victoire	5	11-9	144	10/1	P Hobbs	15	3rd Aintree Hurdle (22)
2013	212	Dell' Arca	4	10-5	128	12/1	D Pipe	18	2nd Auteuil Hurdle (157)
2012		Olofi	6	10-11	136	8/1	T George	18	16th Gr.3 County Hurdle (247)
2011	1	Brampour	4	11-4	149	12/1	P Nicholls	24	1st Listed Ascot Hurdle (15)
2010		Menorah	5	11-12	151	6/1	P Hobbs	17	2nd Gr.2 Aintree Nov. Hurdle (219)
2009	5	Khyber Kim	7	11-9	143	9/1	N Twiston-Davies	15	5th Gr.3 Haydock Hurdle (190)

LEADING TEN-YEAR GUIDES

Previous season's Supreme Novices' Hurdle 3 (*Khyber Kim* 10th, *Menorah* 1st, *North Hill Harvey* 9th)
Previous season's Top Novices' Hurdle 3 (*Menorah* 2nd, *Brampour* 9th, *North Hill Harvey* 4th)
Bet With Ascot Handicap Hurdle 2 (*Brampour* 1st, *Elgin* 1st)

* *Nietzsche had two Flat runs, at Ayr (23rd June) and Newmarket (2nd November), prior to the Greatwood*

Rooster Booster - won the Greatwood Hurdle en route to Champion Hurdle glory

BIG-RACE TRENDS

SAAL *racing* **makes owning a horse simple, transparent, affordable and most of all fun**

Horses running for **SAAL** *racing* this season include our super mare SHANTEWE to be aimed at the top novice hurdle races, BOREAS DUKE an exciting juvenile hurdler and TROPICAL WORLD our bumper horse

Costs start from £100/month for 5% shares

For more information visit www.**saal**racing.**com** or contact

834 949692 matt@saalracing.com ● 07900 000464 andy@saalracing.com

THE RACING MANAGER

SAAL *Racing* uses **THE RACING MANAGER**. The leading platform for trainers and syndicate managers to communicate with owners

- **APP AND WEB BASED**
- **SEND VIDEO, AUDIO OR TEXT POSTS TO OWNERS AT THE CLICK OF A BUTTON**
- **AUTOMATIC ALERTS FOR ENTRIES AND DECLARATIONS**
- **TIMEFORM RACE PREVIEWS AND REVIEWS**
- **RACE RESULTS AND FULL REPLAYS AUTOMATICALLY SENT TO OWNERS**

Contact Anna Rowlinson **to arrange a demonstration**
anna@theracingmanager.com 0203 848 1880

Betfair Exchange Stayers' Handicap Hurdle
(Grade 3) 3m 58y – Haydock Park
Saturday 23rd November 2019

OVERVIEW

First run in 2005, the Betfair Exchange Stayers' Handicap Hurdle – run on the same Haydock Park card as the Grade 1 Betfair Chase – was handed Listed status in 2009, when *Diamond Harry* successfully carried top-weight under a confident Timmy Murphy ride. Awarded Grade 3 status in 2011, this race used the fixed brush hurdles between 2007 and 2016, after which those obstacles were no longer used at the Merseyside track.

The race remains a valuable contest, and since it reverted to the use of standard hurdles, the two winners – *Sam Spinner* and *Paisley Park* – were both successful in the Grade 1 Long Walk Hurdle at Ascot on their respective next starts, and they did, of course, also finish first and second in last season's Stayers' Hurdle at the Cheltenham Festival.

LIGHTLY-RACED/SECOND-SEASON HURDLERS

This is yet another early-season handicap which tends to go the way of a lightly-raced hurdler, with nine of the past 10 winners having had seven hurdles starts or less. Of the nine, seven – including the past two winners – were second-season hurdlers and this septet had an average of five hurdles starts apiece.

CLASS WILL OUT

As stated in the 'Overview', the past two winners went on to win the Grade 1 Long Walk Hurdle on their next start, and there were another two subsequent Grade 1 winners – *Grands Crus* and *Dynaste* – successful in this race during the past 10 years. In addition to this, *Diamond Harry* was a Grade 1-winning novice hurdler the previous season, whilst French raider *Millenium Royal* had already scored at the top level. Obviously, foreseeing the future is never easy, but this suggests that we should be looking for an improving young and unexposed hurdler with aspirations beyond handicap company when assessing this race.

Given that the fixed brush hurdles are no longer in the equation – and the subsequent exploits of recent winners *Sam Spinner* and *Paisley Park* – it could be that this race continues to grow in terms of a stepping stone for second-season stayers. One horse who might well fit the profile is the Warren Greatrex-trained **Emitom**, who begins

the season on a mark of 147 and is clearly held in the highest regard. He had just the four hurdles starts last term and finished runner-up in the Grade 1 Sefton Novices' Hurdle at Aintree on his final start. One place behind him at the Grand National meeting, **Lisnagar Oscar** also chased home Emitom earlier in the season in a maiden hurdle at Ffos Las and is another likely contender for this. An impressive Grade 2 winner here at Haydock, Rebecca Curtis has suggested that he will be chasing before too long, but a mark of 141 might well tempt the Pembrokeshire-based trainer back to the Merseyside track.

WEIGHT AND BHA RATINGS

Four horses have carried top weight (11-12) to success to date, those being *Millenium Royal, Diamond Harry, Trustan Times* and last year's winner, *Paisley Park*. The first-named was winning from a mark of 156, whilst *Diamond Harry* and *Paisley Park* both put up fine efforts in terms of official ratings, scoring off 149 and 147 respectively.

The past eight winners have fallen into the bracket between 136 and 147, with the average winning mark during this period being 140/141.

MARKET FORCES

There were three winning favourites during the first six years of this race – the last being 6/4 shot *Grands Crus* – and although we haven't seen another since, the top of the market has continued to dominate. In total, 10 of the 14 winners were sent off at single figures, with seven of the 10 starting at 6/1 or shorter.

Last year's race was slightly unusual in that only seven horses went to post, but even when we have seen much bigger fields, it can pay to focus on the top end of the market. *Trustan Times* (10/1) and *Baradari* (12/1) were still among the top half-dozen in the betting, and only two of the 14 winners to date were sent off at odds greater than 12/1.

BEEN CHASING

Five of the first 12 winners of this race had been chasing, either earlier in the season or earlier in their career. This might be a trend that begins to decrease in its relevance, with the race now reverting to standard hurdles (possible that chasing types were favoured by the former

BIG-RACE TRENDS

fixed brush hurdles) but I thought it worthwhile mentioning briefly. Three of the five – *St Matthew, Halcon Genelardais* and *According To Pete* (the first two-named before the introduction of the fixed brush hurdles, incidentally) – had run over fences on their previous run, with the former successful in a Wetherby handicap chase and the latter in a novice event at Hexham. *Halcon Genelardais* was having his first start of the season, having finished fifth in the Scottish Grand National in the April, and was running off a much lower hurdles mark.

CURRENT FORM/RECENT RUN

Nine of the 14 winners had finished in the first three on their previous start, be it during the current season or, in the case of *Diamond Harry*, who had finished third in the Ballymore Novices' Hurdle at the Cheltenham Festival, at the end of the previous campaign. The other eight had run during the current campaign and all had finished first, second or third, so if a horse is arriving at Haydock on the back of a 'prep' run, look for one who has shaped extremely well and arrives in Merseyside in good form. Only *Millenium Royal* has won this race having had a run earlier in the campaign which didn't result in a first-three finish, although his sixth just 21 days earlier did come in a Grade 1 event at Auteuil.

Of those who were arriving at Haydock on the back of a recent win, *Grands Crus* was carrying a 6lb penalty for his victory at Cheltenham's November meeting just six days earlier. As this is an early-closing race, it can often be the case that we see a recent winner heading the betting under a penalty, as was the case with Volnay de Thaix (finished 4th) in 2014 and First Assignment last year, who was sent off 11/10 on the back of a nine-length win at Cheltenham a week earlier. He could finish only third of seven, so be slightly cautious of those carrying a penalty.

In terms of races being used as a 'prep' for this, both *Aubusson* and *Sam Spinner* finished runner-up in the **Silver Trophy Handicap Hurdle** over 2m3½f at Chepstow in mid-October. Last year, Captain Cattistock was sent off at 7/2 for this race, having finished sixth at Chepstow on his reappearance and given the emergence of that two-day fixture at the Welsh venue, it could well continue to be a key trial for this race.

KEY TRENDS

 9 of the past 10 winners had 7 or less hurdles starts (7 of the 9 were second-season hurdlers)

 4 subsequent Grade 1 winners have won during the past 9 years

 9 of the 14 winners finished 1st, 2nd or 3rd last time out (8 of the 9 had run the same season)

 10 of the 14 winners were sent off at single figures (7 of the 10 were sent off at 6/1 or shorter)

 The past 8 winners were rated 136-147

 5 winners had been chasing earlier in season/career

 Respect David Pipe's runners

 Respect Nick (and Jane) Williams' runners

 Only 2 of the 14 winners were sent off bigger than 12/1

 Only 1 of the past 10 winners had won over 3m

STAMINA NOT ASSURED

Several recent winners of this race had yet to prove their stamina. Indeed, last year's winner *Paisley Park* – who would go on to prove himself the best staying hurdler in the country – had only had one try at 3m, when only 13th of 20 in the previous season's Albert Bartlett. Haydock's sharp course (particularly over hurdles, which is on the inside of the chase course) requires a horse nimble enough for the bends and also quick enough to hold a position throughout. Therefore, it isn't too surprising that it isn't an out-and-out stayer that we should be looking for. Also, given that several recent winners were unexposed second-season hurdlers, they simply haven't had the time or experience to have been upped this far at this stage of their careers.

In total, six of the past 10 winners were having their first run over further than 2m5f. The only winner in the past decade to have previously won over 3m (or thereabouts) was *Kruzhlinin*. When he won the race – and until last year – the race was run over 2m6½f whereas the distance has now been increased to 3m½f (was originally an extended 2m7f prior to the introduction of the fixed brush hurdles). Again, this might have an impact on this trend, going forward.

TRAINERS TO NOTE

With three wins in the space of four years – all with grey horses – **David Pipe** boasts a fine record in this race. In total, Pipe has saddled 10 runners in the race, with Batavir hitting the frame (3rd in 2015) for him recently. Prior to the victories of *Grands Crus, Dynaste* and *Gevrey Chambertin*, Pipe's father, Martin, saddled Standin Obligation in the very first running of the race (sent off 2/1F), so it is clear that the race has always been a consideration of the stable. Backing David Pipe-trained horses blindly would have yielded a profit of £7.50 to a level-stake of £1.

Three winners from 10 runners is a fine strike rate, whilst **Nick Williams** boasts a 40% strike rate in the race, having won it twice from just five runners. *Diamond Harry* was a very taking winner of the race back in 2009, and the stable struck again just five years later when *Aubusson* made virtually all under a-then-7lb claimer, Lizzie Kelly. A lot of the stable's horses now run in the name of Lizzie's mother, **Jane Williams**, and a couple who might be considered for this race are **Erick Le Rouge** and **Moonlighter**, who both showed plenty of promise last term. Whoever's name is alongside the horse, respect any runner from their stable in George Nympton and, again, backing the Williams horses in this race would have produced a healthy profit of £10.50 to a £1 stake. Nick Williams did saddle the beaten favourite in 2015 in the shape of Tea For Two, but he was another subsequent

Grade 1-winning chaser, so it's clear that the yard are happy to aim their better youngsters at the race. Just two races after finishing seventh in this race, Tea For Two won the Kauto Star Novices' Chase at Kempton and would go on to win the 2017 Bowl at Aintree.

In contrast, several of the high-profile trainers have yet to strike in this valuable event.

Firstly, **Paul Nicholls**' record currently stands at 0/10, following the fall of Captain Cattistock (beaten at the time) last year. He was sent off 7/2 second-favourite, and Nicholls' 10 losers in the race include three favourites (one was joint-favourite), the shortest-priced being Taranis, who was sent off at 7/4 when only fourth in 2007.

Nicky Henderson has seen four of his eight runners in the race hit the frame (saddled two seconds) but he has also yet to win the race, whilst **Jonjo O'Neill**'s record is 0/9 to date. The pair have saddled just one runner between them in the past four seasons, but were clearly happy to target the race more regularly prior to that. Subsequent dual-Cheltenham Festival winner Holywell finished runner-up for O'Neill in 2012, whilst that year's Gold Cup winner, Synchronised, had finished third just four months before his blue-riband success.

ROLL OF HONOUR

Year	Season Form	Winner	Age	Weight	OR	SP	Trainer	Runners	Last race (No. of days)
2018	1	Paisley Park	6	11-12	147	4/1	E Lavelle	7	1st Aintree Hurdle (27)
2017	2	Sam Spinner	5	10-9	139	6/1	J O'Keefe	16	2nd Gr.3 Chepstow Hurdle (42)
2016	P3	Kruzhlinin	9	10-13	136	9/1	P Hobbs	13	3rd Aintree Hurdle (14)
2015		Baradari	5	11-2	136	12/1	D Skelton	16	15th Gr.3 Aintree Hurdle (225)
2014	2	Aubusson	5	10-13	141	9/1	N Williams	16	2nd Gr.3 Chepstow Hurdle (28)
2013		Gevrey Chambertin	5	11-7	143	6/1	D Pipe	17	6th Gr.1 Sefton Hurdle (232)
2012	1	Trustan Times	6	11-12	142	10/1	T Easterby	16	1st Wetherby Hurdle (21)
2011		Dynaste	5	10-13	141	7/1	D Pipe	20	6th Sandown Nov. Hurdle (252)
2010	1	Grands Crus	5	10-10 (6 ex)	132	6/4F	D Pipe	18	1st Cheltenham Hurdle (6)
2009		Diamond Harry	6	11-12	149	9/2	N Williams	16	3rd Gr.1 Ballymore Nov. Hurdle (255)

LEADING TEN-YEAR GUIDE

Silver Trophy Handicap Hurdle 2 (*Aubusson* 2nd, *Sam Spinner* 2nd)

BIG-RACE TRENDS

SIRES IN FOCUS - PART 1

Given that five of this year's 40 *Leading Prospects* are offspring of the sadly ill-fated **Jeremy**, he seemed the obvious place to start when taking a closer look at some of the National Hunt sires, who have been performing particularly well of late.

The top six jumps sires last season – in terms of prize money earned – were the familiar names of Flemensfirth, Oscar, Milan, Beneficial, Presenting and King's Theatre, but there are plenty more who performed well in particular areas.

Jeremy sired 36 individual winners last season in Britain and Ireland (from 127 runners (28%)) but he lead the way in terms of bumper winners, with 23 in that sphere. Fifteen horses contributed to that total and, interestingly, he sired three mares to win Graded bumpers. *Leading Prospects* **Gypsy Island** (these results include the Punchestown Festival) and **The Glancing Queen** both fell into that category, whilst the Paul Nicholls-trained grey *Silver Forever* twice hit the frame in Listed races and appeals as the type to flourish once sent jumping. The other Graded winner was *Santa Rossa*, who won a Grade 2 at the Dublin Racing Festival, before taking on the boys at both Aintree and Punchestown. She ran with great credit at Aintree, travelling strongly for a long way, and despite the apparent depth to the mares' novice hurdle division in Ireland (which also includes Willie Mullins' *Colreevy*), Santa Rossa should certainly make her presence felt.

Like Gypsy Island, **Ard Abhainn** was successful at Punchestown in early-May, staying on really strongly to score for the connections of 2017 Champion Bumper winner Fayonagh. Another mare to score in Ireland – albeit at a lesser level – on debut was **Scarlet And Dove**, who ran out a taking winner of a Limerick bumper last November. We didn't get to see Joseph O'Brien's five-year-old again, but it is hoped that she returns in the autumn, as she had made a highly promising start to her career. In total, nine of his 15 bumper winners from last season were mares, and that is a very strong statistic.

Jeremy died as an 11-year-old in 2014, so there won't be too many more of his progeny coming through the ranks, although one of the more exciting recruits from the Irish Point-to-Point scene – *Lets Go Champ*, who features in the *Point-to-Point Graduates* section and is now in training with Tom George – could well further enhance his impressive record in the bumper division. He is actually a full brother to Scarlet And Dove and is a horse who I am particularly looking forward to seeing under Rules this winter.

Jeremy only had 11 horses race over fences last season, but three were successful (he was still only just making his mark as a young sire when he died) and his other trio of *Leading Prospects* – **Birchdale**, **Bold Plan** and **Reserve Tank** – will be looking to add to that tally during 2019-20. All three are chasers on looks and the Nicky Henderson-trained *Mister Fisher* would be another good case-in-point of a good-looking son of Jeremy. Tall, lengthy and with bags of scope, he could also do well if heading down the novice chase route.

The Glancing Queen - enhanced the fine record of Jeremy with mares in bumpers

Ladbrokes Trophy
(Grade 3) 3m 1f 214y – Newbury
Saturday 30th November 2019

OVERVIEW

Formerly known as the Hennessy Gold Cup – and still often referred to as such by many, myself included – the Ladbrokes Trophy is arguably the most prestigious staying handicap chase aside from the Grand National. In fairly recent years, we have seen both *Denman* and *Bobs Worth* win this race on their first start out of novice company and later the same season claim the Cheltenham Gold Cup. Even more recently, *Native River* also won the Ladbrokes Trophy as a second-season chaser – before winning his Gold Cup the following season – and it is yet another early-season contest in which second-season chasers boast a fine record.

LIGHTLY-RACED/SECOND-SEASON CHASERS

Fourteen of the past 20 winners had raced no more than nine times over fences, with 13 of those having had just seven or less starts over larger obstacles. Again, as with many of the high-profile early-season handicaps, this race really does tend to favour the up-and-coming improver, rather than the more exposed chaser.

Thirteen winners during the past 20 years – if using *Be My Royal* (first past the post, later to be disqualified and the race awarded to *Gingembre*) as the 2002 winner – were second-season chasers, although only five fell into this category in the past decade. Three of the past six winners were in their third season over fences, so were still far from being fully exposed, whilst *Strong Flow* won the race as a novice, back in 2003.

PREP RUN BECOMING MORE POPULAR

There was a spell between 2005 and 2012 when six of the eight winners were victorious on their seasonal reappearance, with five of the six also falling into the second-season category. Since then, however, the past six winners have all arrived at Newbury on the back of a prep run. Following the fifth-place finish of *Smad Place* in 2014 (finished behind subsequent Grand National winner *Many Clouds*), Alan King stated that he believed a prep run to be advantageous – despite the recent results at that time not necessarily suggesting this – and he returned to win 12 months later, having won a graduation chase at Kempton 26 days earlier.

In total during the past 20 years, 13 of the winners had a run earlier in the campaign and, significantly, all bar one (*Madison du Berlais*) recorded a top-three finish, with eight (if once again using *Be My Royal* as the 2002 winner) last-time-out winners. Interestingly, during the past 20 years, 12 winners (again using *Be My Royal*) had won their previous start.

PREVIOUS SEASON'S CHELTENHAM FORM

Two of the past three winners – *Native River* and *Sizing Tennessee* – had finished placed in the 4m **National Hunt Chase**. Last year's winner was a second-season novice when finishing third behind Rathvinden at Cheltenham, so again he was effectively in his first season out of novice company when winning the Ladbrokes Trophy, on the back of an easy success at Fontwell. *Native River* had finished runner-up to Minella Rocco in the National Hunt Chase, before going on to win the Grade 1 Mildmay Novices' Chase at Aintree. He warmed up for his win in this, by finishing runner-up in the West Yorkshire Hurdle at Wetherby. Given the exploits of 2017 National Hunt Chase winner Tiger Roll, the four-miler is clearly becoming a key guide to subsequent top-end staying chases. As stated in last season's *Cheltenham Festival Betting Guide*, that race continues to improve in terms of quality.

Going back a little further, it was the **RSA Insurance Chase** which was even more key in terms of providing future Ladbrokes Trophy winners. In all, five of the past 14 winners contested the previous season's RSA Chase, with *Trabolgan, Denman* and *Bobs Worth* all successful in the Cheltenham Festival contest. *Diamond Harry* was pulled up in the RSA on his final run as a novice, whilst subsequent Grand National winner *Many Clouds* was brought down in the RSA three starts before winning this. Incidentally, in the same renewal of the RSA, *Smad Place* finished runner-up – beaten a neck by O'Faolains Boy – before winning the Ladbrokes Trophy some 20 months later. *Carruthers* is another to have contested the RSA in his novice campaign, finishing fourth to Cooldine.

Many Clouds went on to finish fourth in the **Mildmay Novices' Chase**, so the Aintree novice event has also thrown up a couple of winners in the past five years. Going back a little further, *What's Up Boys* won the Mildmay, whilst *Ever Blessed* was a faller in the race. Basically, looking for a smart

BIG-RACE TRENDS

novice with Graded form in the book is a good place to start.

Nicky Henderson's **Santini** looks the ideal type for the Ladbrokes Trophy, in that he is a strong-looking stayer and the trip ought to really suit. Runner-up in the RSA in March, he is two-from-two at Newbury (at this two-day fixture), having won a novice hurdle and a Grade 2 novice chase. His long stride is clearly well-suited to this galloping track and it would appeal as the obvious race for him in the early part of the season. The question with him is whether or not he can defy a handicap mark of 163, in order to provide trainer Nicky Henderson with a fourth win in the race in 15 years.

Another smart novice last season was the Warren Greatrex-trained **La Bague Au Roi**, who is also unbeaten at the track. A Listed novice hurdle winner at this meeting in 2016, she won her first two chases at Newbury, latterly in a Grade 2 over 2m4f at this fixture, a race (**Berkshire Novices' Chase**) that both *Denman* and *Bobs Worth* won as novices. She finished three-and-a-half lengths in front of Santini when winning the Kauto Star at Kempton last Christmas and given she was receiving a 7lb mares' allowance on that occasion, it could be argued that she is potentially the better handicapped on a mark of 151. The question with her will be the trip, with this race being run over the best part of 3m2f.

COURSE FORM

The proven course form of both Santini and La Bague Au Roi should be viewed upon as a positive should either turn up, as 10 of the past 20 winners had previously won at Newbury. In addition to this, two other winners during this period – *Ever Blessed* and *Gingembre* (if using him as the 2002 winner) – had finished runner-up at the course, the latter in this very race 12 months earlier.

PROVEN STAMINA

Seventeen of the past 20 winners had already won over 3m or further. Of the four who hadn't, *Triolo d'Alene* had scored over an extended 2m7f, whilst *Many Clouds* and *Madison du Berlais* were the other pair. Both had placed form over 3m

A proper National Hunt background can also be viewed upon as a positive, with no fewer than 14 of the past 20 winners (again if using *Be My Royal* as the 2002 winner) having won a Point-to-Point or a National Hunt Flat Race at the beginning of their careers. Looking back at bumper form can prove quite informative, with both *Many Clouds* (9th) and *Trabolgan* (2nd) having contested the

KEY TRENDS

 14 of the past 20 winners had 9 or less chase starts (13 of them had 7 or less)

 10 of the past 20 winners had won at Newbury previously

 13 of the past 20 winners were second-season chasers

 13 of the past 20 winners (including the past 6 winners) had a prep run

 12 of the past 20 winners won last time out

 5 of the past 14 winners contested the previous season's RSA Chase

 17 of the past 20 winners had won over 3m or further

 14 of the past 20 winners had won a Point-to-Point or bumper

 Respect Grade 1 or Grade 2 novice hurdle form

 Every winner since 2005 was rated 145 or higher (9 of which won from 150+)

 13 of the past 20 winners were sent off 8/1 or shorter (7 favourites have won)

 Colin Tizzard has trained 2 of the past 3 winners (he has also saddled a further 3 placed horses, from just 9 runners in total)

 Only 4 of the past 20 winners weren't in their first three seasons over fences

 Of the 13 recent winners who had a prep run, only 1 didn't finish in the top 3 last time out

 Only 2 of the past 20 winners were not aged 6-8

Champion Bumper at Cheltenham, whilst *Diamond Harry* was a dual winner of the valuable sales bumper here at Newbury. *King's Road* was a Grade 1 bumper winner at the Punchestown Festival and also scored at the top level as a novice hurdler. Graded novice hurdle form also crops up among several recent winners, so pay healthy respect to those with obvious back-class.

OFFICIAL BHA RATINGS

Clearly, given the points made above and earlier about Graded form in bumpers, novice hurdles and novice chases, it usually takes a classy horse to win a Ladbrokes Trophy. Therefore, it shouldn't be too surprising that the past 14 winners were all rated 145 or higher. During this period, nine scored from a mark of 150 or higher.

Denman – who won from 161 and 174 – scored from the highest rating, whilst *Bobs Worth* (160), *Diamond Harry* (156), *Smad Place* (155) and *Native River* (155) all defied lofty marks. Class clearly can come to the fore in this event. In terms of weights carried, *Denman* (twice) and *Trabolgan* have both carried top-weight of 11-12 to success in that 14-year period.

AGE

Only two of the past 20 winners weren't aged six, seven or eight. They were *Denman* – when winning for a second time as a nine-year-old in 2009 – and last year's winner, the 10-year-old *Sizing Tennessee*. Seven has proven to be the most popular age during the past 20 years, with nine winners falling into that age group.

MARKET FORCES

Again, *Sizing Tennessee* proved to be a bit of a trends-buster in terms of starting price, being sent off at odds of 12/1. Seven of the past 10 winners were sent off at single-figures, all 8/1 or shorter. During this period, four favourites have won and a further three market leaders were successful between 1999 and 2004. In total during the past 20 years, 13 winners were sent off 8/1 or shorter and a further two winners started at 10/1. So that is 15 from 20 to have started 10-1 or shorter; therefore, it can pay to focus on the top of the market, despite the odd 'upset'.

TRAINERS TO NOTE

Having saddled two of the past three winners, **Colin Tizzard** is as good a place to start as any in terms of trainers to note. Tizzard saddled three horses last year – including the second, Elegant Escape – and, in total, his record stands at two winners from nine runners in the race, which would have produced a profit of £8.50 to a level-stake £1. He has also saddled Theatre Guide to finish third (33/1) in 2013 and second (12/1) in 2011, so only four of his runners have failed to win or place.

Both **Paul Nicholls** and Nicky Henderson have won the race on three occasions. The former has had the more runners, 31 since he first won the race with *Strong Flow* in 2003. His other two victories came courtesy of *Denman*, although Big Buck's unseated Sam Thomas when holding every chance in 2008, which resulted in him reverting to hurdles to great success. Nicholls has also saddled a further seven horses to finish in the frame, with What A Friend, Tidal Bay and Rocky Creek all finishing runner-up for the stable. Given the number of runners and the fact that all three winners were sent off at 5/1 or less, backing Nicholls' runners blindly would have proven costly.

Nicky Henderson had to wait until 2005 for his first victory in the then-Hennessy, a race which clearly means a lot to the Lambourn-based stables. During the same 16-year period as Nicholls (since 2003), Henderson has saddled 10 less runners (21) and backing his runners would have yielded a level-stake profit of £12.50. Since the victory of *Trabolgan*, Henderson has been responsible for six more horses to finish second, third or fourth, with Juveigneur, Burton Port and Whisper filling the runner-up spot.

ROLL OF HONOUR

Year	Season Form	Winner	Age	Weight	OR	SP	Trainer	Runners	Last race (No. of days)
2018	1	Sizing Tennessee	10	11-3	148	12/1	C Tizzard	12	1st Fontwell Chase (57)
2017	1	Total Recall	8	10-8	147	9/2F	W Mullins (IRE)	20	1st Gr.3 Munster National (55)
2016	2	Native River	6	11-1	155	7/2F	C Tizzard	19	2nd Gr.2 Wetherby Hurdle (28)
2015	1	Smad Place	8	11-4	155	7/1	A King	15	1st Kempton Chase (26)
2014	1	Many Clouds	7	11-6	151	8/1	O Sherwood	19	1st Listed Carlisle Chase (27)
2013	13	Triolo d'Alene	6	11-1	147	20/1	N Henderson	20	3rd Gr.3 Ascot Chase (28)
2012		Bobs Worth	7	11-6	160	4/1F	N Henderson	19	1st Gr.1 RSA Chase (262)
2011	3	Carruthers	8	10-4	146	10/1	M Bradstock	18	3rd Gr.3 Cheltenham Chase (14)
2010		Diamond Harry	7	10-0	156	6/1	N Williams	18	p.u. Gr.1 RSA Chase (255)
2009		Denman	9	11-12	174	11/4F	P Nicholls	19	fell Gr.2 Aintree Chase (260)

LEADING TEN-YEAR GUIDES

Previous season's RSA Insurance Chase 3 (*Diamond Harry* p.u., *Bobs Worth* 1st, *Many Clouds* b.d.)
Previous season's National Hunt Chase 2 (*Native River* 2nd, *Sizing Tennessee* 3rd)
Previous season's Mildmay Novices' Chase 2 (*Many Clouds* 4th, *Native River* 1st)

Santini - looks the ideal type for a Ladbrokes Trophy

Becher Chase
(Grade 3) 3m 1f 188y – Aintree (Grand National)
Saturday 7th December 2019

OVERVIEW

First run in 1992, the Becher Chase is one of two races run over the famous Grand National course on the same card, the other being the Grand Sefton Chase, which is run over the Topham Chase trip of 2m5f. As the race grew in stature, it was handed Listed status in 2005 and upgraded again in 2013. Now a Grade 3, the valuable handicap is run over a distance just shy of 3m2f and was won last year by *Walk In The Mill*, who returned to Aintree in April when finishing fourth behind Tiger Roll.

COURSE FORM

Last year's winner was the first since 2009 who hadn't had any sort of previous experience over the big fences. There was a spell between 2004 and 2009 when experience of the course didn't appear to be necessary, but overall since 1994, 19 of the 25 winners had previously run on the Grand National course. Of those 19 winners, only four had tasted victory around here earlier in their career, with both *Into The Red* (1994 & 1996) and, more recently, *Hello Bud* both dual winners of the race. 1998 Grand National winner *Earth Summit* returned to Liverpool some seven-and-a-half months later to land the Becher, whilst *Clan Royal* won the Becher in 2003, having won the Topham in the April of the same year. He, of course, went on to finish runner-up in the Grand National later that season, before being carried out – when travelling powerfully in front – the following year. The course specialist also finished third in the 2006 Grand National.

The most recent winner to win a Grand National subsequently was *Silver Birch*, who won the 2004 Becher for Paul Nicholls, before winning the 'big one' for a relatively unknown (at the time) Gordon Elliott in 2007. The only other horse to complete the Becher-Grand National double (in that order) was *Amberleigh House*, who won the Becher in 2001 and the Grand National in 2004.

Seven of the 19 winners in question had failed to complete the course previously, so don't be put off by a horse who has previously fallen, unseated or been brought down at Aintree. This experience can clearly still be advantageous.

EXPERIENCED CHASERS DOMINATE

In contrast to the races which we have already looked at in the early part of the season, the Becher generally goes the way or a more experienced chaser. Of the 27 winners to date, 22 had at least 13 previous chase starts to their name, of which 12 had 20 or more (and nine had 25+).

Of the five 'lesser experienced' winners, *Indian Tonic* had previously raced 10 times over fences, and *Vieux Lion Rouge* – the only winner in the past 11 years to have raced less than 13 times over fences previously – was having his eighth run over fences when winning three years ago. The other trio – *Silver Birch*, *Eurotrek* and *Mr Pointment* – were all trained by **Paul Nicholls** and won in the space of four years between 2004 and 2007. They had six, six and four runs over fences, respectively, so Nicholls clearly liked to target a lightly-raced chaser at the race at that stage. He also went close with a similar type in 2012, when Join Together finished runner-up to *Hello Bud* (beaten just a neck) on what was his seventh start over fences. **Give Me A Copper** is a possible contender from the Nicholls camp who seems cut from a similar cloth, in that he remains very lightly-raced as a chaser.

In general, however, it can pay to focus on horses with plenty of experience of jumping fences. Despite the fact that the fences at Aintree are nowhere near as big as once was the case, they still take some jumping.

POINT-TO-POINT/BUMPER BACKGROUND & BREEDING

Last year's winner *Walk In The Mill* started his racing career in France and was sent chasing as a four-year-old. However, 10 of the previous 11 Becher Chase winners had a more traditional National Hunt background, in that they had won either a Point-to-Point or a National Hunt Flat Race at the start of their careers.

In the early years of the Becher, the race was dominated by British-bred winners. Nine of the first 12 winners were bred on home soil, before the Irish took control. During the next 12 years, the only non-Irish-bred winner was *Chance du Roy*, and earlier winners such as *Samlee* (1997), *Feels Like Gold* (1999) and *Amberleigh House* (2001) were also bred in Ireland. More recently, however, and since that victory of *Chance du Roy*, three of the past six winners were French-bred.

 BIG-RACE TRENDS

The precociousness of such horses was something I highlighted in detail in last season's *Cheltenham Festival Betting Guide*, and it is no coincidence that the *Vieux Lion Rouge* (seven) and *Walk In The Mill* (eight) are amongst the younger winners of the race. During the past six years, only 25 of the 119 runners (21%) were French-bred, so it is a fine record from a small representation, and backing the French-bred runners blindly during this period would have produced a profit of £10 to a level-stake of £1. There were three French-bred horses in last year's race and they finished first, second and third, with the Trifecta returning a mere £2,375.90 to a £1 stake.

Touching upon ages, *Vieux Lion Rouge* is one of only three seven-year-olds to have been successful in the Becher, the others being *Indian Tonic* back in 1993 and *Silver Birch* in 2004.

WEIGHTS AND BHA RATINGS

Young Hustler, *Earth Summit* and *Young Kenny* all carried 12st and top-weight to success between 1995 and 2000, but since then only *Vic Venturi* has shouldered top-weight (now 11-12) to victory. *Eurotrek* would have carried the same, but Liam Heard took 5lb off and along with stablemate *Mr Pointment* and 2017 winner *Blaklion* (who is the only horse to do so in the past nine years), that completes the list of seven horses who have carried more than 10-12 to success in the Becher.

Given that the ground is often testing in early-December at Aintree, it makes sense that the lower-weighted horses often come to the fore, and seven winners were actually racing from out of the handicap. Backing horses from outside of the handicap isn't something that I am an advocate of, but if there is a time when I will consider it, it will be mid-winter in long-distance races in deep ground.

MARKET FORCES

Although we have seen winners of the Becher priced at 33/1 (x2), 25/1 (x2), 20/1 and 14/1 (x3), the other 19 winners were sent off at 10/1 or shorter, with 17 of them starting at single figures. Fifteen of these winners were sent off at 15/2 or shorter, so the top end of the market has dominated overall. In terms of outright market leaders, *Young Hustler*, *Young Kenny*, *Silver Birch*, *Hello Bud*, *Vieux Lion Rouge* and *Blaklion* have all justified favouritism.

KEY RACES

The **previous season's Grand National** has proven to be a good guide to the Becher Chase over the years, and three times in the past decade the

KEY TRENDS

 19 of the past 25 winners had previous course experience

 22 of the 27 winners had already had at least 13 chase starts (12 of which had run 20+ times over fences)

 10 of the past 12 winners had won a Point-to-Point or Bumper

 11 of the past 15 winners were Irish-bred

 3 of the past 6 winners were French-bred (from just 21% representation)

 7 winners were out of the handicap

 19 of the 27 winners were sent off at 10/1 or shorter (17 of which were single figures and 15 were sent off 15/2 or shorter)

 20 of the 27 winners had already run during the current season

 Nigel Twiston-Davies has won the race 6 times

 Only 3 winners had previously had 6 or less chase starts (all trained by Paul Nicholls)

 Only 3 seven-year-olds have been successful in the 27 years

 Only 7 of the 27 winners carried more than 10-12

 Only 3 of the past 12 winners were making their seasonal reappearance

winner has contested the 'big one' the previous April. These were *West End Rocker* – who was brought down in the National – along with *Vieux Lion Rouge* and *Blaklion*, who finished seventh and fourth respectively.

Blaklion made his seasonal reappearance in Wetherby's **Charlie Hall Chase**, and whilst he is the only recent winner to have run in that Grade 2 contest, three of the first nine winners of the race had run in the Charlie Hall last time out.

In terms of the past decade, four of the past eight winners had run at Cheltenham's November meeting. Two of those winners – *Oscar Time* and *Walk In The Mill* – contested the **Markel Insurance Amateur Riders' Handicap Chase** over 3m1f.

In terms of Becher winners having a 'prep run' beforehand, nine of the last 12 winners had run at least once earlier in the season, with only *Hello Bud*, *Vieux Lion Rouge* and *Chance du Roy* winning on their seasonal reappearance. In total, only seven of the 27 winners were successful on reappearance.

TRAINERS TO NOTE

The three-wins-in-four-years of **Paul Nicholls** has already been highlighted, and it should also be noted that he also saddled the runner-up in 2005 (the year during that short spell in which he wasn't responsible for the winner) in the shape of Le Duc.

However, the most successful trainer in the Becher is, without doubt, **Nigel Twiston-Davies**, who has saddled a remarkable six winners. His first winner was his very first runner in the race, *Indian Tonic*, after which *Young Hustler* and *Earth Summit* made it three winners in the space of six years for the trainer. After 11 years without a winner, Twiston-Davies saddled *Hello Bud* to win the race twice in the space of three years and made it six winners when *Blaklion* justified heavy market support (sent off 7/4F) two years ago. Interestingly, Twiston-Davies was responsible for the two shortest-priced winners of the race, the other being the 2/1 shot *Young Hustler*, in 1995. In total, Twiston-Davies has run 26 horses in the Becher and backing his horses blindly would have yielded a profit of £15.25 to a level-stake of £1.

ROLL OF HONOUR

Year	Season Form	Winner	Age	Weight	OR	SP	Trainer	Runners	Last race (No. of days)
2018	3	Walk In The Mill	8	10-3	137	10/1	R Walford	18	3rd Cheltenham Chase (22)
2017	2	Blaklion	8	11-6	153	7/4F	N Twiston-Davies	15	2nd Gr.2 Charlie Hall Chase (35)
2016		Vieux Lion Rouge	7	10-9	142	8/1F	D Pipe	20	7th Gr.3 Grand National (238)
2015	72	Highland Lodge	9	10-7 (7oh)	132	20/1	J Moffatt	17	2nd Sedgefield Chase (54)
2014	11U	Oscar Time	13	10-12	136	25/1	R Waley-Cohen	20	u.r. Cheltenham Chase (22)
2013		Chance du Roy	9	10-6	135	14/1	P Hobbs	20	8th Cheltenham Chase (233)
2012	35	Hello Bud	14	10-0 (5oh)	130	14/1	N Twiston-Davies	16	5th Cheltenham Cross-Country (22)
2011	P	West End Rocker	9	10-10	137	10/1	A King	14	p.u. Gr.3 Cheltenham Chase (21)
2010		Hello Bud	12	10-5	133	15/2F	N Twiston-Davies	17	p.u. Gr.3 bet365 Gold Cup (211)
2009	21	Vic Venturi	9	11-12	148	7/1	D Hughes (IRE)	8	1st Clonmel Chase (24)

LEADING TEN-YEAR GUIDES

Previous season's Grand National 3 (*West End Rocker* b.d., *Vieux Lion Rouge* 7th, *Blaklion* 4th)
Market Insurance Amateur Riders' Handicap Chase 2 (*Oscar Time* u.r., *Walk In The Mill* 3rd)

Nigel Twiston-Davies - boasts a tremendous record in the Becher Chase

BIG-RACE TRENDS

SIRES IN FOCUS - PART 2

Despite being responsible for producing none other than dual Grand National winner *Tiger Roll*, 2007 Derby winner **Authorized** isn't necessarily a name that springs to mind when thinking of a National Hunt sire. However, he did extremely well in bumpers last season, with five of his seven runners (71%) in that sphere proving successful.

Nobby – who boasts the strongest form – and *Laughing Luis* both won twice, whilst *We've Got Payet* and *Surin* were both successful on debut. Laughing Luis went on to win twice over hurdles, whilst Surin won at Fairyhouse for 'Team Tiger Roll', before finishing third in the Grade 1 Spring Juvenile Hurdle.

With the notable exception of the Aintree and Cheltenham Festival specialist, progeny of Authorized haven't really gone on to develop into chasers, but if there is a youngster who could be capable of bucking that trend in the near future, it could be **Mister Coffey**, who made a winning debut for Harry Whittington, in a bumper at Huntingdon. A month later, he was purchased for £340,000 by Tom Lacey. A tall, leggy individual, he certainly looks to possess a lot more size than your standard Authorized and it will be fascinating to see how he progresses over hurdles. At the time of writing, his new connections are not known, but given the strike rate of Authorized in bumpers, he would be of interest if pitched into a decent contest on reappearance – perhaps at Cheltenham in October or November – before he is sent hurdling.

Leading Prospect **Midnight Run** was the pick of the crop of bumper horses representing **Well Chosen** last season, who was responsible for two more winners in Ireland. Those three winners – who won five times between them – came from just 12 runners (25%) and the other pair were both trained by Noel Meade.

Sellarbridge, who boasts a Flat pedigree, defied greenness to make a winning debut at Punchestown in February, whilst stablemate **Sixshooter** – who, like Midnight Run, represents Gigginstown House Stud – was two-from-two in bumpers last term. Having won at Leopardstown on debut, the four-year-old followed up at the Punchestown Festival, beating The Big Getaway in a slowly-run, four-runner contest. He actually carried the trainer's silks to victory on debut, when he had Dewcup (won next time, before finishing fourth at Aintree) back in third, in atrocious conditions. Ridden patiently at Punchestown, he showed a good turn of foot in the closing stages and is a full-brother to She's A Star (won her first two starts over hurdles and was also trained by Noel Meade, who clearly rates the sire).

Sixshooter should be himself capable of winning over hurdles, although it is noteworthy that Well Chosen boasted a much better strike rate over fences last season. Five of his 29 runners over hurdles were successful (17%) whereas eight of his 13 runners over fences (62%) won at least once. One horse who could be looking to make his mark for the sire over fences this season is the Willie Mullins-trained **Carefully Selected**, Midnight Run's full-brother, who also briefly features in this year's *Across The Sea* section. Placed in Grade 1 company in both bumpers and a novice hurdle, the imposing seven-year-old has the physique of a chaser and remains unexposed, having had just two starts over hurdles.

Like Carefully Selected, **Chosen Mate** is a former Point-to-Point winner and another who could well make an impact over fences, over shorter distances. Pulled up after enduring a troubled passage in the Galway Hurdle, he won twice over hurdles last term and ended the campaign by finishing fifth behind Reserve Tank at Aintree.

Looking at the more up-and-coming sires, **No Risk At All** is very much of interest. He produced just three bumper winners last season (from 18 runners), but I suspect that strike rate will improve, and *Leading Prospect* **Nickolson** – and his full-brother **L'Incorrigible**, who won at Warwick – were his pair of winners in England.

The Liz Doyle-trained **Cayd Boy** impressed when winning a four-year-old bumper at Limerick and was subsequently purchased by JP McManus. He was due to make his debut in the green and gold at the Punchestown Festival, but was pulled out of the race won by the aforementioned Sixshooter, on veterinary advice.

One unraced son of No Risk At All to put in the notebook is **No Risk des Flos**, a half-brother to both Vision des Flos and Umndeni. I saw the four-year-old at the pre-training yard of Francesca Nimmo and Charlie Poste last summer – having been purchased by Aiden Murphy for €200,000 – and he really took the eye, being an athletic-looking individual.

Caspian Caviar Gold Cup
(Grade 3) 2m 4f 127y – Cheltenham (New)
Saturday 14th December 2019

OVERVIEW

The December Gold Cup, as it is often referred to, has been run under various names in recent seasons, latterly the Caspian Caviar Gold Cup. A similar contest to the BetVictor Gold Cup at the November meeting, this race is slightly less valuable in terms of prize-money and, some might say in prestige, too. The main difference in terms of the race itself is that this contest is run over an extra half-furlong (83 yards to be precise) and staged on the New Course, rather than the sharper Old Course. Given that it forms part of the mid-December meeting, the ground is often soft, and added to the more demanding track, stamina is required.

PAUL NICHOLLS

I wouldn't normally touch upon the 'Trainers to Note' until the foot of a race, but such is the recent record of **Paul Nicholls** in this contest, it seems the logical starting point. The current Champion Trainer has won this event no fewer than five times in the past 10 years, from 19 runners. Given the starting prices of *Poquelin* (second win) and *Frodon* (first win), it isn't surprising that his runners during this period have proven profitable to follow, and backing all 19 would have yielded a tasty £34 profit to a £1 stake.

Prior to the start of his dominant run, Nicholls saddled either the second or third in the race in four successive seasons between 2004 and 2007, with Thisthatandtother, Le Passing, Taranis and Le Volfoni all hitting the frame for the stable. His chosen runner(s) warrant utmost respect.

AGE

No horse older than eight has won this race since 1993, when *Fragrant Dawn* was successful for Martin Pipe. The next three winners – *Dublin Flyer*, *Addington Boy* and *Senor el Betrutti* – were all eight-year-olds, and a further four of that age group have won during 19 subsequent renewals (there was no race in either 2001 or 2008).

However, more recently the race has been dominated by six- and seven-year-olds, with that age group responsible for 11 of the 16 winners from 2002 onwards. This would appear to be the age range to pay most attention to.

The record of Paul Nicholls in the race has been highlighted in the subsection above, and another issue that links the trainer with this race is his apparent willingness to pitch in youngsters. In the past decade, seven five-year-olds have taken their chance in the Caspian Caviar Gold Cup, and all bar one were trained by Nicholls, the other being Nicky Henderson's Ma Filleule. His sextet included joint-favourite Caid du Berlais and Clan des Obeaux, who finished runner-up under top-weight in 2017, when sent off the 3/1 favourite. Therefore, with a record of 0/7 in the past decade, be wary of five-year-olds.

In contrast, Nicholls is the only trainer to saddle a four-year-old in the race. In fact, he has saddled two – *Unioniste* and *Frodon* – and both won. Given the record of the five-year-olds, you might find this surprising; however, the four-year-olds receive a massive weight allowance – which now stands at 7lb – and that is clearly advantageous. Both horses were French-bred (more of which shortly), so if Nicholls sees fit to run another similar type in the race, sit up and take note. Backing both four-year-olds from the stable would have yielded a profit of £21.50 to a £1 stake.

FRENCH-BRED WINNERS

That leads me nicely on to the fact that the race has been dominated by French-bred horses in recent years. Ten of the last 16 winners in total were French-bred, from just 37% representation. During this period (going back to 2002 inclusive), 221 horses have contested this race and only 81 of them (37%) were bred in France. Therefore, 10 winners in 16 years is a very good strike rate.

Between 2002 and 2012, only one winner wasn't bred in France and, after three years without success between 2013 and 2015 (only nine ran during this three-year period), Frodon has put the French back on the map, by winning two of the past three runnings. Backing all French-bred horses during the period in question would have yielded a profit of £23 to a £1 stake.

LIGHTLY-RACED CHASERS

Although the past two winners don't fall into the category, it had previously paid to follow the up-and-coming unexposed chasers in this race. Rather like the aforementioned BetVictor Gold Cup – which I will come to in more detail shortly – this is yet another handicap in the early part of the

 BIG-RACE TRENDS

season which has tended to favour 'the improver'. Between 2002 and 2016, only two of the winners had run more than nine times over fences.

Three novices – *Unioniste, Double Ross* and *Frodon* – have proven successful in the past seven years, whilst it is generally a race which favours those who were racing in novice company in the previous season. Between 2002 and 2013, lightly-raced horses were at their most dominant, with only one horse – *Poquelin*, who was winning the race for a second-successive season in 2010 – not fitting the profile of nine or less chase starts.

I'm a big advocate of backing novices in open handicap company later in the season, and the fact that I keep highlighting lightly-raced chasers for many of these early-season handicaps ties in. Such horses can continue to progress in their first season out of novice company, and these early-season races gives many the opportunity to win a valuable handicap, before going up in class. Apologies for the repetition!

PREVIOUS COURSE FORM

Every winner of the Caspian Caviar Gold Cup in the past 20 years had run at Cheltenham previously. Seven of the 18 (on two occasions the race was lost to the weather) winners had been successful at the track, with six of those – starting with *Legal Right* back in 1999 – winners over fences. Only *Monkerhostin* – who won the Coral Cup just nine months earlier – was a hurdles winner, rather than a chase winner, at the track. A further eight winners had previously hit the frame at Cheltenham, so good course form seems essential when assessing this race. Only one winner in the past 15 had failed to win or place at the course.

The key trial for this race is, without doubt, the **BetVictor Gold Cup** at the previous month's meeting. Last year, *Frodon* became the third winner in a row to have contested the BetVictor and the eighth winner in the past 14 renewals to hail from that race. *Frodon* went one place better than he had done a month previous, and it is worth remembering that his two earlier course wins came on the New Course. Following the victory in last year's race, he, of course, went on to win the Cotswold Chase and the Ryanair Chase at the festival, so all five course wins have been secured on the New Course. This is something to bear in mind; some horses do act better on one of the tracks, due to the demands being different. Look for form on the New Course, especially on similar (usually soft) ground.

Back to the BetVictor Gold Cup, and both *Poquelin* (first win in 2009) and *Quantitativeeasing* had also finished runner-up before going one place

better in this. *Monkerhostin* had finished third in the BetVictor, whilst *Exotic Dancer* – who would later go on to prove himself to be a Grade 1 winner – is the only horse this century to complete the famous double. During the 90s, *Senor el Betrutti* completed the feat, as did *Pegwell Bay* in 1988.

MARKET FORCES

Whilst only *Poquelin* has justified favouritism in the past 20 years, this is yet another race in which the top of the market has dominated, so focus on those just in behind the favourite. Of the 18 winners since 1999, 13 were sent off at single-figures and 12 of those were priced at 8/1 or lower.

(OTHER) TRAINERS TO NOTE

The case for Paul Nicholls has already been made, but there are a couple more current trainers who have won the race more than once in the past 20 years.

Firstly, **Jonjo O'Neill** struck with *Legal Right* in 1999 and *Exotic Dancer* in 2006. Both horses went on to prove themselves in Graded company, so O'Neill clearly likes to use this race as a stepping-stone to bigger and better things with an unexposed young chaser (both were six). It is also worth remembering that O'Neill has a fine record in the BetVictor Gold Cup (already highlighted), so his runners in these kind of events clearly warrant respect.

Nicky Henderson saddled back-to-back winners of the race in 2002 and 2003 – *Fondmort* and *Iris Royal* – and although he has managed to win it just once since (*Quantitativeeasing*), his record stands at a very respectable three winners from 15 runners this century. Since that latest win in 2011, Henderson has actually only saddled six runners and hasn't been represented at all twice in the past four seasons. He was responsible for last year's beaten favourite, Rather Be, who ticked plenty of boxes but could finish only fifth. Backing the Henderson runners blindly in the race during this century would have produced a profit of £6 to a £1 stake.

ROLL OF HONOUR

Year	Season Form	Winner	Age	Weight	OR	SP	Trainer	Runners	Last race (No. of days)
2018	12	Frodon	6	11-12	164	7/1	P Nicholls	12	2nd Gr.3 BetVictor Gold Cup (28)
2017	22219	Guitar Pete	7	10-2	134	9/1	N Richards	10	9th Gr.3 BetVictor Gold Cup (28)
2016	1110	Frodon	4	10-10	149	14/1	P Nicholls	16	10th Gr.3 BetVictor Gold Cup (28)
2015	11	Village Vic	8	10-0	136	8/1	P Hobbs	14	1st Musselburgh Chase (23)
2014	1	Niceonefrankie	8	11-5	142	16/1	V Williams	12	1st Ascot Chase (22)
2013	6132	Double Ross	7	10-8	133	7/1	N Twiston-Davies	13	2nd Ascot Chase (22)
2012	113	Unioniste	4	9-9 (6oh)	143	15/2	P Nicholls	14	3rd Cheltenham Nov. Chase (29)
2011	02	Quantitativeeasing	6	10-7	145	6/1	N Henderson	17	2nd Paddy Power Gold Cup (28)
2010	25	Poquelin	7	11-7	163	16/1	P Nicholls	16	5th Paddy Power Gold Cup (28)
2009	12	Poquelin	6	11-8	151	7/2F	P Nicholls	17	2nd Paddy Power Gold Cup (28)

LEADING TEN-YEAR GUIDE

BetVictor Gold Cup 6 (*Poquelin* 2nd & 5th, *Quantitativeeasing* 2nd, *Frodon* 10th & 2nd, *Guitar Pete* 9th)

Poquelin - won back-to-back renewals of the race for trainer Paul Nicholls

BIG-RACE TRENDS

Betfair Exchange Trophy
(Grade 3) 1m 7f 152y – Ascot
Saturday 21st December 2019

OVERVIEW

First run in 2001, the Betfair Exchange Trophy was known as 'The Ladbroke' until 2015, when the race was a dead-heat between *Sternrubin* and *Jolly's Cracked It*. Staged on the Saturday before Christmas, this is another valuable 2m handicap in which lightly-raced hurdlers have a fine record.

It is worth noting that the 2004 and 2005 renewals were run at Sandown in January 2005 and 2006 respectively.

WEIGHTS AND MEASURES

We have seen a wide range of weights carried to success here, but twice in the past three years – with *Brain Power* and *Mohaayed* – we have seen a big weight carried to success. In the last nine runnings of the race, going back to 2006 (there was no race in either 2009 or 2010) a further three winners carried 11-3 or more, those being *Acambo* (11-9), *Sentry Duty* (11-9) and *Bayan* (11-5). *Jolly's Cracked It* also shouldered 11-3 when dead-heating four years ago, so big weights can be carried to success, despite this race often being staged on soft ground.

LIGHTLY-RACED HURDLERS

Once again, this is a handicap that has – over the years – favoured the lightly-raced types. *Mohaayed* was a little more experienced than is often the case, but was still only having his 13th start over hurdles when winning the race last year, as 10 previous winners fell into the 'nine hurdles starts or less' category. Four of the other five had run either 10 or 11 times over hurdles, so only one winner of this race – *Desert Air* in 2015 – had previously run more than 12 times over hurdles.

Eight of those 10 winners had run seven or less times over hurdles and this is correct whether you use *Sternrubin* or *Jolly's Cracked It* as the 2015 winner, as both were having their eighth hurdles start when dead-heating.

Six of these winners were second-season hurdlers, whilst the very first winner – *Marble Arch*, who had previously run 10 times over hurdles – was also having his first start out of novice company, having been a novice for two seasons. *Chauvinist, Thesis, Cause of Causes, Willow's Saviour* and *Sternrubin* were all second-season novices at the time they won this race.

IN-FORM HORSES & KEY RACES

Last year's winner *Mohaayed* was just the second winner to have failed to arrive at Ascot on the back of a top-three finish. So, 14 of the 16 winners (again, both *Sternrubin* and *Jolly's Cracked It* tick this box) arrived on the back of either a win (8 were last-time-out winners) a second, or a third.

Of the pair that failed to record a top-three finish last time, one was having his first outing of the campaign and he – *Tamarinbleu* – is the only winner to date who hadn't run earlier in the campaign. He was having his first start since finishing unplaced in Aintree's Top Novices' Hurdle the previous spring, whilst 2017 winner *Hunters Call* arrived here on the back of a small break. He was having his first start for Olly Murphy and his first start since finishing third at Sligo in August. *Bayan* – who hadn't run since finishing runner-up in the Galway Hurdle – arrived at Ascot on the back of a similar break.

Mohaayed – who had won the County Hurdle at the previous season's Cheltenham Festival – arrived at Ascot on the back of a seventh place in the **Greatwood Hurdle** and he was the third winner in the past seven years to have contested that race at Cheltenham the previous month. *Brain Power* could finish only eighth in the Greatwood (did win a Listed handicap at Sandown in between), whilst *Cause of Causes* hit the frame in the same race, finishing third behind Olofi.

Sternrubin and *Raya Star* both arrived at Ascot on the back of running in Newbury's Gerry Feilden, with the former winning the intermediate event and the latter finishing third behind subsequent Champion Hurdle winner Rock On Ruby. The Listed event is now run under the banner of the **Ladbrokes Intermediate Hurdle** and was won last year by Global Citizen, who had earlier finished runner-up in a Listed event at Ascot's opening National Hunt fixture. That race – the **Bet With Ascot Handicap Hurdle** – was won by Fidux, who could finish only mid-division in this race, but it has supplied a couple of winners of this since 2008. *Sentry Duty* won both races 11 years ago, whilst *Jolly's Cracked It* – who was previously two-from-two at the track as a novice – finished third, on what was his first start outside of novice company.

As well as those two winners who hailed from the Gerry Feilden Hurdle, both the first two winners of this race – *Marble Arch* and *Chauvinist* – had also won at Newbury's Winter Carnival (or Hennessy meeting as it was then). The former had won a handicap hurdle and the latter a maiden, again highlighting the 'in-form' horse angle and also highlighting that form at the bigger tracks is a plus.

TRAINERS TO NOTE

With four wins on the board, **Nicky Henderson** is the most successful trainer in this race to date. *Chauvinist, Sentry Duty, Jack The Giant* and *Brain Power* have all scored for the Master of Seven Barrows, who has also seen Saintsaire, Tarlac, Petit Robin, Consul de Thaix (had the 1-2 in 2016) and Verdana Blue finish second or third. In total, Henderson has saddled 25 runners spread across 13 years (three times – including last year and in 2015 – he hasn't had a runner) and backing his runners blindly would have yielded a profit of £12.75 to a level-stake of £1.

Dan Skelton has a fine record with 2m handicap hurdles – as three wins in the past four County Hurdles will testify – and he has won this race twice in the past six years from just seven runners. *Willow's Saviour* and *Mohaayed* have won this at odds of 10/1 and 16/1 respectively, so backing the Skelton runners blindly would have yielded a profit of £21. Shelford also finished fourth for the stable in 2014, so pay healthy respect to any representative from the yard.

The same comment applies to **Gordon Elliott**, who has only had five runners in the race, which has resulted in two winners and Flaxen Flare finishing third at 16/1. *Cause of Causes* (25/1) and *Bayan* (14/1) were also overlooked in the market, so his level-stakes profit stands at a very tasty £36. On each occasion that he has had a runner, Elliott has saddled just the one horse, so it is not as if he is taking the scattergun approach either.

Elliott's former assistant **Olly Murphy** has only been training for a couple of seasons, but *Hunters Call* provided him with his first really big moment as a trainer when successful in 2017. He also had a runner in the race 12 months ago, and it will be fascinating to see how he progresses, not just in terms of this race but as a whole during the 2019-20 season. Given his record with his novice hurdlers at Cheltenham and Aintree last season, it is quickly becoming clear that Murphy doesn't tend to enter horses for the sake of it in big races and his yard would appear to be one on a rapid ascent towards the top.

MARKET FORCES

Four of the first seven winners of this race started at 15-2 or less, and these included *Jack The Giant* who was sent off the well-backed 9/4 market leader in 2007. Since then, only two winners (again, both *Sternrubin* and *Jolly's Cracked It* meet this criteria, with the other being *Hunters Call*) have started at single-figure odds. The average starting price in the past decade is 12/1, with *Jolly's Cracked It* (joint-favourite at 7/1 in 2015) only the second market leader to win the race. Or, dead-heat it, in his case.

 BIG-RACE TRENDS

ROLL OF HONOUR

Year	Season Form	Winner	Age	Weight	OR	SP	Trainer	Runners	Last race (No. of days)
2018	47	Mohaayed	6	11-10	145	16/1	D Skelton	21	7th Gr.3 Greatwood Hurdle (34)
2017	9453	Hunters Call	7	10-3	128	9/1	O Murphy	17	3rd Sligo Hurdle (135)
2016	381	Brain Power	6	11-11	149	12/1	N Henderson	19	1st Listed Sandown. Hurdle (14)
2015	**DEAD-HEAT**								
	1	Sternrubin	4	10-10	134	9/1	P Hobbs	21	1st Newbury Hurdle (23)
	3	Jolly's Cracked It	6	11-3	141	7/1JF	H Fry		3rd Listed Ascot Hurdle (67)
2014	124	Bayan	5	11-5	146	14/1	G Elliott (IRE)	18	4th Leopardstown Handicap (98)
2013	11	Willow's Saviour	6	10-5	130	10/1	D Skelton	20	1st Musselburgh Hurdle (43)
2012	12613	Cause of Causes	4	10-13	142	25/1	G Elliott (IRE)	21	3rd Gr.3 Cheltenham Hurdle (34)
2011	213	Raya Star	5	10-1	134	12/1	A King	16	3rd Newbury Hurdle (21)
2010	**NO RACE**								
2009	**NO RACE**								

LEADING TEN-YEAR GUIDES

Greatwood Hurdle 3 (*Cause of Causes* 3rd, *Brain Power* 8th, *Mohaayed* 7th)
Ladbrokes Intermediate Hurdle 2 (*Raya Star* 3rd, *Sternrubin* 1st)

Brain Power - emerges from the gloom to win under David Mullins

King George VI Chase

(Grade 1) 3m – Kempton Park

Thursday 26th December 2019

OVERVIEW

Not only is the King George VI Chase the highlight of a busy festive period, but it is one of the most prestigious races in the National Hunt calendar. The roll of honour includes the likes of *Mill House* and *Arkle*, whilst *Pendil, Captain Christy, Silver Buck, Wayward Lad, Desert Orchid, The Fellow, One Man, See More Business, Kicking King* and, of course, *Kauto Star* were all multiple winners of the race. More recently, *Long Run* and *Silviniaco Conti* added their names to that illustrious list, and it is a race that *Silvinaco Conti*'s trainer, Paul Nicholls, has won on no fewer than 10 occasions since 1997.

Kempton is a course which requires a good jumper and a horse who can travel well at pace, holding their position. This is often why we see top-class two-milers attempt to go up in trip, and it could be that we see that again this year, with the race having been mentioned as a probable target for Altior. Often described as a 'speed track', you still need to see out the trip in full at Kempton, and we have seen the likes of Azertyuiop and Master Minded fail in similar bids in recent seasons.

STAMINA

Given that last point, proven stamina is probably as good a place to start as any. Last year, *Clan des Obeaux* became the first winner since subsequent Gold Cup winner *Kicking King* in 2004 who had yet to prove himself over 3m. Every winner in between had already won at least once over a minimum of 3m, with 2m5½f as far as *Clan des Obeaux* had previously won. He had twice run over 3m+, when third in the Bowl at Aintree and fourth in the Betfair Chase, whilst *Kicking King* had finished runner-up over 3m in the James Nicholson Wine Merchant Champion Chase at Down Royal.

The other winner during the past 20 years without proven stamina in the book was *Edredon Bleu*, who had only ever raced over 3m once previously, when sixth of nine in the 2000 King George. Despite being most well-known as a two-miler, he had won 11 times previously at trips ranging between 2m4f-2m5f.

GRADE 1 CLASS

Clan des Obeaux also broke a key trend in that he became the first winner in the past 20 years – the last being *Teeton Mill* in 1998 – who hadn't previously won a Grade 1. A Grade 2 novice chase

winner two seasons earlier, he had finished sixth in the Triumph Hurdle in 2016 and had contested three Grade 1s over fences prior to his King George success, finishing placed in the Bowl at Aintree the previous April. The majority of the winners during this 20-year period were multiple Grade 1 winners, so class comes to the fore here.

Going back to *Teeton Mill*, he had risen through the Point-to-Point and hunter chase ranks before bursting onto the scene under Rules with victories in the Badger Ales at Wincanton and the then-Hennessy Cognac Gold Cup at Newbury (both handicaps). His rise was quite meteoric and rarely seen, so he can be treated as an exception.

MARKET FORCES

We have only really seen three relative 'shocks' in the past 20 years, again *Clan des Obeaux* being a trends-buster in that he was sent off at odds of 12/1. Classing *Florida Pearl* as a 'shock' in 2001 (sent off at 8/1) might be harsh, whilst *Edredon Bleu* was a 25/1 shot when securing back-to-back King Georges for Henrietta Knight and Jim Lewis, who saw their *Best Mate* land the prize 12 months earlier.

Best Mate was one of 12 winning favourites during the past 20 years, whilst a further five were either second or third in the betting. All 17 winners started at 9/2 or shorter, again emphasising the fact that the cream usually rises to the top in the King George. Look for a proven Grade 1 performer, preferably with top-class form at 3m already in the book.

COURSE FORM

Previous form at Kempton seems to be advantageous, too. Obviously, given the number of multiple winners of the race, **last year's renewal** is an obvious place to start. Interestingly, the past three winners were having their first run in the race, but seven of the previous nine winners had run in the race the previous year.

On the same card, the **Kauto Star Novices' Chase** (or the Feltham to many of us) has proven to be another 'key trial' for the following season's King George, with three winners in the past nine years having contested that race 12 months earlier. *Long Run* won the Feltham as a four-year-old (*note he was a six-year-old when winning the King George, but it was run on 15th January 2011 that year, due to the weather causing a Boxing

BIG-RACE TRENDS

Day abandonment), whilst *Silviniaco Conti* finished runner-up to classy hurdler Grands Crus. The most recent graduate from the Feltham to win the following year's King George was *Might Bite*, who would have bolted up but for crashing out at the final fence. He was also a winner at Kempton over hurdles, landing the 2016 running of the Silver Plate, the consolation race for those who miss the cut for the Cheltenham Festival handicaps.

Last year's Kauto Star was won by Warren Greatrex's classy mare **La Bague Au Roi**, who fended off subsequent RSA Chase winner **Topofthegame** (and Santini) up the home straight, whilst last year's King George winner *Clan des Obeaux* had run once at Kempton previously, when runner-up in a two-horse graduation chase. He was narrowly beaten by Whisper.

Thistlecrack is the only King George winner in the last 12 years who hadn't won or finished second at the track previously. The top-class hurdler – who was still a novice chaser at the time – was having his first run at Kempton, when winning in 2016.

OTHER KEY RACES

Since the introduction of the **Betfair Chase** in 2005, no fewer than 11 of the 14 King George winners contested the Haydock race earlier in the campaign. Six of the 11 were successful in the Betfair Chase, whilst three finished either second or third. Only two failed to hit the frame, with *Kauto Star* (2008) unseating at Haydock and last year's winner only finishing fourth of five on unseasonably quick ground.

Four years ago, *Cue Card* emulated 1999 winner *See More Business* in having won the **Charlie Hall Chase** at Wetherby at the start of the campaign. *Silviniaco Conti* also finished unplaced in the Grade 2 prior to winning his second King George.

The last two Irish-trained winners of the King George – *Florida Pearl* and *Kicking King* (before his first win in 2004) – followed a similar path to Kempton, by running in the **JNWine.com Champion Chase** at Down Royal, before winning the 2m4f **John Durkan Memorial Chase** at Punchestown. *Kauto Star* also contested the former (won) before winning his third King George in 2008, whilst the John Durkan is often a shade close in the calendar. There are 18 days between the two races in this year's calendar.

Looking back at the previous season and the **Betway Bowl** – won in impressive fashion this year by **Kemboy**, who went on to follow up at Punchestown – has thrown up four King George winners in the past six years. Obviously, there are only so many races these Grade 1 staying chasers

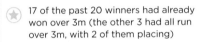
can run in, but there are similarities between Kempton and Aintree – highlighted in the most recent edition of the *Cheltenham Festival Betting Guide* – especially on the chase tracks. *Silviniaco Conti* (twice), *Cue Card* and *Clan des Obeaux* all ran in the Bowl the previous spring.

THE CHELTENHAM GOLD CUP

Again, the programme book for King George horses is a rather obvious one, and five of the past 10 winners had run in the **Cheltenham Gold Cup** earlier in the calendar year. Of those five winners during the past decade, only *Kauto Star* (2009) was successful in the Gold Cup.

Winners of the Gold Cup have a fine recent record in the King George overall. In the past 20 years, seven Gold Cup winners have attempted to win at Kempton some nine months later, and five have proven up to the task. *See More Business* (1999),

Best Mate (2002), *Kicking King* (2005) and *Kauto Star* (2007 & 2009) all won both races in the same calendar year, and since then only two Gold Cup winners have tried to win the King George. Long Run finished runner-up in 2011 and Native River finished third last year.

Therefore, a record of five winners from seven runners bodes well for **Al Boum Photo**, should he travel over from Ireland. The 20-year record of Gold Cup winners in the King George reads 1111123, and the track does suit a smooth-traveller such as him. If we had a dry winter, it could be that his stablemate Kemboy is considered for the trip.

OFFICIAL BHA RATINGS

Another point which highlights that class comes to the fore in the King George is that between 1999 and 2009 the seven British-trained winners were officially top-rated on BHA ratings. The other four winners during this period – *First Gold, Florida Pearl* and *Kicking King* (twice) – weren't handed an official rating prior to the race; neither was *Thistlecrack*, who was still a novice when scoring three years ago.

The next five winners were all rated in the 170s and among the top-three-rated in each renewal. The past two winners were less-exposed than that quintet, so had only achieved an official rating of 162 (*Might Bite*) and 160 (*Clan des Obeaux*), but if you are looking at the seasoned staying chasers, it can pay to focus on those rated 170 or above.

AGE

In the past 20 years, *Kicking King, Kauto Star, Long Run* and *Clan des Obeaux* have won the King George at the age of six, although Long Run should officially be considered a five-year-old winner, as the King George of that season had to be run on 15th January. It, therefore, bodes well for fans of last year's winner that the three previous 'young' winners of this came back to win it again.

The age bracket to focus on would be seven to nine, with *Kauto Star* the only double-digit aged winner in the past 15 years. Prior to his remarkable fifth success in the race, *Edredon Bleu* is the only other 'older' horse to win the King George in the past 28 years. Every other winner during this period were nine or younger.

KING NICHOLLS

With 10 victories to his name in the race, **Paul Nicholls** is certainly a trainer who warrants utmost respect with his runners. Given that *See More Business* (2), *Kauto Star* (5) and *Silviniaco Conti* (2) were all multiple winners of the race, *Clan des Obeaux* was actually just the fourth individual horse who Nicholls has won with, but this also bodes well for last year's winner, should he return for a repeat bid. Nicholls' record with returning horses in this contest – and, in general, the longevity he seems to instil into his stayers – has to be commended, and it is no coincidence that many of his leading lights have been able to perform at the top level for several seasons. Denman and Big Buck's are another pair of obvious examples.

Since 1997, Nicholls has saddled 30 runners in 20 renewals (only twice – in 2002 and 2017 – has he not had a runner), and as well as his 10 winners, he has seen five horses finish in third place. Backing his horses blindly during the past 22 years would have yielded a profit of £15.70 to a level-stake of £1.

The Nicholls stable could be represented this Boxing Day by last year's winner **Clan des Obeaux** and/or last season's RSA winner **Topofthegame**, who, of course, finished runner-up in last year's Kauto Star. The giant chestnut remains very lightly raced over fences and he finished fourth in the 2018 Lanzarote Hurdle, on his only other start at Kempton.

There is also **Cyrname** to consider and he boasts an unblemished record of two-from-two at the track to date, having won the Wayward Lad and Pendil the season before last. Nicholls clearly has plenty of options for the race and it could be that last season's Ascot Chase winner ends up being his main contender.

Looking at other trainers, **Nicky Henderson** is another with a decent recent record in the King George, having won the race on three occasions during the past nine years, from just 11 runners. As well as saddling *Long Run* (twice) and *Might Bite* to land the big prize, Henderson has also seen the former finish runner-up in 2011 and Riverside Theatre made it a 1-2 for the stable 12 months earlier.

 BIG-RACE TRENDS

ROLL OF HONOUR

Year	Season Form	Winner	Age	Weight	OR	SP	Trainer	Runners	Last race (No. of days)
2018	4	Clan des Obeaux	6	11-10	160	12/1	P Nicholls	10	4th Gr.1 Betfair Chase (32)
2017	1	Might Bite	8	11-10	162	6/4F	N Henderson	8	1st Listed Sandown Chase (44)
2016	111	Thistlecrack	8	11-10	-	11/10F	C Tizzard	5	1st Newbury Nov. Chase (30)
2015	11	Cue Card	9	11-10	172	9/2	C Tizzard	9	1st Gr.1 Betfair Chase (35)
2014	51	Silviniaco Conti	8	11-10	174	15/8F	P Nicholls	10	1st Gr.1 Betfair Chase (34)
2013	3	Silviniaco Conti	7	11-10	173	7/2	P Nicholls	9	3rd Gr.1 Betfair Chase (31)
2012	2	Long Run	7	11-10	172	15/8F	N Henderson	9	2nd Gr.1 Betfair Chase (32)
2011	P1	Kauto Star	11	11-10	174	3/1	P Nicholls	7	1st Gr.1 Betfair Chase (37)
*2010	3	Long Run	6	11-10	162	9/2	N Henderson	9	3rd Gr.3 Paddy Power Gold Cup (63)
2009	1	Kauto Star	9	11-10	186	8/13F	P Nicholls	13	1st Gr.1 Betfair Chase (35)

LEADING TEN-YEAR GUIDES

Betfair Chase 7 (*Kauto Star* 1st & 1st, *Long Run* 2nd, *Silviniaco Conti* 3rd & 1st, *Cue Card* 1st, *Clan des Obeaux* 4th)
Last season's Cheltenham Gold Cup 5 (*Kauto Star* 1st & 3rd, *Long Run* 3rd, *Silviniaco Conti* fell & 4th)
Last year's renewal 5 (*Kauto Star* 1st & 3rd., *Long Run* 2nd, *Silviniaco Conti* 1st, *Cue Card* 5th)
Last season's Betway Bowl 4 (*Silviniaco Conti* 3rd & 1st, *Cue Card* 2nd, *Clan des Obeaux* 3rd)
Last year's Kauto Star Novices' Chase 3 (*Long Run* 1st, *Silviniaco Conti* 2nd, *Might Bite* fell)
Charlie Hall Chase 2 (*Silviniaco Conti* 5th., *Cue Card* 1st)

* Run in January 2011

La Bague Au Roi & Topofthegame - could renew Kempton rivalry in this year's King George

Challow Novices' Hurdle
(Grade 1) 2m 4f 118y – Newbury
Saturday 28th December 2019

OVERVIEW

The first Grade 1 novice hurdle of the season in England, the winner of the Challow has a notoriously poor record in the Ballymore Novices' Hurdle at Cheltenham, although that almost changed last season, when *Champ* went on to finish runner-up at the festival. Last year's race was run at a crawl and on much quicker ground than is usually the case, so speed came to the fore in the end, whereas it is often won by a hardened novice who has no trouble in handling deep ground. The likes of *Diamond Harry, Wichita Lineman, Bindaree, King's Road* and, most notably, *Denman* have all won this race in the past 21 years before going on to make up into very smart staying chasers.

SECOND-SEASON/EXPERIENCED NOVICES

Last season's winner *Champ* had run four times over hurdles prior to his victory in the Challow and was the third successive second-season novice winner of the race. Nicky Henderson's subsequent Aintree winner had only had one start the season before – when runner-up to *Vinndication* at Ascot – before winning a couple of small races in May. He returned from his summer break to win a handicap at Newbury's winter carnival, so had plenty of experience under his belt before tackling the Challow. The most experienced of the first four home, only one runner in last year's race boasted more experience than Champ (that being *Coolanly*) and it is something that shouldn't be underestimated.

Three of the four previous winners – *Parlour Games, Messire des Obeaux* and *Poetic Rhythm* – had all had either six or seven starts over hurdles prior to the Challow, again showing the benefit of experience in what can sometimes be a tough race for youngsters. The only anomaly during the past five years was *Barters Hill*, who was successful on just his second start over hurdles, although he faced just two rivals who were both only four-year-olds. He had also won four bumpers, so wasn't lacking in racecourse experience.

Going back a little further, *Coolnagorna, Brewster* (who was actually in his third season over hurdles) and *Reve de Sivola* also fit a similar profile. Pay healthy respect to those with considerable experience, especially those with winning form in Graded novice company. Of the six horses

highlighted, only *Champ* had failed to win a Grade 2 prior to the Challow.

GRADED FORM

Champ became the first horse in five years, and just the third in the past 11 years, to have won the Challow without having earlier recorded a Graded win. Seven of the eight had won a Grade 2 novice hurdle, whilst *Barters Hill* had won the Grade 2 bumper at Aintree's Grand National meeting the previous season. Going back a little further, *Cornish Rebel* is another to have recorded a Grade 2 bumper success, having won at Newbury the previous February (the race is now a Listed event and had also been won by Barters Hill, incidentally).

Cornish Rebel was one of four winners in the space of five years to have recorded a Grade 2 success earlier in their careers, so in total during the past 20 years, 12 of the 19 winners (no race in 2000) had already scored at Grade 2 level.

KEY RACES

Three Graded novice hurdles have proven to be 'key races' in terms of the Challow in the past decade, with four recent winners having contested Cheltenham's **Hyde Novices' Hurdle** at the November meeting. *Fingal Bay* and *Parlour Games* were both successful in the 2m5f race, whilst *Reve de Sivola* finished runner-up and *Poetic Rhythm* third. Going back a little further, both *Brewster* and *Diamond Harry* also won this race earlier in the campaign. Incidentally, the Hyde was given Grade 2 status in 2008 when *Diamond Harry* won, and *Wichita Lineman* was yet another winner to have contested this race, prior to it being upgraded, when runner-up under a penalty. Therefore, seven of the past 15 winners hail from that particular Cheltenham race – a strong statistic.

Before moving onto the other two prominently featured races, there was another Cheltenham novices' hurdle – the **Bristol Novices' Hurdle**, a 3m contest staged at the December meeting – which produced three Challow winners between 1999 and 2007. *Bindaree* and *Brewster* both won that race on their previous outing, whilst *Souffleur* finished third before going two places better at Newbury. I don't think that it is coincidental that since the Hyde was upgraded, the Bristol has become less of a factor in terms of a 'trial'. It tends to be that Albert Bartlett types are more inclined to head down that route nowadays.

BIG-RACE TRENDS

Another race during December to have thrown up a trio of winners – more recently – is Sandown's **Winter Novices' Hurdle**, staged on the first day of the two-day Tingle Creek meeting. This race is run over a similar distance to the Challow and is also often run on soft ground, with the stiff Sandown finish also bringing stamina into play. *Fingal Bay* and *Taquin du Seuil* were back-to-back winners of both the Winter and Challow in 2011 and 2012, respectively, whilst four-year-old *Messire des Obeaux* repeated the feat in 2016.

Finally, the **Persian War Novices' Hurdle** at Chepstow in October has also provided three Challow winners in the past decade, with *Reve de Sivola*, *Fingal Bay* and *Poetic Rhythm* all successful at the Welsh track. That Grade 2 is often an early-season target for second-season novices, with experience gained during the previous campaign often beneficial.

NEWBURY FORM

Five of the past 16 Challow winners had been successful at Newbury previously (and two of those renewals were run at Cheltenham), but surprisingly *Champ* is the only one to have won over hurdles at the course. He landed a handicap off a mark of 139 on his final outing before winning this race last year, whereas four other Challow winners were bumper winners at the track.

Cornish Rebel and *Barters Hill* – as stated previously – had won the bumper at the Betfair Hurdle meeting, whilst *Wichita Lineman* and *Diamond Harry* were both dual bumper winners at the Berkshire venue. The latter won the valuable Goffs UK Spring Sale Bumper twice (a fine piece of training by Nick Williams), a race which was won this year by **Get In The Queue** and which will always be remembered as Noel Fehily's swansong. He could easily develop into a Graded novice hurdler this winter, whilst another Newbury bumper winner from last season who could do likewise is **McFabulous**. He won under a penalty on 2nd March, before going on to score in the Grade 2 bumper at Aintree's Grand National meeting.

MARKET FORCES

Ten of the 18 winners since the turn of the century (again, no race in 2000) were sent off favourite. Four of the 10 were sent off odds-on, with the starting price of the other six ranging from Evens to 5/2. A further four winners during this period were sent off second in the market (15/8 to 100/30), as was *Bindaree* in 1999, whilst the other four winners were priced at 7/1, 5/1, 8/1 and 6/1 respectively. The top of the market tends to dominate.

CONNECTIONS TO NOTE

Following last year's victory of *Champ*, leading owner **JP McManus** has now seen his famous green and gold hooped silks carried to victory on four occasions since 2006. *Wichita Lineman* got the ball rolling for McManus, before *Backspin* followed suit some four years later. *Captain Cutter* made it three wins in the race for the owner in 2013, before *Champ* made it four winners from just five runners in the space of 13 years. The only McManus 'loser' during this period was the Gordon Elliott-trained Baltazar d'Allier, who finished runner-up in 2016. Backing the McManus runners blindly during this 13-year period would have yielded a tidy profit of £15.75 to a level-stake of £1.

McManus' two latest winners were trained by Nicky Henderson, whilst his first two came from the **Jonjo O'Neill** stable, and O'Neill has saddled four winners in total since 2002. *Coolnagorna* and *Taquin du Seuil* were the other two winners to come from Jackdaws Castle, and O'Neill hasn't had a runner since the latter was successful in 2012. Clearly very selective in what he runs in the Challow, O'Neill boasts an unblemished record in the race this century, with all four of his runners proving successful. As stated, he has been without a runner in the race in the past six renewals, but should he deem a horse good enough to take their chance come late-December, sit up and take note.

OFFICIAL BHA RATINGS

The past three winners were either top- or joint-top-rated on official BHA Ratings, as were *Reve de Sivola* and *Fingal Bay*. Both *Backspin* and *Barters Hill* (who had run only once apiece over hurdles previously) hadn't been handed an official mark, so five winners this decade – and four were clear top-rated – is a decent strike rate.

Last year's winner *Champ* was already officially rated 150 ahead of the Challow, and that is the highest obtained by any winner in recent years. *Fingal Bay* was next-best, having achieved a rating of 149 to that point.

ROLL OF HONOUR

Year	Season Form	Winner	Age	Weight	OR	SP	Trainer	Runners	Last race (No. of days)
2018	111	Champ	6	11-7	150	EvensF	N Henderson	7	1st Newbury Hurdle (28)
2017	13	Poetic Rhythm	6	11-7	147	15/8F	F O'Brien	6	3rd Gr.2 Cheltenham Nov. Hurdle (43)
2016	11	Messire des Obeaux	4	11-7	143	100/30	A King	8	1st Gr.2 Sandown Nov. Hurdle (29)
2015	1	Barters Hill	5	11-7	-	4/11F	B Pauling	3	1st Huntingdon Nov. Hurdle (58)
2014	21021	Parlour Games	6	11-7	145	6/1	J Ferguson	6	1st Gr.2 Cheltenham Nov. Hurdle (45)
2013	11	Captain Cutter	6	11-7	130	8/1	N Henderson	6	1st Market Rasen Nov. Hurdle (23)
2012	121	Taquin du Seuil	5	11-7	137	13/8F	J O'Neill	6	1st Gr.2 Sandown Nov. Hurdle (22)
2011	111	Fingal Bay	5	11-7	149	1/4F	P Hobbs	5	1st Gr.2 Sandown Nov. Hurdle (29)
2010	1	Backspin	5	11-7	-	5/1	J O'Neill	9	1st Bangor Nov. Hurdle (14)
2009	12121	Reve de Sivola	4	11-7	143	15/8	N Williams	11	2nd Gr.2 Cheltenham Nov. Hurdle (44)

LEADING TEN-YEAR GUIDES

Hyde Novices' Hurdle 4 (*Reve de Sivola* 2nd, *Fingal Bay* 1st, *Parlour Games* 1st, *Poetic Rhythm* 3rd)
Winter Novices' Hurdle 3 (*Fingal Bay* 1st, *Taquin du Seuil* 1st, *Messire des Obeaux* 1st)
Persian War Novices' Hurdle 3 (*Reve de Sivola* 1st, *Fingal Bay* 1st, *Poetic Rhythm* 1st)

Denman - seen here winning the Challow by 22 lengths

BIG-RACE TRENDS

Tolworth Novices' Hurdle
(Grade 1) 1m 7f 216y - Sandown Park
Saturday 4th January 2020

OVERVIEW

The second domestic Grade 1 novice hurdle comes hot on the heels of the Challow from Newbury, with Sandown staging the 2m Tolworth Novices' Hurdle on the first Saturday of the year. Despite being run over the minimum trip, the ground is often soft and, therefore, can become a test of stamina at the distance, especially given the uphill finish. As a consequence, National Hunt horses – those with Point-to-Point and/or Bumper backgrounds – have a fine recent record.

The race was lost in both 2009 and 2010, and has been rearranged to four different tracks since the turn of the century, due to the weather: Kempton (2014), Wincanton (2003), Warwick (2002) and Ascot (2001).

SECOND-SEASON NOVICES VS UNEXPOSED TYPES

Although experience doesn't seem as important in the Tolworth as it does in the Challow, *Elixir de Nutz* last season became the sixth second-season novice winner in the past 13. He had run in a Grade 2 juvenile contest (Finesse on trials day) for Philip Hobbs and was a faller in a maiden hurdle at Uttoxeter last May, before switching stables. The grey showed considerable improvement during the first half of last season and had run five times over hurdles in all, prior to winning the Tolworth.

Breedsbreeze had run twice over hurdles the season before he won the Tolworth, whilst the Nicky Henderson-trained *Royal Boy* had done the same and actually finished third in the race 12 months prior to winning it. Another Henderson winner, *Minella Class*, had run once over hurdles in Ireland (prior to running in a couple of bumpers), whilst *L'Ami Serge* – yet another recent winner from Seven Barrows – boasted considerably more experience, winning the Tolworth on his ninth start, having run six times over hurdles in France.

The other recent winner with plenty of experience under his belt was multiple-winner *Marcel*, who had also run in France and was having his 13th hurdles start when winning this race in 2005.

In stark contrast, 10 of the past 20 winners were successful after just one (3) or two (7) hurdles starts. *Behrajan* – who was successful as a four-year-old, on the back of a wide-margin juvenile hurdle win – and, more recently, *Yorkhill* and *Finian's Oscar* were all able to win the Tolworth

on the back of just one run over timber. The rise of the latter was quite dramatic, as he went from winning an Irish Point-to-Point, to the sales ring at Cheltenham, to winning a Hereford maiden, then onto Sandown in the space of just two-and-a-half months. Sadly, we did not get to see him fulfil his huge potential.

CHELTENHAM FESTIVAL WINNERS

Whilst the ill-fated *Finian's Oscar* would miss that season's Cheltenham Festival, he would return in time to win the Grade 1 Mersey Novices' Hurdle just three months after his Tolworth success. Other recent winners have fared well at the festival, however, with the Tolworth boasting a much better record as a Cheltenham trial than the aforementioned Challow. Five of the past 20 Tolworth winners have gone on to win either the Supreme (2) or Ballymore (3), and whilst this doesn't exactly help in finding the winner of the Sandown race, it gives you an indication of the calibre of horse often required.

Interestingly, of those 20 winners only 12 went on to take their chance in one of the festival novice hurdles, so a record of five-from-12 is very good. The past two winners to have run at Cheltenham – *Yorkhill* and *Summerville Boy* – have won, whilst *Noland* scored in the 2006 Supreme Novices' Hurdle, before which both *French Holly* and *Monsignor* completed the Tolworth-Ballymore double, both in emphatic fashion at Cheltenham. This might help from an antepost point of view; if you are keen on a horse for Cheltenham who is set to line up in the Tolworth, it certainly shouldn't be viewed upon as a negative and, again, it just gives you an idea of the level of ability that can be required in certain years.

It is also worth noting that those five subsequent Cheltenham Festival winners formed part of the less-exposed crop of Tolworth winners, with all five having had just one (1), two (3), or three (1) starts over hurdles previously. Therefore, if looking at the class angle, you should probably focus on the lightly-raced types, as opposed to those hardened, more-exposed novices, as covered in the previous subsection.

BUMPER & POINT-TO-POINT WINNERS

Having won an AQPS race at Argentan in France, *Elixir de Nutz* became the fifth winner in the past eight years to have won a bumper at the start of their career. *Minella Class* and *Summerville Boy* both won bumpers in Ireland before joining their

Tolworth-winning connections, whilst *Yorkhill* was also a bumper winner on home soil in Ireland, having scored twice, latterly at the Punchestown Festival the previous April. *Melodic Rendezvous* had won a Chepstow bumper before finishing runner-up in a Grade 1, also at the Punchestown Festival.

Going back a little further, five of the 10 winners between 1998 and 2007 had also won at least one bumper and, interestingly, four of those five had run in one (or three in *French Holly*'s case) of the Graded bumpers at one of the three spring festivals. *Monsignor* had, of course, won the previous season's Champion Bumper, whilst *Thisthatandtother* and *Noland* had both shaped well in the Grade 2 at Aintree.

Yorkhill is the only winner in the past 20 to have won a bumper and an Irish Point, whilst another trio of fairly recent winners hailed from the Pointing ranks. Both *Royal Boy* and *Finian's Oscar* were successful 'between the flags' in Ireland, as was 2008 winner *Breedsbreeze*.

RESPECT EARLY-SEASON CHELTENHAM FORM

The past two winners both contested the Grade 2 **Sharp Novices' Hurdle** at Cheltenham's November meeting and returned to the same venue to contest the **British Stallions Studs EBF 'National Hunt' Novices' Hurdle** at the December meeting. *Elixir de Nutz* was successful in both races, whilst *Summerville Boy* finished second in the Sharp and third in the December race.

Going back a little further, both *Noland* and *Melodic Rendezvous* also won the race at the December fixture, which is staged on the New Course and over 2m1f, so is often a similar test in terms of stamina to the Tolworth, and, in 2005, *Marcel* won the Sharp Novices' Hurdle.

There aren't any other races which you would highlight as 'key trials' for the Tolworth, although two of the past 10 winners had run in handicap company earlier in the season. *L'Ami Serge* had won the Gerry Feilden at Newbury on his penultimate start (won the Grade 2 Kennel Gate after that) and *Breedsbreeze* had finished runner-up in a Listed handicap over course and distance on his previous outing.

MARKET FORCES

The Tolworth is traditionally a small-field novice hurdle and, rather like the Challow, it has been dominated by the top end of the market in recent years. During the past 20 runnings, 14 winners were either favourite (9) or second-favourite (5).

KEY TRENDS

 14 of the past 20 winners were sent off favourite (9) or second-favourite (5)

 5 of the past 8 winners had won a bumper

 4 of the past 10 winners had won an Irish Point-to-Point

 6 of the past 13 winners were second-season novices

 5 of the past 20 winners went on to win at the Cheltenham Festival

 4 of the past 13 winners had finished 1st or 2nd at Cheltenham in November (G2 Sharp) or December

 Nicky Henderson has won the race 5 times

 Only 4 of the past 20 winners were sent off bigger than 5/1

 Summerville Boy is the only recent winner who was a maiden over hurdles

Melodic Rendezvous (7/2) and *Silverburn* (5/1) were another pair sent off quite short in the market, whilst the other four winners during this period had starting prices ranging from 8/1 to 11/1.

TRAINERS TO NOTE

With four winners in the space of five years between 2011 and 2015, **Nicky Henderson** is the most successful trainer in the Tolworth Hurdle, having earlier won it with *New York Rainbow*, back in 1992. Since 2011, Henderson has saddled nine runners in the race and also been responsible for a couple of seconds, as well as those four winners. Backing his horses blindly during this period would have yielded a healthy-profit of £16.88, mainly thanks to *Royal Boy* and *Captain Conan* both being sent off at 9/1. His runner(s) warrant utmost respect, although he was responsible for last year's beaten favourite Rathhill, who appeared to fail to give his running and wasn't seen thereafter.

Paul Nicholls also enjoyed a fine spell shortly after the turn of the century, winning the race four times in the space of six years, between 2003 and 2008. *Thisthatandtother, Noland, Silverburn* and *Breedsbreeze* were all successful for the Champion Trainer, who then didn't saddle a runner between 2013 and 2016. Since then, Capitaine finished second for the yard in 2017; Mont des Avaloirs finished third in 2018; and he saddled the second and third last year. Only one of Nicholls' nine runners since 2006 has failed to finish in the first three.

Interestingly, two of Nicholls' winners – *Thisthatandtother* and *Noland* – ran in a Grade 2 bumper at Aintree, and he won that race last season with **McFabulous**. I have already touched upon him under the Challow Hurdle and as stated there, it wouldn't be a surprise if he made the grade over hurdles and developed into a leading contender for Grade 1 honours.

More recently, **Colin Tizzard** – with two winners in the past three years – has been the man to follow in the Tolworth. *Finian's Oscar* was his first runner in the race and *Elixir de Nutz* made it two winners from three runners in the race for the Dorset-based trainer, who was actually said to be targeting Eldorado Allen at the race after his victory at Sandown (mentioned by Joe Tizzard in a post-race interview) last November. This clearly shows that the race is to the forefront of the stable's thinking, and I suspect that is likely to continue.

ROLL OF HONOUR

Year	Season Form	Winner	Age	Weight	OR	SP	Trainer	Runners	Last race (No. of days)
2019	F211	Elixir de Nutz	5	11-7	140	3/1	C Tizzard	5	1st Cheltenham Nov. Hurdle (22)
2018	1223	Summerville Boy	6	11-7	142	8/1	T George	5	3rd Cheltenham Nov. Hurdle (22)
2017	1	Finian's Oscar	5	11-7	-	11/10F	C Tizzard	6	1st Hereford Nov. Hurdle (19)
2016	11	Yorkhill	6	11-7	-	4/9F	W Mullins (IRE)	5	1st Punchestown Hurdle (27)
2015	11	L'Ami Serge	5	11-7	149	4/9F	N Henderson	4	1st Gr.2 Ascot Nov. Hurdle (15)
2014*	31	Royal Boy	7	11-7	138	9/1	N Henderson	6	1st Ascot Hurdle (22)
2013	1231	Melodic Rendezvous	7	11-7	135	7/2	J Scott	7	1st Cheltenham Nov. Hurdle (22)
2012	341	Captain Conan	5	11-7	-	9/1	N Henderson	5	1st Auteuil Hurdle (198)
2011	1	Minella Class	6	11-7	-	6/4F	N Henderson	5	1st Newbury Hurdle (24)
2010	**NO RACE**								

LEADING TEN-YEAR GUIDES

British Stallion Studs EBF 'National Hunt' Novices' Hurdle 3
(*Melodic Rendezvous* 1st, *Summerville Boy* 3rd, *Elixir de Nutz* 1st)
Sharp Novices' Hurdle 2 (*Summerville Boy* 2nd, *Elixir de Nutz* 1st)

* Run at Kempton Park

Colin Tizzard - has won the Tolworth twice in the past three seasons

Lanzarote Hurdle
(Listed) 2m 5f – Kempton Park
Saturday 11th January 2020

OVERVIEW

A Listed handicap hurdle, the Lanzarote was run over 2m until 2007 when the race returned to Kempton – had spent one year at Carlisle – and has since been run over 2m5f. Therefore, for the purposes of this race, I think it makes sense to focus on the 12 runnings (race abandoned in 2009) over the current distance. This is yet another handicap in which lightly-raced, unexposed hurdlers boast a good recent record, and form on right-handed tracks seems essential.

RIGHT-HANDED FORM

Since the race was upped in distance (2007), four of the 12 winners had previously won at Kempton. *Nycteos* had won a handicap over course and distance on his previous start; *Micheal Flips* was a novice hurdle winner at the track; *Tea For Two* was a winner over course and distance earlier in the season, on his hurdling debut, and he was actually four-from-four on right-handed tracks prior to his win in the Lanzarote; and *William Henry* had won a bumper at the track earlier in his career – he actually hadn't run on a right-handed track since.

The other eight winners since the race changed distance had all won on right-handed tracks. Last season's winner, *Big Time Dancer,* might not have won over hurdles on a right-handed track, but his three wins on the Flat had all come on right-handed turning tracks (Beverley, Hamilton and Leicester).

NOVICES & LIGHTLY-RACED HURDLERS

Big Time Dancer became the fourth winning novice in the past eight years, and the second during this time who was a second-season novice. *Yala Enki* was the other with a similar profile – although he had only had the six starts, compared with the nine of last season's winner – whilst the Nick Williams-trained pairing of *Swincombe Flame* and *Tea For Two* were both in their first year over hurdles and winning this on their fourth start over timber.

Nicky Henderson's pair of recent winners – *Oscara Dara* and *William Henry* – had only had three and four hurdles starts respectively, whilst the other four winners during the past decade had run either seven or eight times over hurdles previously.

Nine of the past 10 winners had recorded two wins over hurdles prior to winning the Lanzarote, the exception being *Yala Enki* who had won just once. It should be pointed out that he did boast a fair bit of racing experience in France and had won a couple of chases prior to joining the Venetia Williams stable, but he only had an Exeter novice hurdle win to his name from three starts in Britain.

CONDITIONAL JOCKEYS

This might well be coincidental, but six of the past 12 winners were ridden by conditional jockeys claiming an allowance and, more significantly, five of the past six winners tick this box. As well as six winners, conditionals have ridden eight of the 12 runners-up. The fact that the Lanzarote is staged on a Kempton card which often shares a date in the calendar with Warwick's Classic Chase could mean that many of the leading jockeys are riding there, but it is certainly a noteworthy trend.

In the case of the five winners during the past six years, the winning riders were Harry Derham, Lizzie Kelly, Charlie Deutsch, James Bowen, and last year Jonjo O'Neill Junior landed his biggest prize at that stage of his career. He, of course, went on to win the Martin Pipe a couple of months later aboard Early Doors and also carried the famous JP McManus silks to victory at the Punchestown Festival, when successful on Musical Slave. The previous year, young James Bowen was the hottest property in terms of up-and-coming conditionals, so look out for a well-touted young jockey being booked.

During the past six years, 22 horses have been ridden by claiming conditionals in the Lanzarote. That is only 28% of the field-sizes (total number of runners = 78), so it is a very good strike rate, and backing all 22 would have yielded a profit of £19.25 to a level-stake of £1.

For the record, the other conditional jockey-ridden winner since the race distance was increased was *Verasi*, who was partnered by Eamon Dehdashti when winning at 20/1 in 2007.

AGE

Nicky Henderson's two recent winners – *Oscara Dara* and *William Henry* – were aged eight, and since the race distance was increased, only one five-year-old has been successful, that being the Paul Nicholls-trained *Saphir du Rheu*. Both *William Henry* and *Saphir du Rheu* would have shouldered top-weight but for being ridden by 5lb claimers.

 BIG-RACE TRENDS

The other nine winners were all aged six (7) or seven (2), so that is the age bracket to pay most attention to. Five-year-olds had a much better record in the race when it was run as a 2m contest, with that age group successful three times in the space of five years between 1998 and 2003.

MARKET FORCES

The past 12 winners have been book-ended with big-priced winners, with *Verasi* scoring at 20/1 and *Big Time Dancer* at 16s. The 10 winners in between, however, were all sent off at single-figure odds. Four horses have justified favouritism (*Tea For Two* was joint-favourite in 2015) and a further five winners hailed from the front three in the market.

KEY RACES

There aren't many standout races to feature here, but the race formerly known as the Fixed Brush Hurdle at Haydock has popped up twice during the past nine years. *James de Vassy* was unplaced behind Grands Crus at Haydock before winning this, and *Yala Enki* finished fifth behind the ill-fated Baradari on Betfair Chase day, before winning his Lanzarote. At the time of both renewals, the Haydock race was run over an extended 2m6f, whereas the Betfair Exchange Stayers' Handicap Hurdle (covered earlier) is now run over an extended 3m, so it is possible that is might not have an impact on the Lanzarote going forward.

Another small point worth noting is that Nicky Henderson's two most recent winners – *Oscara Dara* and *William Henry* – were winning the Lanzarote on the back of running in a novice chase. The former – who was two-from-two over hurdles when racing right-handed, incidentally – was beaten on his chase debut at Plumpton in mid-December, before reverting to hurdles, and the latter was pulled up in the Steel Plate And Sections Novices' Chase at Cheltenham's November meeting. He jumped badly from the off and was pulled up after his saddle slipped, before being given a couple of months off prior to winning the Lanzarote in 2018. Therefore, it is clear that Henderson is happy to admit when a novice chase plan doesn't seem to be working out – Buveur d'Air being an even more high-profile example of this, with him winning twice over fences before switching back to the smaller obstacles ahead of his first Champion Hurdle win.

TRAINERS TO NOTE

As touched upon already – in various subsections – **Nicky Henderson** has won the Lanzarote twice in the past seven years, thanks to *Oscara Dara* and

KEY TRENDS

 All 12 winners since the race changed distance had won on right-handed tracks

 The past 10 winners had 9 or less starts over hurdles

 5 of the past 6 winners were ridden by conditional jockeys

 9 of the past 10 winners had won twice over hurdles

 9 of the past 12 winners were aged 6 or 7

 9 of the past 12 winners were in the top 3 of the betting (4 winning favourites)

 Nick Williams has won the race 3 times from just 5 runners

 4 of the past 8 winners were novices

 4 of the past 12 winners had won at Kempton

 Only 1 winning 5yo since the distance was increased

Only 2 of the past 12 winners were sent off at double-figures

William Henry. Henderson also saddled *Non So* to win the race in 2003, when the race was still a 2m contest, and he was another lightly-raced sort (seven previous starts). Since the distance of the race was increased, Henderson has saddled 15 runners and had two winners. In addition, Duc de Regniere finished runner-up for the stable in 2010, whilst Royals Darling and Afrad filled the places behind Verasi in 2007.

Paul Nicholls has also enjoyed three victories in the Lanzarote, with all three coming between 2008 and 2017. Since 2007, Nicholls has saddled 13 runners in all and as well as those three winners, he has seen Organisateur, Ibis du Rheu, Old Guard and Topofthegame finish in the first four.

The trainer with the best recent record – strike rate-wise – is **Nick Williams**, who has won the race three times from just five runners. His first three runners in the race all won and since the success of *Tea For Two* in 2015, he has saddled just the two runners, both in 2018. Both horses were sent off at 25/1, whereas the stable's three winners were sent off at 9/2, 9/2 and 8/1 respectively. As stated in the preview of the Betfair Exchange Stayers' Handicap Hurdle, several of the yard's horses now run under the name **Jane Williams**. Respect any horse sent out of their Devon base.

ROLL OF HONOUR

Year	Season Form	Winner	Age	Weight	OR	SP	Trainer	Runners	Last race (No. of days)
2019	36421	Big Time Dancer	6	10-10 (5)	125	16/1	J Candish	14	1st Doncaster Hurdle (42)
2018	P	William Henry	8	11-7 (5)	145	7/1	N Henderson	16	p.u. Cheltenham Nov. Hurdle (57)
2017	327	Modus	7	11-4	145	7/1	P Nicholls	13	7th Gr.3 Ascot Hurdle (28)
2016	15	Yala Enki	6	9-12 (5)	130	11/4F	V Williams	9	5th Gr.3 Haydock Hurdle (49)
2015	131	Tea For Two	6	9-12 (7)	134	9/2JF	N Williams	13	1st Towcester Nov. Hurdle (15)
2014	541	Saphir du Rheu	5	11-7 (5)	145	6/1	P Nicholls	13	1st Sandown Hurdle (35)
2013	12	Oscara Dara	8	11-0	140	5/1	N Henderson	18	2nd Plumpton Nov. Chase (26)
2012	211	Swincombe Flame	6	10-4	123	9/2	N Williams	19	1st Wincanton Nov. Hurdle (19)
2011	0	James de Vassy	6	11-2	144	8/1	N Williams	19	13th Listed Haydock Hurdle (56)
2010	36	Micheal Flips	6	10-11	137	9/1	A Turnell	13	6th Listed Newbury Hurdle (49)

Tea For Two - bolted up in the Lanzarote on just his fourth start over hurdles

BIG-RACE TRENDS

Betfair Hurdle
(Grade 3) 2m 92y – Newbury
Saturday 8th February 2020

OVERVIEW

Formerly known as the Schweppes Gold Trophy, then the Tote Gold Trophy, Newbury's Betfair Hurdle figures prominently in the 2m-handicap hurdle calendar. It has actually proven to be a springboard to Champion Hurdle success in the past, with both *Persian War* and *Make A Stand* successful at Cheltenham the following month.

The latter was only a novice when scoring in 1997 for Martin Pipe, and it is novices that have dominated the race in the past decade. This really does appear to be a race that trainers are targeting with lightly-raced up-and-coming hurdlers, en route to the Cheltenham Festival. Interestingly – as pointed out in last season's *Cheltenham Festival Betting Guide* – the winner doesn't tend to have a good record when going onto the Supreme Novices' Hurdle, and that trend continued last season, with *Al Dancer* disappointing in the festival curtain-raiser.

It should be noted that last season's race was lost due to the Equine Influenza outbreak and restaged at Ascot the following weekend. The prize fund was down considerably and as a consequence, it could be that last season's renewal wasn't quite as strong as usually is the case, although the winner certainly matched the profile of recent winners.

NOVICE DOMINATION

As stated in the 'Overview', *Make A Stand* was a novice when scoring in 1997, although he had run nine times over hurdles previously. After rattling up a hat-trick the previous May, he reverted to the Flat during June and July, before switching back to hurdles in October, when winning his first handicap. He arrived at Newbury on the back of another three straight wins, including the Grade 2 Kennel Gate Novices' Hurdle at Ascot, so was a very experienced horse despite him falling into the novice category.

Pipe went close to repeating the trick in 2000, when the thrice-raced *Copeland* – who would return to win the race in 2002 – finished runner-up, and the next novice to win the race after Make A Stand was *Get Me Out Of Here* in 2010. Since then, the tide has well and truly turned in favour of the novices, with eight of the past 10 winners being first-season hurdlers. Six of the eight – including the last three – were all winning the Betfair Hurdle on their fourth start over hurdles. Five of that sextet had won at least twice previously, whilst *Ballyandy* arrived at Newbury as a maiden over hurdles.

The more 'experienced' novice winners were *Splash of Ginge*, who had run six times, and *Agrapart*, who had had four starts over hurdles beforehand.

LIGHTLY-RACED HURDLERS

Of the past 20 winners – going back to 1998 (as the race was lost to the weather in both 2006 and 2009) – only three had run more than 10 times over hurdles. Therefore, it isn't just the novices that have dominated, but lightly-raced types in general. *Violet Dancer* (10 runs) and *Zarkandar* (3 runs) were the two non-novice winners during the past decade, and the latter certainly falls into the lightly-raced category, having had just the three starts the previous season. His Betfair Hurdle win was his first start since winning the Grade 1 Anniversary 4YO Hurdle at Aintree the previous April.

The previous 10 winners included *Sharpical* (8), *Decoupage* (6), *Geos* (8), *Landing Light* (3), *Essex* (4), *Heathcote* (10) and *Wingman* (8), who all scored on the back 10 or less previous runs over hurdles. *Geos*, of course, won the race again in 2004 (four years after his first victory), and *Copeland* – another of the 'experienced' winners (having had 15 starts) – had also finished runner-up in the race previously. Therefore, unless you are looking at a horse who has performed extremely well in the race previously, it can certainly pay to focus on the unexposed types.

AGE

Rather in keeping with the lightly-raced theme, the past 13 winners were all aged five (7) or six (6), with *Geos* (when successful for a second time) the only winner older than seven in the past 24.

OFFICIAL BHA RATINGS & WEIGHT

Seven of the past 10 winners – including the past four – were officially rated between 134 and 141, the exceptions during the past decade being *Violet Dancer* (132) and the more highly-rated pairing of *Zarkandar* (151) and *My Tent Or Yours* (149).

In terms of weight carried, five of the past 10 winners carried more than 11 stone, and this again includes the three most recent winners. There appears to be a wide range in terms of weight, often determined by the quality of the race.

MARKET FORCES

Splash of Ginge, Violet Dancer and *Agrapart* were successive big-price winners between 2014 and 2016, but either side of that three-year period saw winning favourites. Five of the past eight winners – when including co-favourite *Kalashnikov* – justified favouritism, with *Zarkandar, Ballyandy* and *Al Dancer* the shortest-priced. Going back a little further, both *Landing Light* and *Essex* were also sent off favourite (both 4/1), whilst in all, 11 of the past 20 winners started at 8/1 or lower.

KEY RACES

Five of the past eight winners contested a Grade 1 or Grade 2 on their previous start. The five includes *Zarkandar*, who was making his belated seasonal reappearance, whilst the other four were novices. Two of those novices – *Agrapart* and *Kalashnikov* – arrived at Newbury on the back of contesting the **Tolworth Novices' Hurdle** at Sandown the previous month. Both were beaten in the Grade 1, but would later go on to prove themselves to be better than handicappers.

The previous season's Grade 2 **Weatherbys Racing Bank Bumper** at Aintree's Grand National meeting – won last season by Paul Nicholls' McFabulous, who fended off Thebannerkingrebel – has produced three winners from the past seven years. *My Tent Or Yours* finished runner-up to The New One at Aintree, whilst both *Ballyandy* and *Al Dancer* finished fourth in the same event.

Al Dancer and *Recession Proof* both won the same early-season novice hurdle at Carlisle (at their midweek mid-October meeting), whilst both *Splash of Ginge* and *Agrapart* scored at Aintree's Becher Chase meeting (early-December). The race was a maiden hurdle when the former won and a novice event when the latter was successful.

TRAINERS TO NOTE

Having won five of the past 20 runnings of the race, local Lambourn-based trainer **Nicky Henderson** is the obvious place to start. Henderson enjoyed a fine time of it in this race between 1998 and 2004, saddling four winners in that seven-year spell. *Sharpical, Geos* (twice) and *Landing Light* were the horses in question, whilst his next – and last – winner came courtesy of subsequent three-time Champion Hurdle runner-up, *My Tent Or Yours*. Whilst five winners is hugely impressive and clearly hints at Henderson targeting the race, it has to be noted that he has run no less than 49 horses in the race during this period and backing them blindly would still have left you at a loss.

KEY TRENDS

- ⭐ 8 of the past 10 winners were novices
- ⭐ 15 of the past 20 winners had 8 or less hurdles starts
- ⭐ Nigel Twiston-Davies has saddled 3 of the past 6 winners
- ✓ The past 13 winners were aged 5 or 6
- ✓ 7 of the past 10 winners rated between 134–141
- ✓ 5 of the past 8 winners were favourite
- ✓ 11 of the past 20 winners were sent off 8/1 or lower
- ✓ 5 of the past 8 winners ran in a Grade 1 or Grade 2 last time out
- ✓ Nicky Henderson has won the race 5 times
- ✗ Only 1 winner since 1998 has won more than 3 times over hurdles previously
- ✗ Only 3 of the past 20 winners had run more than 10 times over hurdles
- ✗ Only 1 winner since 1994 older than 7
- ✗ Philip Hobbs is 0/25 this century
- ✗ Willie Mullins is 0/17 in the past 20 runnings

More recently, **Nigel Twiston-Davies** has been the trainer to follow in the Betfair Hurdle, saddling three winners in the past six years. All three were novices and he also saddled Flying Angel – a novice who would go on to win the Imperial Cup on his next start – to finish third at 25/1 in 2016. Twiston-Davies has only run six horses in the race during the past six years, so his record is very strong indeed. During the past decade, he has saddled eight runners in total and backing them all would have yielded a profit of £33.50 to a level-stake of £1.

Even more profitable to follow has been **Gary Moore**, who won the race three times from eight renewals between 2007 and 2015. *Heathcote* got the ball rolling when springing a 50/1 shock, which was followed 12 months later by *Wingman*. *Violet Dancer* provided the trainer with a third Betfair Hurdle in 2015 and he has only saddled three runners in the race since. In total during the last 20 runnings, Moore has saddled 16 horses in the Betfair, including Nahrawali (4th in 1998), Tikram (3rd in 2003) and Sire de Grugy (4th in

2012). Backing all the Moore horses during this time would have pocketed you a very healthy profit of £71 to a level-stake of £1.

One trainer who hasn't enjoyed success in the Betfair Hurdle is **Philip Hobbs**. This century, Hobbs has saddled 25 runners in the race without success, although he has seen 10 of his runners finish in the first four, including four seconds. Three of those seconds came courtesy of Rooster Booster, who finished runner-up in the race in three successive seasons. Hobbs didn't have a runner in the race last year, but Wait For Me (2017), Sternrubin and War Sound (both 2016) were sent off at 8/1, 8/1 and 12/1, respectively, in recent seasons.

In last season's *Cheltenham Festival Betting Guide*, I highlighted that **Willie Mullins** had – at that point – yet to win the Gold Cup. I was also quick to point out that I wouldn't back against it happening and it is a similar story here. Of course, Al Boum Photo corrected the Gold Cup statistic back in March, and if Mullins continues to send runners over for the race, it is likely that he will win the Betfair Hurdle at some stage, too, given the firepower at his disposal. However, with a record

of 0-17 since 1998, it was something that had to be highlighted and as you would expect, several of his runners have gone off at short odds. Blazer was sent off at 3-1 favourite in 2016, whilst another six of his runners were sent off at 10/1 or shorter, including Blue et Rouge, who finished runner-up to *Kalashnikov* in 2018. Mullins didn't have a runner in last year's rearranged race.

The Irish – in general – have struggled since *Spirit Leader* and *Essex* won in the space of three years, and another Irish trainer who has had a few stabs at the Betfair Hurdle is **Noel Meade**. His runners have been more spread out over the years, but he has yet to go close from six runners, including Native Dara (14/1), Power Elite (12/1) and De Name Escapes Me (14/1). Power Elite finished fifth in 2005 and was Meade's best effort to date.

ROLL OF HONOUR

Year	Season Form	Winner	Age	Weight	OR	SP	Trainer	Runners	Last race (No. of days)
2019*	111	Al Dancer	6	11-8	141	5/2F	N Twiston-Davies	14	1st Cheltenham Hurdle (64)
2018	112	Kalashnikov	5	11-5	141	8/1CF	A Murphy	24	2nd Gr.1 Tolworth Hurdle (35)
2017	232	Ballyandy	6	11-1	135	3/1F	N Twiston-Davies	16	2nd Gr.2 Sandown Nov. Hurdle (71)
2016	5213	Agrapart	5	10-5	137	16/1	N Williams	22	3rd Gr.1 Tolworth Hurdle (42)
2015	49322	Violet Dancer	5	10-9	132	20/1	G Moore	23	2nd Lingfield Maiden (17)
2014	24133	Splash of Ginge	6	10-3	134	33/1	N Twiston-Davies	20	3rd Gr.2 Leamington Hurdle (28)
2013	121	My Tent Or Yours	6	11-2	149	5/1F	N Henderson	21	1st Huntingdon Nov. Hurdle (29)
2012		Zarkandar	5	11-1	151	11/4F	P Nicholls	20	1st Gr.1 Anniversary Hurdle (316)
2011	1211	Recession Proof	5	10-8	134	12/1	J Quinn	15	1st Southwell Bumper (52)
2010	1111	Get Me Out of Here	6	10-6	135	6/1	J O'Neill	23	1st Newbury Hurdle (79)

LEADING TEN-YEAR GUIDES

The previous season's **Weatherbys Racing Bank Bumper** 3
(*My Tent Or Yours* 2nd, *Ballyandy* 4th, *Al Dancer* 4th)
Tolworth Novices' Hurdle 2 (*Agrapart* 3rd, *Kalashnikov* 2nd)

* *Run at Ascot*

INDEX

CALENDAR COLLECTION 2020

£9.99

£8.99

BiRDiE

2020 CALENDAR

ORDER NOW

WALL CALENDAR **£9.99**

DESK CALENDAR **£8.99**

BIRDIE BUNDLE (BOTH) **£15.99**

🏛 WEATHERBYS

CHELTENHAM
FESTIVAL
Betting Guide

AVAILABLE TO PRE-ORDER, JANUARY

- Includes exclusive Jumpers to Follow update for Cheltenham
- Published in association with the Sporting life
- Extensive trends analysis of all 28 races
- Positive and negative trends boxes for quick and easy referencing
- Spring Horses To Follow
- Feature articles from the Sporting life team and other Guest Authors
- FREE 1st class p&p • Includes FREE Aintree Guide & Grand National preview

♪bettrends

HOW TO ORDER

online **www.bettrendsshop.co.uk** | by phone **+44(0)1933 304776**

(Mon-Fri 8.30am-5.30pm)